Microsoft® Word 5.0 Simplified
for the IBM® PC

Microsoft® Word 5.0 Simplified
for the IBM® PC

David Bolocan
Robert Bixby

For Kathy, Jenny, and Steve

Windcrest books are published by Windcrest Books, an imprint of TAB BOOKS. The name "Windcrest" is a registered trademark of TAB BOOKS.

Published by **Windcrest Books**
FIRST EDITION/FIRST PRINTING

© 1990 by **David Bolocan and Robert Bixby**. Reproduction or publication of the content in any manner, without express permission of the publisher, is prohibited. The publisher takes no responsibility for the use of any of the materials or methods described in this book, or for the products thereof. Printed in the United States of America.

Library of Congress Cataloging-in-Publication Data

Bolocan, David.
    Microsoft Word 5.0 simplified for the IBM PC / by David Bolocan,
  Robert Bixby.
      p.   cm.
    ISBN 0-8306-3318-9
    1. Microsoft Word (Computer program) 2. IBM Personal Computer-
-Programming. 3. Word processing. I. Bixby, Robert, 1952–
II. Title.
Z52.5.M52B644 1990
652.5'536—dc20   89-49412
                                                                                                                             CIP

TAB BOOKS offers software for sale. For information and a catalog, please contact
TAB Software Department, Blue Ridge Summit, PA 17294-0850.

Questions regarding the content of this book should be addressed to:

    Windcrest Books
    Imprint of TAB BOOKS
    Blue Ridge Summit, PA 17294-0850

Acquisitions Editor: Ron Powers
Technical Editor: Sandra L. Johnson
Production: Katherine Brown
Book Design: Jacyln J. Boone
Cover Design: Lori E. Schlosser

Contents

Acknowledgments xiii

Introduction xv

    Typewriters and word processors *xv*
    Special features of Word *xvi*
    Philosophy and organization of the book *xvii*
    Notation *xviii*

Chapter 1. Word system requirements 1

    CPU requirements *1*
    Monitor requirements *2*
    Additional requirements *2*
    Printer requirements *2*
    Optional equipment *4*
    Summary *6*

Chapter 2. The keyboard and loading the operating system 7

    The IBM keyboard *7*
    Care and handling of disks *10*
    Loading the operating system *11*

Entering the date and time *12*
Making and maintaining backups *13*
Summary *14*

Chapter 3. Installing Word 15

Installing Word version 5.0 *16*
Installing Word for a hard disk *17*
Installing printer drivers *18*
Installing the mouse *19*
Modifying your Autoexecute and Configuration files *19*
Summary *20*

Chapter 4. Entering a document 21

The keyboard *21*
Running Word *22*
The Word screen *23*
Entering text *26*
Editing keys *28*
Moving the cursor *29*
Scrolling text *31*
Summary *33*

Chapter 5. Editing text 35

Highlighting blocks of text *35*
Procedure for selecting text *39*
Extending selections *41*
Selecting columns *41*
Deleting text *41*
The Insert command *42*
Deleting and inserting with the mouse *43*
The Undo command *43*
Summary *45*

Chapter 6. Word commands and menus 47

Command selection *47*
The self help feature *50*
Printing a document *53*
Saving text *56*
Clearing a document from Word *57*
Retrieving a document *58*
Exiting Word *59*
Summary *59*

Chapter 7. Formatting paragraphs 61

On-screen formatting *61*
Selecting paragraphs *62*
Direct keyboard formatting *62*
Paragraph alignment *63*
Indention *64*
Combining paragraph formats *66*
Double-spaced and open paragraphs *67*
The Format Paragraph command *67*
Joining and splitting paragraphs *68*
Hyphens, spaces, and word wrap *69*
Advanced Paragraph Format options *71*
Summary *75*

Chapter 8. Character format options 77

Hardware capabilities *77*
Selection of text *78*
Formatting with format keys *78*
The Format Character command *79*
Summary *83*

Chapter 9. Setting tabs, margins, and page numbers 85

Default page settings *86*
Changing default settings *86*
Entering and deleting divisions *86*
The ruler line *87*
The Format Division command *88*
Tabs *91*
Erasing or resetting tabs *96*
Activating page numbering *98*
Summary *99*

Chapter 10. Manipulating blocks of text 101

Moving text *101*
Copying text *102*
Managing the scrap *102*
Replacing blocks of text *103*
The Overtype option *103*
The glossary *105*
The F3 (ref) key *107*
Glossary files *109*
Summary *111*

Chapter 11. Searching and replacing text   113
    The Search command   *114*
    The Replace command   *117*
    Default values of Search and Repeat commands   *119*
    The Repeat Search Key   *119*
    The Redo key   *120*
    Searching and replacing formats and styles   *120*
    Summary   *122*

Chapter 12. Window operations   123
    Opening windows   *123*
    Moving between windows   *126*
    Changing window dimensions   *127*
    Options   *129*
    Closing windows   *130*
    Working with windows   *131*
    Controlling windows with the mouse   *135*
    Summary   *136*

Chapter 13. The Jump and Option commands   137
    The Jump command   *137*
    Rapid cursor movement with the mouse   *140*
    Word options   *141*
    Summary   *144*

Chapter 14. Advanced page formatting   145
    Starting a new division   *145*
    The Format Division Layout command   *146*
    Document dimensions   *147*
    Footnotes   *149*
    Annotations   *154*
    Bookmarks   *154*
    Running heads   *155*
    Summary   *158*

Chapter 15. Advanced Transfer and Print commands   161
    The default drive   *162*
    File directories   *163*
    Using wildcards   *163*
    Loading the document   *164*
    Clearing the document   *166*
    Saving documents   *166*
    Word processing for programmers   *167*
    Deleting files   *168*

Renaming files *168*
Merging documents *168*
Print commands *169*
Print preView *173*
Summary *174*

Chapter 16. Using style sheets 175

Indirect formatting with style sheets *175*
Attaching and detaching style sheets *176*
The Gallery menu *177*
Formatting documents with style sheets *179*
Summary *182*

Chapter 17. Creating style sheets 183

Entering the Gallery *183*
Creating a key code *184*
Formatting styles *186*
Recording styles from a document *188*
Editing styles *189*
Saving and retrieving style sheets *190*
Other Gallery commands *192*
Summary *192*

Chapter 18. Merging documents 193

Designating Merge commands *194*
Merge variables *195*
Creating a data file with Word *195*
Printing a merged document *197*
Printing to a disk file *197*
Commas and quotation marks *197*
Using header files *198*
Merging data files from other programs *199*
Summary *200*

Chapter 19. Merge commands 201

The Set and Ask commands *201*
The If command *205*
The Skip command *208*
The Next command *208*
The Include command *209*
Summary *210*

Chapter 20. Word to WordStar and back again 211

Making the conversion *211*
Other options *212*

Chapter 21. The spelling checker   213

How Spell works   *214*
Starting Spell   *214*
The main menu   *214*
Summary   *216*

Chapter 22. Dictionary management   217

Changing corrections   *217*
Adding words to the dictionaries   *218*
The three dictionaries   *218*
General principles   *219*
The options   *220*
Editing your dictionaries   *221*
Summary   *221*

Chapter 23. Other library commands   223

Automatic hyphenation   *223*
Operating system commands from Word   *225*
Summary   *225*

Chapter 24. The thesaurus   227

Looking up words in the thesaurus   *227*
A hands-on example   *229*
Advanced options   *229*
Summary   *230*

Chapter 25. Drawing lines   231

Line drawing with the arrow keys   *231*
Paragraph borders   *233*
Shading, color and background shading   *235*
Summary   *236*

Chapter 26. Sorting   237

The Library Autosort options   *239*
Sorting paragraphs   *240*
Undoing a sort   *240*
Summary   *240*

Chapter 27. Mathematical calculations   243

Columns   *245*
How Word performs calculations   *245*
Summary   *246*

Chapter 28. Using outlines 247
Outlining *248*
Converting an existing document to an outline *253*
Using the outline style sheet *254*
Printing *254*
Summary *254*

Chapter 29. The document retrieval system 255
Entering the document retrieval menu *256*
Entering and editing summary sheets *258*
Selecting files with the Query command *260*
Changing the arrangement of the document list *262*
Summary *262*

Chapter 30. Indexes and tables of contents 263
Entries for tables of contents *264*
Creating indexes *267*
Compiling tables and indexes *268*
Formatting tables and indexes *269*
Summary *270*

Chapter 31. Printing line numbers and revision marks 273
Line numbers *273*
Adding revision marks *275*
Searching for revision marks and cancelling revisions *277*
Summary *277*

Chapter 32. Macros 279
Running a macro *279*
Creating macros by recording *279*
Saving and retrieving macro programs *282*
Writing and editing macros *282*
Testing and debugging macros *284*
Macro formatting and notes about macros *284*
Adding comments to a macro *286*
Summary *286*

Chapter 33. Macro instructions 287
The Ask instruction *287*
The Comment-Endcomment instruction *288*
The If-Else-Endif instruction *288*
The Message instruction *291*
The Pause instruction *291*
The Quit instruction *292*

The Repeat-Endrepeat instruction *292*
The Set instruction *293*
The While-Endwhile instruction *293*
Combining macro commands in macro programs *294*
Arrays *301*
Functions *301*
Summary *302*

Chapter 34. Page layout 305

Importing graphics *305*
CAPTURE.COM *307*
Positioning and formatting graphics *308*
Summary *309*

Chapter 35. Importing data from other programs 311

Placing a spreadsheet in a Word document *312*
Updating imported spreadsheets *313*
Formatting imported tables *313*
Linking a document *314*
Summary *315*

APPENDICES

A. Macro keystrokes 317

B. Editing commands 321

C. Useful DOS commands 329

D. Starting Word 333

E. The mouse 335

F. Network notes 339

Index 341

Acknowledgments

My thanks to:

Kathleen, Jennifer, and Steven, the family that holds me together.

Star Micronics for the use of a Laserprinter 8, which produced many of the illustrations in this book. It proved to be a fast, reliable laser printer for which I was most grateful.

Bill Gladstone, superagent.

Robert Bixby

Introduction

Microsoft Word is an extremely powerful and flexible word processor which runs on the IBM PC, PC-XT, PC-AT, PS/2 models, and true IBM compatible machines. A word processor, at first glance, seems similar to a typewriter. Both word processors and typewriters are used to write letters, memos, papers, and other documents. Furthermore, both machines utilize a keyboard to enter text.

The surface similarities between typewriters and word processors end there. A typewriter records information on sheets of paper, while a word processor records information in the memory of a computer. From this subtle difference evolves all the advantages of word processors.

Typewriters and word processors

If typewriters and word processors are similar, why buy a word processor? Typewriters are generally less expensive and better suited for typing short documents. A good word processing system requires an expensive computer and costly word processing software. A complete system can cost nearly three thousand dollars, substantially more than an IBM Selectric with a backspace erase key.

Not only are typewriters relatively cheap, they are also faster at short jobs like writing memos, filling forms, and typing addresses. Loading and running a word processing program takes time. The overhead required to start the computer, run the word processor, load the printer, and eventually print out the document makes a word processor impractical for small typing jobs.

So, what are the advantages of a word processor? Because word processors store information in an electronic memory, you can edit your writing with incredible ease. With a word processor, you can dump the correction fluid, forget about the half-space key, and put away your pencil and ruler. Instead of leaving drops of white-out all over a document, you can cleanly remove any typographical errors from memory. The computer automatically fills in the space with new text.

Similarly, you no longer need to retype a document to make space to insert text. Instead, you can simply type in the new text wherever you wish. The computer then automatically makes room for the incoming text. Word processors copy, move, format, and replace text at the push of a few keys. After the document has been edited, it can be printed with a printer.

Word processors are also able to do far more complicated things, like formatting text, checking spelling, and creating tables of contents and indexes. Word processors are much better than typewriters at writing anything but short documents.

Furthermore, technical breakthroughs and assembly-line production have significantly lowered the price of personal computers and increased their speed and storage capabilities. It's now possible to buy a powerful word processing system for under three thousand dollars. You can have in your home a word processor with features and capabilities which, just a few years ago, were found only in expensive dedicated word processors owned by Fortune 500 companies and firms.

Special features of word

About three years ago, most personal computers had 64K or less of memory and one single-sided disk drive. Word processors were constrained by the limited memory, slow speed, and small disk storage of these computers. Word processors designed for these personal computers were often complex and difficult to learn.

As personal computers became more powerful, word processors were designed to exploit the increased memory and storage abilities. A new generation of word processors was designed to provide powerful functions and common-sense commands. Chief among this new breed of word processors is Microsoft Word. If you know how to use a typewriter, you can quickly learn how to use Word.

Word is a state-of-the-art word processor. It has many features previously found only on dedicated word processors costing $6000 or more. One such feature is on-screen formatting.

In Word, paragraph and page formats, such as indentions and line spacing, are displayed exactly as they will appear in the printed copy. Furthermore, Word does not use embedded control characters to indicate character formats. Word displays character formats such as boldface, italics, and underlining exactly as they would appear in print.

Word offers a merge facility. The merge facility simplifies the development and printing of form letters. The Word merge option can be used in conjunction with dBASE, Lotus 1-2-3, and other popular software packages to add an additional dimension to your documents.

Word features a spelling checker and an electronic tutorial. The tutorial can introduce you to the Word program and teach you basic word processing skills. The spelling checker can read a document and find the misspelled words in it, as well as questionable punctuation.

Word is designed to work with an electronic mouse. A *mouse* is a small, hand-held computer-input device. There has been much research into the ergonomics of electronic mice. Reports state that mice make it easier for people to operate a computer system. Many writers agree that though writing itself is not aided by the mouse, it can be invaluable in the editing process.

Word also has commands that control style sheets, windows, direct printing, footnoting commands, different character sizes, running heads, gutter widths, orphaned lines, and much more. Word also utilizes the function keys to select words, sentences, lines, paragraphs, and groups of paragraphs. Once these units are selected, they can be formatted, deleted, or copied quickly.

Philosophy and organization of the book

This book was written to provide users of Word with a comprehensive tutorial. The Word manual offers a detailed reference guide for all of Word's features. It provides technical details on all Word commands, but the manual does not teach the user how to use Word. Just as you would not try to learn English by reading *Webster's Unabridged Dictionary of the English Language*, you should not try to learn Word from the manual.

This book has been divided into four parts. The first part introduces you to Word and helps you install Word on your computer system. The first part also covers formatting blank disks, making backup copies of files, and installing the mouse; in short, the first section tells you everything you need to know to run Word.

The second part of the book provides a crash course in word processing with Word. All the fundamental word processing functions are covered, including creating, editing, saving, and printing documents. If you are familiar with word processors, you might wish to skim these sections. The point of the crash course is to teach you everything you need in order to start using Word to write letters, reports, and other short documents. Once you have finished the crash course, you can learn about the more powerful features of Word at your leisure.

The third part of this book covers some more advanced features of Word. Topics such as formatting paragraphs, characters, and divisions are covered. This part also explores moving blocks and the search and replace commands to help you gain an intermediate understanding of Word's various options.

The fourth and final part of this book examines advanced topics such as window operations, setting options, adding footnotes, designing running heads, constructing style sheets, and page layout. Unless you write a very broad range of material, you probably do not need to read this part of the book. Consult these topics only when you need or desire to employ these advanced functions.

Notation

Certain conventions are used in this book to mark information displayed on the screen and data you should enter at the keyboard. Although you need not memorize all the conventions at this point, you can refer back to this section as you read the book.

Keys on the keyboard are shown with the first letter capitalized such as Del and Return. When two or more keys are to be pressed simultaneously, a dash (−) is employed to connect the two keys. For example, pressing the Ctrl and Return keys together is expressed as Ctrl−Return.

When a key is to be pressed with a certain toggle key active, a plus sign (+) joins the two keys. For example, hitting the Home key with the Num Lock toggle switched on is shown as Num Lock+Home.

Any prompts from Word or material for you to type in are expressed in another font such as Edit document or press Esc to use menu or type Esc, P, O (Esc would be a key you would press rather than typing the letters). Any text that you should type something else for is set in italics, such as COPY A:*FILENAME* B: where you would fill in the appropriate file name.

CHAPTER 1

Word system requirements

Software is machine-specific. Word only runs on a certain kind of computer. You should therefore verify that your system contains the proper components to run Word. If your system lacks some of these essential components, you must upgrade your system or obtain the necessary components from your local computer dealer.

Even if your computer meets Word's minimum requirements, you might wish to purchase additional equipment. This equipment can increase your productivity. For instance, obtaining a hard disk drive would allow Word to load and save files faster than is possible with a floppy disk.

CPU requirements

Word is a powerful software package and needs to run on a powrful computer. Word will run on an IBM Personal Computer (PC), IBM PC-XT, IBM PC-AT, PS/2, or any 100 percent compatible. The computer should have at least 384K. In addition, one double-sided floppy disk drive is needed.

Many IBM-compatible computers will run Word. You should, however, check with a dealer to see whether Word is compatible with your non-IBM computer before purchasing the Word package. Most computer dealers will not give refunds on software purchases.

Monitor requirements

Word demands at minimum an 80-column monochrome monitor. There are two kinds of monochrome video cards: text-only and Hercules-compatible. They use almost identical methods of putting information on the screen, but the Hercules-compatible video card is capable of displaying monochrome graphics as well as text. The text-only card can only display text. Word will function with either of these cards, though such graphics features as page preview will be impossible with a text-only monitor.

The text-only card can produce boldface and underlined characters but cannot display any other special character formats (such as italic, small caps, strikethrough, double underline, superscript, and subscript).

Other cards and monitors supported by Word's programmers include CGA, EGA, VGA, 8514A adapter and 8514 monitor, Hercules Plus, InColor, HP Vectra, AT&T 6300, Genius adapter and full-page monitor, and any built-in adapter and monitor on an IBM system.

Additional requirements

In addition to Microsoft Word, you will need the IBM PC Disk Operating System (also called PC-DOS, Microsoft DOS, and MS-DOS) or the new operating system recently developed by Microsoft, OS/2. PC-DOS and OS/2 will be referred to collectively as *the operating system*. The operating system is normally sold with the computer system. There are a number of different versions of DOS. Word versions 1.15 through 5.0 will run under DOS versions 2.0 or later.

Before installing Word, you should have at least 14 blank disks available: 13 for backup copies of the Word disks and 1 for storing your documents.

Printer requirements

A computer system need not include a printer in order to run Word. A printer is only necessary to produce printed copies (called *hard copies*) in the industry) of your work. Word supports a number of printers, including the most popular ones.

The list of printers is not complete, because many printers use similar control codes.

Dot matrix, letter quality, and non-impact printers

The three main types of printers available for use with Microsoft Word are dot matrix printers, letter quality (also known as daisy wheel) printers, and non-impact printers.

A dot matrix printer uses an array of dots to create letters. Different printers use different size arrays. The larger the array, the better the quality of the printed character. A 9 × 11 array, for example is better than a 7 × 9 array. New 24-pin printers provide printouts that rival the letter quality printers.

A letter quality printer produces letters just like a typewriter (in fact, some letter quality printers are nothing more than modified typewriters). A printing element produces the characters. The printing element is often a wheel with spokes that some people think resemble petals on a flower, hence the name "daisy wheel printer."

Dot matrix printers are generally much faster, less expensive, and more flexible than letter quality printers. Dot matrix printers can also produce underlines, boldface characters, double underlines, subscripts, superscripts, italics, small caps, and a plethora of font types. A letter quality printer can produce different fonts, but only by manually changing the printing element. Changing the printing element several times while printing a document can be time-consuming and result in ink smudges on your document.

In addition, dot matrix printers can also produce graphs, charts, and pictures, while letter quality printers are limited to the characters on the printing element. Dot matrix printers are considerably cheaper than letter quality printers. The only redeeming feature of letter quality printers is that they produce crisp, clear characters.

Non-impact printers such as laser printers have brought together the speed of the photocopier with the flexibility of the dot matrix printer. Virtually silent and troublefree, producing near-typeset-quality print, laser printers have changed the way professional offices do their work. Laser printers are much faster than dot matrix printers and can provide sharp graphics without the jagged lines that dot matrix printers produce on curves and obliques. Laser printers can provide text as clean as that produced by a letter quality printer, but they change fonts automatically in response to codes sent by the computer.

The laser printer's work is performed by the *print engine*. Though laser printers in one form or another date from the late 1970s, the first affordable print engine appeared in the early 1980s. Thus the door was opened for laser printing. The print engine consists primarily of a laser beam and a drum (some printer drums are actually belts). The drum is coated with a compound that is ionized by light. The drum is scanned by the laser, which charges the scanned area with an electrical potential.

The drum is exposed to a fine powder called *toner* which clings to the scanned, charged areas of the drum. Electrically charged paper passes by the drum. The paper is more highly charged than the drum, so the toner is transferred to the paper electrostatically. The paper is heated until the toner melts, which binds the toner to the paper. The drum is then scraped clean and its residual charge is led away by tiny wires. After this process, the drum is ready to be scanned by the laser to create the next page.

The other type of non-impact printer is the ink jet printer. This creates a printout by spraying tiny, strategically aimed droplets of ink at the paper. These printers are fast, silent, and produce printouts as fine as those of laser printers. Unfortunately, they create their printout with water soluble ink, so the final product is prone to smear and smudge, particularly when wet.

To print or not to print

Because a computer does not need a printer to run Word, several computers can share a single printer. Documents can be created on one computer and printed on a second computer connected to a printer. This can be accomplished over a network through the use of a *black box* switch, or through "sneaker net" (saving the document to a disk, which is then carried to the computer with the printer).

Some printers can be very expensive. A laser printer can cost thousands of dollars, but the price is coming down. Hewlett-Packard has released a slow laser printer for personal use to be priced close to $1000. The NEC 3550 retails for about $1500, and even a machine as advanced as the Star Micronics Laserprinter B can be purchased for a little over $2000. Considering that a complete IBM PC system can be purchased for about $2000, a printer can represent a sizable investment. However, an expensive printer can actually be a low-cost way to project a quality image to your customers and clients. Many times, the only contact a customer has with a firm is through reports and letters. If the printing on these documents is first-rate, the customer will tend to put more trust in the company that produces them.

It makes sense for computer systems to share expensive printers. Printers are frequently used during word processing, but the majority of a word processor's time is spent composing pages, not printing them. If you are considering the purchase of a number of computers for your office, consider buying one good letter quality or laser printer as well. This printer might be shared by the entire office. You might also purchase inexpensive dot matrix printers for each computer, for printing rough drafts.

With this system, a worker would compose and edit a document on his or her computer. Once the work is in its final form, it can be printed on the letter quality printer. This combination not only saves money, but also time. The office will benefit in two ways: from the speed and flexibility of a dot matrix printer in producing rough drafts, and from a letter quality or laser printer's attractive and professional-looking output.

Optional equipment

There are a number of optional pieces of equipment you might want for your system. These pieces of equipment, although not required by Word, can increase your productivity. Moreover, some of the equipment is required by other programs and will undoubtedly be of much use. This optional equipment includes a mouse, a second disk drive, and extra RAM.

The mouse

Word can be controlled with an electronic mouse (so called because the unit's shape faintly resembles a mouse). Mice are sold by Microsoft, Logitech, and a number of other companies. The Microsoft mouse can be purchased separately or along with Word.

If you are hesitant about buying a mouse, remember that it also works with other popular software packages. The mouse works with Lotus 1-2-3, WordStar, and MultiPlan, and Windows applications. Some programs, however, were not originally designed to work with a mouse, so they do not offer as many mouse-operated features as Microsoft Word. The mouse is helpful if you are a poor typist, but the keyboard is still faster than the mouse at running these programs. For this reason, many writers agree that while a mouse is not very useful as you are entering text, it becomes invaluable at editing time.

The mouse comes with a special utility that enables you to create customized menus for other programs. This facility is useful if you like to tinker with computers. It can also be a boon to computer consultants who want to create special mouse-run programs. If they are willing to spend a few minutes learning to use it, this facility can make itself useful to any mouse user. Microsoft has also provided facilities that incorporate mouse functions in BASIC, Pascal, COBOL, Fortran, and assembly language programs.

The mouse is by no means required to run Word. In fact, as you become more adept with Word, you will tend to use the mouse less and the keyboard more. The keyboard can perform just about every function faster than the mouse. Some people just find the mouse friendlier and more logical.

Two disk drives are better than one

Not so long ago, when personal computers were still a novelty and Apple was king, most people had just one disk drive. Because these early pioneers could only afford one disk drive, word processing programs were designed to operate with just one drive. Limited memory and disk storage imposed draconian restrictions on word processing programs. Consequently, they were very simple and lacked many features, such as on-screen formatting, which we now take for granted.

In those dark days, computer equipment was very costly. Over the years, computer equipment has become more reliable, powerful, and less expensive. Owning two disk drives is no longer a luxury. Microsoft Word will work with a single disk drive, although it works much better with two.

When you work with just one disk drive, you must use the Word program disk for data storage. As a result, data files will quickly fill the program disk. To prevent the program disk from being filled, you must frequently transfer data files from the program disk to a data disk.

Transferring files from one disk to a second disk is cumbersome with one disk drive. To transfer a file, you must frequently swap disks, a time-consuming and frustrating procedure. Moreover, sometimes the mindless swapping of disks leads to errors in copying, causing data to be lost.

Because a second disk drive can be purchased fairly cheaply, you should seriously consider buying one (you might have to hire someone to install the drive if you are not facile with computers). The second disk drive will save you much aggravation in the long run and can be useful with other programs such as 1-2-3 and dBASE.

Random access memory

Word requires a minimum of 384K of RAM. A PC with limited RAM is also severely limited in its usefulness. Furthermore, with additional RAM, you can create RAM drives and printer spoolers that will speed up your computer and make it more versatile.

RAM is available in individual chips for fully populating motherboards, and is also available on add-on boards as EMS memory. Word itself doesn't require expanded memory, but as a general principle, future expansions of programs are putting outward pressure on the 640K limits of most PCs. If you are not now considering increasing your memory capacity, you should be. A few software products like Turbo EMS are also coming available that simulate expanded memory through intelligent use of floppy or hard disk storage. If you find yourself in a RAM crunch, you should consider this software as a stop-gap until additional RAM can be obtained.

Summary

Word runs on IBM PC, IBM PC-XT, IBM PC-AT, and PS/2 computers. You will need an 80-column monitor and at least 384K of available RAM to run Word 5.0. You should consider such optional equipment as printers, extra RAM, a mouse, and a second disk drive in order to get the most out of Word.

CHAPTER 2

The keyboard and loading the operating system

Prior to using Word, in fact prior to using any program, the operating system (DOS or OS/2) must be loaded into the computer. The operating system controls the transfer of information to and from the disk drives. Thus, DOS tells the computer where to find Word on the disk, how the Word program is stored on the disk, and how to load the Word program into memory.

Prior to loading the operating system, you must be familiar with the IBM keyboard. The keyboard is your chief means of sending commands to the computer. Although it is unnecessary to memorize all the keys at this point, it is a good idea to familiarize yourself with the keys.

The IBM keyboard

If you are new to your PC or PS/2, you must familiarize yourself with your keyboard. You communicate commands and data to your computer through the keyboard. You should be familiar with the keyboard before starting the operating system or Word.

This book is written primarily with the PC in mind. If you are using a PS/2 machine or a compatible, it's possible that your keyboard will vary somewhat from the description here. To cover more than one keyboard would require endless lists of exceptions. Generally, the keyboards (even the Tandy) contain approximately the same keys.

The IBM PC keyboard can be divided into three sections: the numeric keypad, the function keys, and the main keyboard. The main keyboard resembles a typewriter keyboard, containing letters, numbers, and symbols. The numeric keypad lies on the right of the keyboard and is used to move the cursor and enter numbers. The function keys lie to the left of the main keyboard or along the top. They are used for cursor movement and editing.

The main keyboard

On the IBM PC keyboard, the Shift keys are in positions familiar to typists, although on some (particularly on the original PC keyboard), the keys are somewhat smaller. This discrepancy was cleared up by the time the XT and AT computers appeared, so your keyboard will probably have normal-sized Shift keys.

Two other keys, the Alt and Ctrl keys, function in a manner similar to the shift keys. Alt stands for *alternate*. Ctrl stands for *control*. These keys are used to modify the action of other keys when they are pressed in combination. The control and alternate keys are either located above and below the left Shift key, respectively, or they are next to the spacebar.

Because Shift, Ctrl, and Alt keys are used in combination with other keys, their use will be indicated by a dash (-) in this book. Using this format, described earlier in the introduction, holding down the Ctrl key while hitting H is shown as Ctrl-H.

By employing the Shift, Alt, and Ctrl keys singly or in combination, programmers multiply the kinds of information you can provide through the keyboard to the computer. In Word, for example, pressing H, Shift-H, Ctrl-H, or Alt-H results in vastly different effects. You will come across their use later in the book.

The Esc key is located in the top left corner of the keyboard. The Esc key cancels the execution of certain commands in Word. For example, it can be used to terminate the execution of the Transfer Load commands.

Another important key is the Tab key. The Tab key is in the upper left corner of the keyboard. On the face of the key are two arrows: one pointing left and one pointing right. Pressing the Tab key produces a tab.

The Tab key has two roles. If you are entering text, Tab operates like a typewriter Tab key, moving your cursor to the next tab stop. If you are navigating the menus, the Tab key moves the selection from option to option within the menu. For example, if you are in the Print Options Menu, pushing the Tab key moves you to the next option. Pressing Shift-Tab moves you to the previous option.

The Return key (also called the Enter key) is located on the right side of the keyboard, where the carriage return of a typewriter would be. There is often a bent arrow on the face of the key itself, or it might be embossed with the word *Return* or *Enter*. In the operating system, the Return key is used to enter data into the computer.

In Word, the Return key has two functions. If you are typing in text, tapping Return marks the end of the old paragraph and the beginning of a new paragraph. If you are in one of the selection menus offered by Word, hitting Return sets the options as they stand and returns you to the parent menu or to editing the document.

The Backspace key is located in the upper right of the keyboard, right above the Return key. The Backspace key erases the character to the left of the cursor. The Backspace can be used in both Word and the operating system.

The function keys

On the far left of the keyboard lie 10 function keys, five each in two columns numbered from top to bottom (some newer keyboards feature 12 function keys arrayed in a single row along the top of the keyboard, numbered left to right). The function keys select text for editing, move the cursor, perform editing, switch between insert and overtype modes, and select the active window. If you have not already done so, attach the appropriate keyboard template to the function keys on your keyboard. The templates are included with Word and will help decipher the roles of the function keys.

Toggle keys

Finally, a group of keys are known as the *toggle keys*. Toggle keys are switched on when first pressed and are switched off when pressed again. Most keyboards feature indicator lights to show what the condition of the toggle keys are. The toggle keys include the Caps Lock key, the Num Lock key, and the Scroll Lock key. The F5 (Overwrite) key is also a toggle key, but only within Word, so of course there is no F5 indicator light.

The Caps Lock key, which locks letters in uppercase, is located in the lower right corner of the keyboard. To activate it, press it once. To deactivate it, press it a second time.

The Caps Lock key only affects the letter keys. For example, to type a dollar sign ($), you must depress one of the Shift keys in combination with the 4 key, whether or not the Caps Lock key is activated. Also note that, if Caps Lock is on and the Shift key is pressed, the letter keys type lowercase letters.

The numeric keypad

A set of keys called the *numeric keypad* is located on the right of the keyboard. The numeric keypad has a dual role: Numbers can be entered, or the cursor can be moved with the keys in the numeric keypad.

The Num Lock key toggles the function of the numeric keypad. Normally the numeric keypad is used for cursor movement. By pressing Num Lock, the keypad can be used for numeric entries. By pressing the Num Lock key a second time, the keys can be used for cursor movement again. The top row of keys on the keyboard can also be used to enter numbers. Thus, the numeric keypad is only used to enter large amounts of numeric data.

The Scroll Lock key has an interesting effect. When it is turned on, it allows you to scroll the screen with the cursor keys rather than moving the cursor. That makes it easier to work with texts wider than the screen can show. To look at areas off-screen, press Scroll Lock and then use the numeric keypad the scroll to the hidden area.

Care and handling of disks

Despite their rigid appearance, floppy disks are extremely susceptible to damage. Because one floppy disk might contain months of work, it is especially prudent to protect your disks.

Never expose disks to dust, because dust particles can reduce the life span of a disk. Floppies should be kept in their protective envelopes to protect the disk surface from flying dust.

A floppy disk is encased in a stiff vinyl jacket. There is an oval hole through which the disk surface may be seen. Never touch the disk surface. Hold the disks by the vinyl jacket.

Finally, do not expose the disk to temperature extremes, magnetic fields, or physical abuse. The office environment is hostile to computer disks. Coffee spills, intense sunlight, uninformed coworkers, and simple carelessness all mean death to your precious data.

Your copy of Word might have arrived on smaller 3½ inch microdiskettes. These disks are even more rigid that the older 5¼ inch disks, but they are just as susceptible to coffee spills, and, if their little sliding door is open, can easily be ruined by a finger print or a loose, magnetized paperclip. Always keep the microdiskette door shut.

Write protection

Floppy disks of the 5¼ inch variety are notched on one side. This is the *write-protect* notch. If the notch is covered, the disk cannot be "written to" by your disk drive (when your computer stores information on the disk, it is said to be "writing to" the diskette). The smaller microdiskettes have a tiny slider that write protects them. Confusingly, the write protection is on when the hole is open in the corner of the microdiskette. The write-protect tab does not protect the disk from physical abuse.

Not every disk requires a write-protect tab. The Word program disk should not have a write-protect tab, nor should disks frequently used for data storage. These disks might not possess write-protect tabs because you need to create and edit documents on them.

Loading the operating system

Before you run Word, in fact before you use the disk drives at all, you must load the operating system. The operating system controls the disk drives and manages the exchange of information between the CPU and the disk drives. Without an operating system, the disk drives would be useless, and you would have no way to store data.

Before proceeding, make sure the computer is turned off. If you boot from a floppy, follow the directions under the section "Running DOS with a floppy disk drive." If you have a hard disk drive, you might follow the directions under "Starting the operating system with a hard drive."

Running DOS with a floppy disk drive

To run DOS from a floppy disk drive (booting OS/2 from a floppy is only possible if you make special preparations; therefore this section is devoted to PC-DOS), take the DOS (Disk Operating System) disk out of its protective jacket. You will see an oval slot and a label on the disk. Look at drive A. Drive A is the left disk drive if the two disk drives are arranged horizontally, or the top disk drive if the two disk drives are arranged vertically. If the *latch* (the disk drive door) to disk drive A is closed, either turn the latch counter-clockwise or lift it up, depending on the drive design. Gently insert the disk into the open disk drive, with the slot entering the drive first and the label turned upwards. Push the disk gently in until you feel resistance, then close the disk drive door.

If the computer is off, turn on the system unit and then the peripherals such as printers. When you do so, the computer will warm up and run a self-diagnostic test. If the checkup indicates any internal maladies, a numeric error code will appear on the screen.

If no error appears, the computer is probably in good health and the disk drive light will go on, indicating that the disk drive is in use. Never remove or seat a disk in the disk drive while the drive is in use. This can destroy information on the disk, and could cause physical harm to the disk itself.

When you activate the computer, the DOS disk or a disk with the DOS files should be in drive A. After the self-diagnostic test, the computer will transfer the DOS files from the disk into RAM. This process is called *booting up* the computer, because the computer is pulling itself up by its own bootstraps.

Starting the operating system with a hard drive

Hard disks have two advantages: They are about six times as fast as floppy disks (some are even faster), and they can store much more data than a floppy disk. A 30 megabyte hard drive can store as much information as 80 double-sided floppies. Because a hard disk can store so much information, it eliminates disk-swapping.

12   *The keyboard and loading the operating system*

If your hard disk has been installed properly, you should be able to load the operating system directly from your hard disk. To load the operating system from a correctly installed hard disk, open the drive door of disk drive A. Next turn on the power to your computer.

After the IBM completes a self-diagnostic test, the A floppy disk drive will whir into motion. Upon finding the drive door open, the computer will search the hard disk for the operating system files. The boot files must be in the opening directory. If they are, the operating system will be loaded.

Entering the date and time

Now that the operating system has been loaded into the computer, the computer is active. Some older PCs will prompt you for the date and time. The date and time are used to date files altered or created. You should always enter the correct date and time because they help organize your files.

The date

Once the operating system has been successfully loaded, some older PCs request the date:

Current date is Tue 1-01-1980

Enter new date: _

When entering the date, the month, day, and year are entered as numbers. Each number is separated by dashes (the dash key is to the right of the zero key). For example, if today were August 17, 1990, the date would be entered as 8-17-90. If the date were December 3, 1991, then you would enter 12-3-91

Let's assume the date is November 9, 1990. To enter the date, type 11-9-90. If you make a mistake while entering the date, use the Backspace key to erase the entry and then reenter the date. Once the date is correct, press the Return key. The computer will display:

Current date is Tue 1-01-1980

Enter new date 11-19-84

Current time is 0:01:32.81

Enter new time: _

Sometimes you might press Return before you realize that you have typed in the incorrect date. If the date has the incorrect format, such as 10:5:91, the operating system will inform you of your error. Likewise, if you enter an impossible date, such as 13-5-90, DOS will again inform you. After you have been told that you've made a mistake, the operating system will prompt you to enter the date again, at which point you can reenter the date. Another option is to press Return, which allows you to skip updating the computer's calendar, but dating files is important, so you should persist until the date displayed is correct.

It is also possible that you will enter a valid date which is the incorrect date. For example, if today were September 17, 1990 and you entered 7-17-80, you would have a problem. In such cases, you must wait until you have entered the time and the DOS prompt appears (see below). After the DOS prompt appears, enter DATE and hit Return, and DOS will request the correct date.

The time

After setting the date, DOS will request the time of day. All the time that the computer is running, it counts hours, minutes, seconds, and hundredths of seconds. For practical purposes, it is only necessary to enter the hours and minutes. The hours and minutes are separated by a colon.

If you enter an invalid time, such as 25:11 or 13/23, DOS will prompt you for a correct time. In such scenarios, simply reenter a valid time.

Occasionally, you enter a valid time that is factually inaccurate. For example, it might be 2:09 PM, and you entered 12:09. To correct this, simply type time, then Return after the A > prompt. DOS will ask again for the time, at which point you can reenter the time.

Most modern PCs are shipped with built-in clock/calendars. The clock/calendar is an option on multifunction cards that eliminates the need to enter the date and time. The clock/calendar automatically keeps track of the date and time when the computer is off. Thus, the date and time are set electronically when the computer is booted.

If you have a PC that lacks this feature, you will probably want to purchase a multifunction card. Make sure to order a clock/calendar option.

Making and maintaining backups

Even if you pamper your floppy disks, a disaster could still befall your disks. A single unexpected accident can result in the loss of hours upon hours of hard work. A disk might be lost in an obscure corner of your filing cabinet, your dog might decide to gnaw on your disk collection, or someone might accidentally erase important files from your disk.

Accidents happen to everyone. You must make backups of active files at regular intervals. These copies should be recorded and stored in a safe place. There are two types of backups. The first is to copy the file on the disk so that two copies of the file exist on the disk. The second is to copy the entire disk onto another disk. The two disks are then separated and one maintained as an backup copy.

How frequently you backup your work depends on how much work you do. If you use Word only a few times each week, it does not make much sense to backup your files more than once a week. If you use Word eight hours each day, then it would make sense to make backups several times a day. Furthermore, it is not necessary to backup all your files, but only the files that have been modified. A good rule of thumb is to backup all altered data files after every two hours of work.

You should also make backups of all the Word disks. The XCOPY, COPY, and DISKCOPY commands are used to backup files and disks. These commands, and other useful operating system commands are explored in Appendix C. Although you do not have to know the operating system commands to use Word, the commands will help you organize your files on floppy disks.

Summary

After reading this chapter, you should know how to:
- Find the important keys on the IBM keyboard.
- Handle and maintain floppy disks.
- Load the operating system.

CHAPTER 3

Installing Word

For those uninitiated to the world of computers, there are a number of steps one must follow before using a software package. Many software packages, including Word, require you to install or configure the package for different computer systems. This process tailors Word to the specific components of your system.

Before installing Word, you must make copies of all the disks. These copies are called *backups* and should always be used in place of the originals. That way, if a disk fails due to overuse, it will be a relatively valueless copy rather than an original.

When you copy the Word disks, keep the copies in a safe place nearby, on a high shelf in a bedroom closet, for instance. Take great pains to protect the originals. If you use Word at home, keep the originals at work; if you use Word at work, keep the originals in a safe or safe deposit box. Under no circumstances should the originals and the backups be under the same roof, and probably not in the same part of town. Word is just too valuable, expensive, and difficult to replace to take any chances with its safety. You should treat the original disks with at least as much care as you would take with an heirloom or a piece of expensive jewelry.

In addition to the 12 disks necessary to copy the Word disks, several data disks should be prepared for use with Word. A thorough understanding of the operating system is required to perform these tasks. Only after these initial preparations can you begin to run Word.

With Word, you also have to install the mouse. Depending on the mouse design, you might have to open up the PC and place the mouse interface card in a slot. Some mice operate through the serial port. With either type of mouse, you will then have to plug in the mouse and install the mouse drivers. This chapter guides you through the installation procedures.

Installing Word version 5.0

Installing Word 5.0 is easy because the manufacturer has provided a setup program that takes care of the most difficult parts of installation. To begin the installation, find the Word disks. Use DISKCOPY to copy the contents of each disk onto a backup. If you have one drive, type DISKCOPY A: A: and press Return and the computer will prompt you to insert the SOURCE disk. The SOURCE disk is the original. Insert the disk and press Return.

After a minute or two, the operating system will prompt you to insert the TARGET disk. The TARGET disk is the backup. Insert the backup and press Return. You might have to swap the disks once or several times depending on several factors, but in any case, when the copy is finished, you will be asked if you want to make more copies. Type Y and press Return and the process will start over again.

Copy the rest of the disks the same way. If you have two floppy disk drives, you won't have to swap the disks at all until the copy is completed. Simply enter DISKCOPY A: B: and press Return and the computer will prompt you to place the SOURCE (original) disk in drive A and the TARGET (backup) in drive B. Press Return, and the copy will be performed for you. Don't get the SOURCE and TARGET disks mixed up, or you will destroy a valuable original disk. You might want to put tape over the write-protect notch in the originals to prevent this kind of accident.

As you make your backups, copy the disk name of the original on the label of the backup. Note that the disk name describes the kinds of files to be found on the disk. This is important.

Before you begin installation, you must be sure you know what kind of printer you are using and to what port it is connected. You must know what kind of computer you are using, as well as the video card and monitor you are using.

If your computer does not have a hard disk, you will find yourself changing disks frequently as you use Word. Hard disks are so inexpensive now that anyone using a PC should seriously consider purchasing one. Of course, operating OS/2 is impossible without a hard disk.

If you are operating a DOS system with floppy drives, you can eliminate a few headaches by placing the DOS boot files on a work disk along with the Word program files. This will enable you to load DOS from the Word Programs Disk and then run Word with no disk swapping. The DOS SYS command will be used to transfer the DOS boot files to the Word Programs Disk.

OS/2 can be booted from a floppy disk, if you know how to do it, but because it requires a hard disk to operate and because it is assumed that a user with a hard disk will also want Word on the hard disk, the floppy installation refers entirely to installing the program under DOS.

Two-disk drive systems

Check that your DOS boot disk is in drive A. Place a blank disk in drive B. Either enter the FORMAT B: /S command or, if the disk is formatted but blank, use SYS B:. Either command will place the DOS boot files on the disk in drive B:. Type COPY A: COMMAND. COM B: and press Return. This copies the COMMAND. COM file from the disk in drive A, the DOS disk, to the disk in drive B. Once the transfer has been completed, you will be informed by a message on the screen.

One-disk drive systems

If your computer has only one disk drive, you must follow a slightly different procedure to transfer the DOS boot files. Find the Word Programs Disk and set it aside. You must have a third disk on hand a formatted but blank work disk to use with Word, called the Word work disk. First, check that the DOS disk is in the disk drive.

1. Type SYS B: and press Return.
2. Remove the DOS disk and insert the Word work disk into the disk drive. Press the Return key.
3. Remove the Word work disk and insert the DOS disk into the disk drive.
4. Type COPY A:COMMAND.COM B: and press Return. Wait a few seconds, then follow the directions on the screen.

The files you have copied onto the Word disk will allow you to load DOS and run Word with just the Word disk. You can also copy other useful DOS files, such as the FORMAT.COM command, onto your Word work disk. However, for now it is better to reserve the disk space for temporary files you will use later in editing documents.

Once the DOS files are transferred, you can copy the Word program onto the Word work disk.

Installing Word for a hard disk

If you have a hard disk, you can transfer the Word files to the hard disk. This eliminates sifting through stacks of floppy disks trying to find the correct floppy disk to perform a given task. Before installing Word, the hard disk must have a capacity of at least 1.5 megabytes. The hard disk must also be compatible with DOS 2.0. To install Word:

1. Place the Word Utilities 1 disk in drive A.
2. Type A:INSTALL and press Return.
3. Follow the directions on the screen.

Formatting blank disks

If you have been following directions up to this point, you might have already formatted a disk. Formatting a disk prepares it for data storage. The computer cannot store or retrieve information from an unformatted disk. The data stored can be programs, such as Word or operating system files, or it can be data files, such as documents created by Word.

A formatted disk is a little like a phonograph record. On a record, the sound vibrations are stored in spiral grooves. When the phonograph needle plays the record (reads data from the record), it follows these grooves. If the sound vibrations were not stored in grooves but were scattered randomly across the record, it would be impossible to play the record.

Similarly, the data on a formatted disk is arranged in concentric circles. Data is stored in these circles, which are called *tracks*. Before using a disk, the disk must be formatted. Formatting a disk destroys all the information stored on a disk. Thus, you must be careful not to format any disks that contain important information.

The DOS FORMAT command is used to format disks. Disks that have been formatted can be reformatted at any time. To format a disk with a floppy-drive system, place the DOS system disk in drive A. Type FORMAT B: and press Return. If you have two floppy disk drives, place the blank disk in drive B and hit the Return key. If you have just one floppy drive, remove the DOS disk and insert the blank disk and hit the Return key. When this disk is formatted, the computer will ask whether you wish to format another disk. Type N to indicate no.

If you have a hard disk, you can run the FORMAT command from the hard disk. Be careful not format the hard disk itself.

Installing printer drivers

If you follow the installation program run from the Utilities 1 disk, menu allows you to install Word and its speller and thesaurus as well as perform other installations. The next item on the installation menu is the installation of printer drivers. With the copying of the program files and the speller and thesaurus, the installation is nearly complete, but you will want to install a printer as well, if you intend to print documents with Word. The installation copies special files called *printer drivers*. Printer drivers contain control codes that govern the operation of different printers. Different printers require different control codes, hence you will find a multitude of different printer drivers.

The installation program presents you with a list of printers. If you don't see your printer, press the Page Down (or Pg Dn or your computer) key until you see the printer. If you go to the end of the list without seeing your printer, you might need the supplemental printer disk provided at a small charge by Microsoft, or your printer might be similar enough to another printer to use its driver. Consult the *Printer Information for Microsoft Word* book included with the package.

When you find the proper printer, type in its number and press Return. You will be asked to which port the printer is attached. Enter this number as well and press Return. You are then prompted to insert a disk that contains your printer driver. If you plan to use several different types of printers, you might transfer several different printer drivers to the Word Programs Disk. the printer drivers can be transferred at any time, so if you do not know what type of printer you will be using, you can install the printer drivers at a future date.

Installing the mouse

Perhaps the most difficult thing about a mouse is its installation procedure. The mouse manual tells you in great detail how to install the mouse. Use the directions in the manual to install the mouse interface board (if it is called for) and the mouse unit.

The installation program will install the mouse for you. Just select the mouse installation option from the installation menu.

Loading the mouse driver

Before the mouse can be used, the mouse driver must be loaded into the computer's memory. The mouse driver must be loaded into the memory each time the computer is turned on or reset. If you do not intend to use the mouse during a session with the computer, you do not have to load the mouse driver for that session.

The mouse driver only needs to be installed once during a session with the computer. If the mouse driver is installed more than once during a single session with the computer, the mouse device is not affected. However, the driver requires about 3K of RAM, so installing the driver more than once uses up a certain amount of memory. If you loaded large numbers of drivers, the situation could get out of hand.

Once the mouse driver has been copied to the hard disk or the Word work disk, loading the mouse driver is an easy procedure. To load the driver, place the Word work disk in disk drive A. Type A:MOUSE. If you are using a hard disk, you must change the directory path to the directory holding the mouse driver. Then type MOUSE.

If the mouse driver is loaded successfully, a message appears to let you know. If a message appears stating that the mouse hardware couldn't be found, the operation was unsuccessful. In such rare circumstances, you should check that the mouse is plugged into the mouse interface board. If the error persists, the mouse might have to be replaced. Check your warranty.

Modifying your Autoexecute and Configuration files

The last step in your installation is to select Quit from the installation menu. Before you are allowed to leave, you are given the option of altering two files that set up your computer's operation when it is started up. One of these is the AUTOEXEC.BAT file and the other is the CONFIG.SYS file (both of these files can have different names under OS/2).

Simply select the option that allows the alteration. The changes won't do your computer any harm, and they make Word run more efficiently. One of the things the installation program will do is add the subdirectory into which you placed the Word program in your path. The path is the list of subdirectories where the operating system looks for programs and commands. Having the Word subdirectory on the path makes it possible to type WORD at any subdirectory location and start the Word word processor.

Summary

Upon completing this chapter, you should be familiar with:

- Placing DOS on the Word work disk.
- Formatting blank disks for data storage and other uses.
- Installing printer drivers.
- Installing the mouse hardware.
- Transferring the mouse drivers to the Word work disk.

4
CHAPTER

Entering a document

This crash course teaches the basics of word processing: creating, editing, and saving/printing a document. With just these rudimentary operations, you will see that Word is far more powerful than an electric typewriter.

First, you will learn how to create a document with Word. To create a document you must know how to start the Word program. After Word is running, you can type in a document.

The keyboard

Before anyone learns how to use Word, he or she must be familiar with the IBM PC keyboard. Chapter 2 has a brief description covering all the special keys on the PC keyboard; if you have not had any experience with the computer keyboard, you should review it.

For the crash course, you must know the position of the Esc (escape or cancel), Backspace, Del (delete), Alt (alternate), and Return keys, as well as the positions of the function keys and the numeric keypad.

Running Word

Now that you have made it this far, running Word should be easy. The manner in which you run Word is determined by the computer system you are using to run Word. There are three basic computer systems: those with one floppy disk drive, those with two floppy disk drives, and those with a hard disk drive.

For one floppy disk drive systems, follow these steps:

1. Load DOS. If DOS is on the Word work disk, load DOS from the Word disk.
2. Insert the Word work disk in the disk drive.
3. Type WORD and hit Return.

For two floppy disk drive systems, follow these steps:

1. Load DOS. If DOS is on the Word work disk, load DOS from the work disk.
2. Insert the Word work disk in drive A.
3. Place a formatted disk in drive B. The formatted disk in drive B serves as a data disk. Document files, style sheets, and glossary archives are stored on the data disk.
4. Type WORD and press Return.

For hard disk drive systems, these steps will start Word.

1. Load the operating system from the hard disk. This probably happens automatically when you start the computer.
2. Type WORD and press Return.

The disk drive light shines for a few seconds, and then the Word Word opening screen (seen in Fig. 4-1) appears. This screen merely states that Word is copyrighted. The computer pauses, and the Word screen appears. A number of different parameters can be used to run Word. These variants are discussed in Appendix D.

```
                    Microsoft (R) Word
                      Version 5.0

          Copyright (C) Microsoft Corporation, 1983-1989
                    All Rights Reserved
        WordFinder Copyright (C) Microlytics, Inc., Selfware, Inc.
                1986-1989.  All Rights Reserved
          Spelling Checker Copyright (C) Soft-Art, 1987-1989
                    All Rights Reserved
```

4-1 The opening Microsoft Word screen.

The Word screen

What you see in Fig. 4-2 is the main menu. The main menu is a major menu containing commands that edit, print, and save documents on a disk. The main menu is also a way station towards the Gallery menu and the Library menu.

The Word screen is divided into two areas: the window area and the command area.

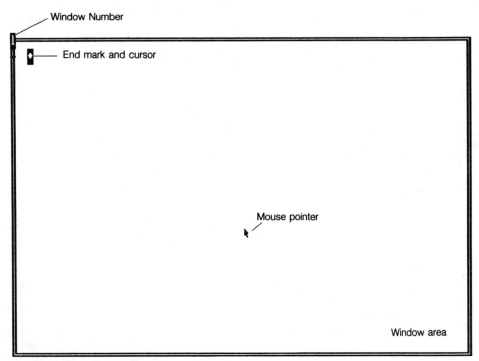

4-2 The important components of the Word screen.

The window

The *window* is the upper portion of the screen and is surrounded by a rectangular border. The window border shows the number of the window in the upper left corner. The window displays the document, style sheet, or glossary being edited. When the window is blank, nothing is loaded in the computer's memory for editing. The tiny mouse pointer in Fig. 4-2 is a solid rectangle if the program is run in text mode. The screen shown is in graphics mode. When the program is running, you can toggle between modes by pressing Alt-F9 or by using the display mode option on the Option menu.

The maximum dimensions for a window are 19 lines high by 77 characters wide. Chapter 13 explains how to divide the current window into a maximum of eight smaller windows by splitting the original window horizontally or vertically.

A new window only contains a cursor and the end marker. The cursor is the highlighted box in the upper left corner of the window. The end marker is a diamond-shaped character that marks the end of the document.

The cursor marks the point of activity within the window. Any new text is entered at the cursor's location. Any text deleted is deleted according to the cursor's position. When the cursor is at the end of the document, it occupies the same location as the end marker.

The command area

The bottom of the screen is the *command area* (Fig. 4-3). The command area consists of four lines. The top two lines form the command menu. The bottom two lines form the message line and the status line. The command menu lists commands that can be executed in Word.

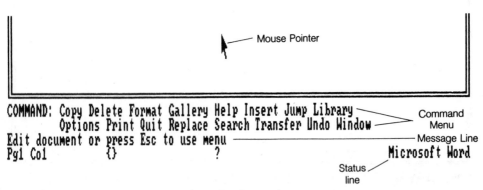

4-3 The command menu, message line, and status line are shown.

The message line   Word displays information for the user on the message line. During normal use, the message line acts as a prompt line. The message line tells you what Word expects you to enter next. It could be asking you to enter additional information, or it could be asking you to enter a command.

For instance, on the current screen the message line reads Edit document or press Esc to use menu. The message shows that Word is waiting for your next action.

If you commit an error, Word beeps and the message line informs you of your mistake. Due to the limited space on the message line, the messages tend to be cryptic. The Word manual supplies a short explanation of each message. However, you will rarely refer to the message line once you become accustomed to Word.

The status line   The *status line* is the third element of the command area. The status line posts the name of the document being edited, your position in the document, the condition of the toggle keys, and the remaining free memory. The extreme left of the status line displays the page number and division number of your position in the document (Fig. 4-4).

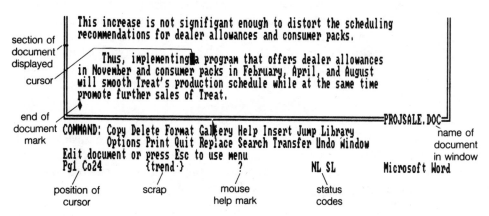

4-4 The status codes, document name, scrap, cursor position, end of document mark, cursor, and other informative items in the Word screen.

If you have more than one division in your document, the status line displays your page number in the format P _D _. The number after P is the page number, and the number after D is the division number. For example, P39 D2 means that you are viewing the thirty-ninth page of the document, which is in the second division. Knowing your position within a document can be helpful when editing long documents.

To the right of the page number are two braces ({}). The braces hold the contents of the *scrap*. The scrap is a place that stores text on a temporary basis. The contents of the scrap can be inserted anywhere in the document, thus facilitating editing. If there is too much text in scrap to be shown on the status line (more than a few characters), only the beginning and ending words of the contents are displayed.

The middle of the status line might contain a question mark (?). The question mark is not visible if the Microsoft Word help file is not available. The help file is called MW.HLP. If you click on the question mark with the mouse pointer, you will trigger the help function. To select help with the mouse, point to the question mark and click the left button.

The next segment of the status line displays the status of the toggle keys (if none of these keys is toggled on, there might be nothing in this area). Toggle keys were described earlier in Chapter 2. Each toggle key has a two-letter code that can be displayed on the status line. The codes for the various toggle keys are EX for Extend, NL for Number Lock, SL for Scroll Lock, CL for Caps Lock, and OT for F5 (overwrite).

Entering text

When you run Word, you are immediately placed in the type-in mode. When you are in the type-in mode, you can start entering text for a document. Thus, at this point, every letter key you press places a letter on your screen.

For your crash course in Word's abilities, you need to create a short document. As you type a document, press Return only where it is marked on the page. You should not press Return at end of each line. A special property called *word wrap* allows Word to start a new line automatically each time you cross the right margin. Only press Return at the end of a paragraph to start a new paragraph.

Word wrap

For practice, type the passage in Fig. 4-5. Do not worry if you make mistakes, just continue typing. Notice as words appear on the screen, the cursor moves to the right. Once the cursor passes the right margin, the word being entered and any succeeding words are pushed to the next line instead.

```
SPECIAL FEATURES OF WORD<Return>
<Return>
Word processors used to be very complex and difficult to
learn.  A new generation of word processors, however,
provides powerful functions without making them impossible
to use.  Chief among this brave new world of word processors
is Microsoft Word.  If you know how to use a typewriter, you
can quickly learn how to use Word.<Return>
<Return>
Microsoft Word is a state of the art word processor.  It has
many features which previously were found only on dedicated
word processors.  One notable feature is on-screen
formatting.  With Word, the claim "what you see is what you
get" is completely realized.<Return>
<Return>
In Microsoft Word, paragraph and page formats, such as
indentations and line spacing, are displayed on the monitor
as they would be in the final draft.  Furthermore, Word does
not employ imbedded control characters to indicate character
formats.  Microsoft Word can display character formats such
as boldface, italics, and underlining on a monitor exactly
as they will appear when printed (See figure I-1).<Return>
```

4-5 This document is used to practice basic editing techniques with Word. When typing the document, press Return where <Return> appears in the figure.

Take a look at how word wrap functions when you are typing the short example document. At the end of the first line, as soon as the word "learn" passes the right margin, Word moves the word and the cursor down to the next line, as shown in Fig. 4-6.

Word wrap allows you to concentrate on entering text rather than worrying about where the end of the line is. With word wrap in operation, the only time Return should be pressed is at the end of a paragraph.

```
┌─────────────────────────────────────────────────┐
│ SPECIAL FEATURES OF WORD                        │
│                                                 │
│ Word processors used to be very complex and difficult to learn─┐
│ learn ─────────────────────────────────────────                │
│                                    Word wrap                    │
│                                 starts a new line               │
│                                  when a word                    │
│                                   passes the                    │
│                                  right margin                   │
└─────────────────────────────────────────────────┘
```

4-6 Word wrap automatically places words within the left and right margins, eliminating the need to press Return at the end of each line.

If you ever need to start a new line and do not want to start a new paragraph, you can avoid using Return by employing the Newline key. The Newline key is actually a combination of the Shift and Return keys (Shift–Return), so you will not find it on the keyboard. It is a useful combination to remember because it starts a new line without starting a new paragraph. The advantage of this will be made clear later.

Automatic screen scrolling

Word also automatically changes the location of text. Suppose you have been faithfully typing into Word the short document for this crash course. Eventually you will fill up the window with text, as in Fig 4-7.

```
┌─────────────────────────────────────────────────────────┐
│ SPECIAL FEATURES OF WORD                                │
│                                                         │
│ Word processors used to be very complex and difficult to│
│ learn. A new generation of word processors, however,    │
│ provides powerful functions without making them impossible│
│ to use. Chief among this brave new world of word processors│
│ is Microsoft Word. If you know how to use a typewriter, you│
│ can quickly learn how to use Word.                      │
│                                                         │
│ Microsoft Word is a state of the art word processor. It has│
│ many features which previously were found only on dedicated│
│ word processors. One notable feature is on-screen       │
│ formatting. With Word, the claim "what you see is what you│
│ get" is completely realized.                            │
│                                                         │
│ In Microsoft Word, paragraph and page formats, such as  │
│ indentations and line spacing, are displayed on the monitor│
│ as they would be in the final draft. Furthermore, Word does│
│ not employ imbedded control characters to indicate character│
└─────────────────────────────────────────────────────────┘
COMMAND: Copy Delete Format Gallery Help Insert Jump Library
         Options Print Quit Replace Search Transfer Undo Window
Edit document or press Esc to use menu
Pg1 Co62        {}                              Microsoft Word
```

4-7 The first half of the sample document as it appears on the screen.

28　*Entering a document*

When the entire screen is filled with text, the next word you type will not have space to be displayed on the screen. Word solves the problem by moving all the text upwards in the screen in a process called *scrolling*. After you type the word format, the window will resemble Fig. 4-8.

As you can see, this movement leaves more space in the window for you to finish typing the document. I explain scrolling in a later section, and you will learn to control it to move the document about on your own.

```
Microsoft Word is a state of the art word processor.  It has
many features which previously were found only on dedicated
word processors.  One notable feature is on-screen
formatting.  With Word, the claim "what you see is what you
get" is completely realized.

In Microsoft Word, paragraph and page formats, such as
indentations and line spacing, are displayed on the monitor
as they would be in the final draft.  Furthermore, Word does
not employ imbedded control characters to indicate character
formats []




                              Window              text
                              scrolls            scrolls
                               down              upwards




COMMAND: Copy Delete Format Gallery Help Insert Jump Library
         Options Print Quit Replace Search Transfer Undo Window
Edit document or press Esc to use menu
Pg1 Co9          {}                                  Microsoft Word
```

4-8　When the document fills the screen and you type in more text, Word automatically scrolls the document to accommodate the additional text and display it on the screen.

Editing keys

If you tend to make mistakes while typing, you will appreciate the many editing features Word offers. The Backspace and Del keys delete characters from the document. With just these two keys, you can bid farewell to the tedious and time-consuming task of correcting mistakes on a conventional typewriter.

The Backspace key on your keyboard erases one character to the left of the cursor. The Backspace key operates much like the backspace-erase key on an IBM Selectric, except that it closes up the text to the right of the cursor, drawing it left with the cursor. If you make any typographical errors, you can correct the errors with the Backspace key as shown in Fig. 4-9. To remove incorrect words or

```
indentations and line spacing, are displayed on the monitor
as they would be in the final draft.  Furthermore, Word does
not employ imbedded control characters to indicate character
formats.  Microsoft Word xan
```

```
COMMAND: Copy Delete Format Gallery Help Insert Jump Library
         Options Print Quit Replace Search Transfer Undo Window
Edit document or press Esc to use menu
Pg1 Co29          {}                                    Microsoft Word
```

4-9 The Backspace key erases the character to the left of the cursor.

characters, continue to use the Backspace key until your errors are erased from the screen.

The Del key is also used for erasing errors. The Del key deletes the character highlighted by the cursor; pressing the Del key repeatedly erases characters to the right of the cursor. You will learn how to use the Del command later.

Moving the cursor

So far, you have been content to leave the cursor alone, letting the cursor mark the location where you are entering your text. Because the cursor automatically remains ahead of the last text typed, there has been no need to move the cursor. You could continue to type, and the new text will be placed in front of the text entered previously. Even when the Backspace key was used to erase text, the cursor has remained in front of the text.

In some situations, however, it would be convenient to be able to move the cursor. Suppose, for example, that you finished typing in your document, and now realize that the phrase costing upwards of six thousand dollars should be appended to the sentence It has many features which were previously found only on dedicated word processors. (the second sentence in the second paragraph). Unfortunately, the cursor is separated from the the end of the place of insertion by two entire paragraphs.

You could use the Backspace key to erase backwards until the cursor was positioned where you wish to insert the text. Unfortunately, this solution requires erasing everything between where you are now and where you wish to be. After you moved back, you would have to retype all the text erased by the Backspace key. This is not only an impractical solution, it is a nightmare.

Arrow keys

Fortunately, there is a better way. You can move the cursor to the spot where you wish to insert (or delete) text with the arrow keys as shown in Fig. 4-10. The arrow keys are located on the numeric keypad and are the most basic means of moving the cursor.

First, you need to be sure that the Num Lock and Scroll Lock keys are off. In this state, each key with an arrow moves the cursor one space in the direction

Entering a document

```
Microsoft Word is a state of the art word processor. It has
many features which previously were found only on dedicated
word processors■. One notable feature is on-screen
formatting. With Word, the claim "what you see is what you
get" is completely realized.         ──── cursor moved back with arrow keys
```

4-10 The arrow keys can move the cursor to any point in the document. This is important when editing a document.

pointed. The left and right arrow keys move your cursor one space left or right, and the up and down arrow keys move your cursor one line up or down. These keys give you great local control over the location of your cursor.

Now, to append your phrase to the sentence, you only need to move the cursor to the location where you wish to begin inserting text. Use the arrow keys to move the cursor. Once at the desired location, you can type in the document. Notice that any text behind the cursor is automatically pushed back to make space for the new text (see Fig. 4-11).

```
                                                            new
Microsoft Word is a state of the art word processor. It has text inserted
many features which previously were found only on dedicated
word processors costing upwards of six thousand dollars.
One notable feature is on-screen formatting. With Word, the
old text  claim "what you see is what you get" is completely realized.
moved to
make room  In Microsoft Word, paragraph and page formats, such as
indentations and line spacing, are displayed on the monitor
as they would be in the final draft. Furthermore, Word does
not employ imbedded control characters to indicate character
formats. Microsoft Word can display character formats such
as boldface, italics, and underlining on a monitor exactly
as they will appear when printed (See figure I-1).♦
```

4-11 When the insert mode is on, Word automatically makes space in a document for any text inserted.

Other cursor keys

A few other keys allow you to move your cursor greater distances at a time. The Home and End keys move your cursor to the beginning and end character in the line, respectively. When used with the Ctrl key, Home and End perform other cursor functions. Ctrl-Home moves the cursor to the first character in the window, and Ctrl-End moves the cursor to the last character in the window.

The PgUp (Page Up) key moves your cursor back 20 lines in the document. The PgDn (Page Down) key moves the cursor forward 20 lines. When used with the Ctrl key, Ctrl-PgUp takes the cursor to the first character in the document, and Ctrl-PgDn sends the cursor to the last character in the document. These cursor movement commands are listed in Fig. 4-12.

Scrolling keys	Scrolls
PgUp	Up page
PgDn	Down page
Ctrl-PgUp	To beginning of document
Ctrl-PgDn	To end of document
Ctrl-right	Right page
Ctrl-left	Left page
Scroll Lock + right	Right 1/3 window
Scroll Lock + left	Left 1/3 window
Scroll Lock + up	Up a line
Scroll Lock + down	Down a line

4-12 These are the keys used to move the cursor in a document.

Using the mouse

The mouse can be used to move the cursor short and long distances. The mouse can move the cursor to any character on the screen by pointing to the character and pressing either the left or right mouse button. Pressing the left button highlights a single character. Pressing the right button highlights a word. Highlighting words is used when deleting unwanted text.

Scrolling text

While you are creating a document, you might wish to review parts of the document not displayed. To do so, you must move the cursor toward the desired text. As you move toward the borders of the window, new text appears on the screen. This process is called *scrolling*, because your text typed on a word processor does not resemble pages in a book so much as a single scroll of text under a rectangular window.

Word scrolls for you when you enter text and when you move the cursor. When the cursor is moved toward text not visible on the screen, the screen is scrolled until the text is visible. When the arrow keys move the cursor past the top or bottom line of text on the screen, the document scrolls up or down a line at a time. Similarly the PgUp and PgDn keys scroll the document up and down 20 lines at a time.

Scrolling with the mouse

The mouse can scroll through text. When you point to text on the screen and hold down the left or right mouse button, a character or word is highlighted by the cursor. If you continue to depress the mouse button and move the mouse pointer past one of the window borders, the text scrolls. At the same time, the highlight expands, encompassing all the text between the first character highlighted and the current position of the mouse pointer.

A document can be scrolled left, right, up, or down with the mouse. If the text does not extend past the left or right window borders, you are not able to scroll text left or right. When you cannot scroll the text in a certain direction, you have reached the end of the document. For example, if you cannot scroll the text upwards, you have reached the bottom of the document. If you cannot scroll the text downwards, you have reached the top of the document.

For practice, point to the i in the word italics on the next to last line of the document. Press the left mouse button and do not release it. Now roll the mouse forward so that the mouse pointer moves to the top of the screen. When the pointer reaches the top window border, the text will scroll forward. Release the mouse button when you reach the beginning of the text.

The scroll bar

Text can be scrolled up or down 1 to 20 lines at a time with the mouse. Scrolling text with the mouse pointer at the position in the scroll bar with the maximum scroll is similar to using the PgUp and PgDn keys. To scroll text up or down with the mouse, move the mouse to the far left of the screen. When the mouse is positioned on the left window border, the shape of the mouse pointer changes. The left window border is called the *scroll bar*.

The pointer resembles two joined arrows (if you are using Word with a text screen, the mouse pointer looks like a large box). When the pointer assumes the shape of two arrows (Fig. 4-13), pressing the left button scrolls the text up and pressing the right button scrolls the text down.

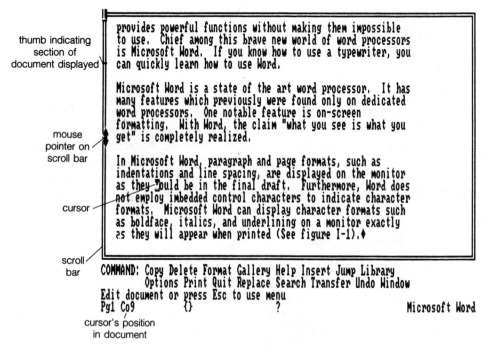

4-13 The mouse can be used to scroll the document, jump to any point in the document, move the cursor, and highlight text.

The number of lines scrolled up or down can be controlled by the position of the double arrow mouse pointer on the left window border. When the double arrow is near the top of the border, pressing either the left or right mouse button only scrolls the text a line or two. When the double arrow mouse pointer is near the bottom of the left window border, pressing either button scrolls the text about 20 lines.

As you scroll the document with the mouse and the scroll bar, you do not change the position of the cursor. If you scrolled from the end of the document to the beginning of the document, the cursor would remain at the end of the document. Thus, if you were to type in a character, the screen would jump back to the position of the cursor and the character would be added to the document.

Thus, to move the cursor great distances with the mouse, first use the mouse and the left window border to scroll to the desired line. Then point to a character in the line and press the left mouse button.

To practice scrolling with the mouse and the left window border, scroll the document until you reach the beginning of the document. Now scroll the document until you reach the end. The cursor has not moved during the entire scrolling operation. Now move the cursor by pointing to a character and pressing the left mouse button.

Summary

At this point, you should be familiar with the following:

- The IBM PC keyboard.
- Running Word, either in text or graphic mode.
- Entering text from type-in mode.
- Employing the Backspace and Del keys for correcting errors.
- Moving the cursor with the arrow keys.
- Moving the cursor with the mouse.
- Scrolling a document with the arrow keys.
- Scrolling a document with the mouse.

CHAPTER 5

Editing text

In the previous chapter, you learned how to enter text. This is sufficient for people who never make mistakes. But if you occasionally make errors (who doesn't?), you will need to know how to edit documents. The two most basic editing functions are inserting and deleting characters in a document. Word has several commands and function keys that control inserting and deleting.

Highlighting blocks of text

Blocks of text can be highlighted (selected) with the function keys and the arrow keys. By controlling the highlighted text, you can increase the power of Word commands that act on highlighted text. Function keys F6 through F10 are utilized to extend the cursor so that it highlights several characters, lines, sentences, paragraphs, or even the entire document.

    To demonstrate the advantages of being able to select blocks of text, suppose that you must delete an entire paragraph. Instead of tediously deleting the paragraph one character at a time, you can highlight it with the cursor in one step and delete it with the Del key. The Del key deletes whatever text is highlighted, whether it is a character, word, sentence, paragraph, or the entire document, and places it in a temporary storage area called the *scrap*.

Selecting text with the function keys

The function keys are used to control the position and size of the cursor. The function keys are found on the left side of the keyboard in 2 columns of 5 keys

36 *Editing text*

each, or in a single row of 10 or 12 keys along the top of the keyboard. Keys F6 through F10 are used to select blocks of text.

If you have the clip-on function key template, put it on the keyboard. The template makes it easier for you to find the appropriate function key. If you have lost your template, inquire at a full-service bookstore or a computer store. Third-party publishers produce replacement templates.

Suppose that you wished to delete the word "Microsoft" from the second paragraph in the short document created in the last chapter (see Fig. 5-1). You can use the F8 (next word) key. The F8 (next word) key highlights the word to the right of the cursor. If the cursor is pointing to a character in a word, it expands to highlight the entire word.

```
┌─────────────────────────────────────────────────┐
│ SPECIAL FEATURES OF WORD                        │
│                                                 │
│ Word processors used to be very complex and difficult to │
│ learn. A new generation of word processors, however, │
│ provides powerful functions without making them impossible │
│ to use. Chief among this brave new world of word processors │
│ is Microsoft Word. If you know how to use a typewriter, you │
│ can quickly learn how to use Word.              │
│                                                 │
│ Microsoft Word is a state of the art word processor. It has │
│ many features which previously were found only on dedicated │
│ word processors costing upwards of six thousand dollars. One │
│ notable feature is on-screen formatting. With Word, the │
│ claim "what you see is what you get" is completely realized. │
│                                                 │
│ In Microsoft Word, paragraph and page formats, such as │
│ indentations and line spacing, are displayed on the monitor │
│ as they would be in the final draft. Furthermore, Word does │
│ not employ imbedded control characters to indicate character │
└─────────────────────────────────────────────────┘
COMMAND: Copy Delete Format Gallery Help Insert Jump Library
         Options Print Quit Replace Search Transfer Undo Window
Edit document or press Esc to use menu
Pg1 Co10        {}                              Microsoft Word
```
Word highlighted by pressing F8

5-1 F8 highlights the current word or the next word. F7 highlights the current word or the previous word.

To employ the F8 (next word) key, move the cursor to any character in the word Microsoft. Press the F8 (next word) key; the cursor leaps to extend over the word. Press the Del key and the entire highlighted word is erased.

The F7 (previous word) key is similar to the F8 (next word) key, but it highlights the word to the left of the cursor. Note that with the F7 and F8 keys, you can move the cursor a single word in either direction each time. It becomes very convenient to move word by word employing the F7 and F8 keys, rather than character by character with the directional arrows.

Extending the cursor

With the addition of the function keys, your ability to delete text has been considerably enhanced. But suppose you wish to erase the sentence With Word, the claim that "what you see is what you get" is completely realized from the second paragraph. You could employ the Del key to erase the sentence one character at a time. However, you can further improve your efficiency by extending the cursor to select the entire sentence at once. To accomplish this goal, you need the assistance of the F6 (Extend selection on/off) key.

The F6 key is a toggle key. (Toggles were explained in Chapter 2.) Pressing F6 once turns on the extend toggle, pressing it again turns it off. Press F6. You should immediately notice the status code EX for "extend" in the status line of the command area.

Once you turn on Extend with the F6 key as shown in Fig. 5-2 you add to the cursor with the cursor keys instead of moving it. Make sure that the the Extend feature is on by checking the status line, then press the F8 (next word) key several times. Instead of moving the cursor several words to the right, the cursor stretches to cover the words on the right including the original word. The cursor has been "extended" to cover both the new words and the old word.

5-2 F6 is used to extend the cursor and highlight text. EX is displayed on the status line when the extend mode is on.

Stretching the cursor

If you have extended the cursor past the end of the sentence, press the F7 (previous word) key. The cursor did not extend its left edge by one word. Instead, the right edge of the cursor shrank by one word. Press the F7 key a few more times until only the original word is highlighted. Press the F7 key a few more times. Notice that the cursor is now extending itself to the left.

To explain this reaction, you can compare extending the cursor to stretching a rubber band. When you press the F6 (extend) key, you fix one end of the cursor to where it is. This end becomes the anchor point, and will remain fixed until the extend feature is turned off with the F6 key.

With one end of the cursor anchored by the extend function, attempts to move the cursor stretch the cursor like a rubber band. In this way, you can highlight blocks of text with the cursor. There is no limit to how much you can extend the cursor. You can stretch it just by a character, or by half the document, or even the entire document.

What happens when you press F7 (previous word) once after pressing F8 several times? With the extend feature on, you can think of it as letting the cursor (or rubber band) slacken. The cursor shrinks by one word. By pressing the F7 (previous word) key several times, you return the cursor to its original location. By pressing F7 several more times, the cursor is stretched to the left as shown in Fig. 5-3.

5-3 The F6 and F7 keys are used here to highlight text. Highlighted text can be deleted, copied, formatted, searched, printed, or checked for spelling errors.

Procedure for selecting text

The general method for selecting a block of text thus comprises of three steps:

1. Move the cursor to one end of the block of text.
2. Turn on the extend feature by pressing the F6 key.
3. Extend the cursor with the arrow keys or function keys to highlight the block of text.

The F7 (previous word) and F8 (next word) keys are not the only keys used to stretch the cursor; the directional arrow keys can be used as well as other cursor-movement keys (like Pg Dn or Home). In this manner, you can enclose any block of text you choose, from two characters to the entire document.

Now go back to the original example. To delete the sentence, With Word, the claim . . . is completely realized., first move the cursor to the beginning character of the sentence. If the extend feature is not on, turn it on by pressing the F6 key. Press the F8 (next word) key until the entire sentence is highlighted as in Fig. 5-4. Now press the Del key. The sentence fragment is then erased.

```
SPECIAL FEATURES OF WORD

Word processors used to be very complex and difficult to
learn. A new generation of word processors, however,
provides powerful functions without making them impossible
to use. Chief among this brave new world of word processors
is Microsoft Word. If you know how to use a typewriter, you
can quickly learn how to use Word.

Word is a state of the art word processor. It has many
features which previously were found only on dedicated word
processors costing upwards of six thousand dollars. One
notable feature is on-screen formatting. With Word, the
claim "what you see is what you get" is completely realized.

In Microsoft Word, paragraph and page formats, such as
indentations and line spacing, are displayed on the monitor
as they would be in the final draft. Furthermore, Word does
not employ imbedded control characters to indicate character
```

```
COMMAND: Copy Delete Format Gallery Help Insert Jump Library
         Options Print Quit Replace Search Transfer Undo Window
Edit document or press Esc to use menu
Pg1 Co60        {Microsoft.}                          Microsoft Word
```

5-4 Shift-F8 highlights the current sentence or the next sentence. Shift–F7 highlights the current sentence or the previous sentence.

Selecting sentences and paragraphs

The Shift-F7 key combination selects the previous sentence. The Shift-F8 key combination selects the next sentence. The F9 (previous paragraph) selects the previous paragraph. The F10 (next paragraph) function key is used to select the next paragraph. To highlight two paragraphs at one time, press F10 twice to select two paragraphs.

The F9 and F10 keys can be used in conjunction with the F6 (extend) key. Suppose, for example, that you wish to select the first part of a paragraph. First press the F6 key; then select the part of the paragraph before the cursor by pressing the F9 (previous paragraph) key. This action selects the first half of the paragraph.

The function of these keys is slightly different from the F7 and F8 (previous word and next word) keys. They expand rather than move the cursor. For example, move the cursor to the middle of your document. By pressing the F7 (next word) key three times, you select the word three words to the left of the current position of the cursor.

Selecting sentences and paragraphs can be very useful when formatting or reformatting text, especially large blocks. When you have selected the section you want to change, you can change the font, or you can change other type attributes. You can also add a box around the text to make a sidebar.

Later in this book, you will learn that graphics are treated as paragraphs. You can use these paragraph selection techniques to select individual graphics or groups of graphics to impose special formatting commands such as boxes surrounding the graphics or a screen over text.

Now move the cursor back to its original location and try to do the same with the Shift-F8 key. Press Shift-F8 three times. Note that you have selected only the third sentence following the cursor's position. You could press Shift-F8 as many times as you like, and it still selects only a single sentence. This is because Shift-F8 expands the cursor only to include the sentence containing the cursor.

Selecting the entire document

One specialized function key combination should be mentioned here: the Shift-F10 (whole document) key combination that selects the entire document. This action is extremely useful when installing global changes like changing font, format, or tab stops.

Selecting text with the mouse

The mouse can also be used to select text. At first you may have difficulty selecting text with the mouse, but after you develop hand-eye coordination, selecting text with the mouse becomes easier. To select text with the mouse, follow these steps:

1. Point to the first character in the passage you wish to select.
2. Press the left mouse button and continue holding it.
3. While holding the left mouse button, move the pointer to the last character in the text you wish to select.

4. Release the left mouse button. The desired text will be highlighted on your screen.

The mouse can also be used to select a word or a sentence at a time. To select a word, point to the desired word and press the right mouse button. To select a sentence, point to the sentence and press both buttons. The cursor can be extended while selecting words or sentences by holding down the button(s), moving the mouse pointer to the end of the text you wish to select, and releasing the button(s).

You can select a line or paragraph quickly with the mouse using the two character spaces that appear between the text and the border (the *selection bar*). If you are working in graphic mode, the mouse pointer tilts to the right when you are within the area. Click the left mouse button to select the line of text next to the mouse pointer. Click the right button to select the paragraph next to the mouse pointer. Click both buttons to select the entire document.

Extending selections

Sometimes you must discover that you selected all but the last word of the section you intended to format, or all but the last character or paragraph. Rather than start the selection all over again, you can simply extend the selection. Turn on the extender by pressing F6. But before you do, look to see if the EX code appears in the lower left corner of the screen. When this code appears, the selection simply follows the cursor, whether you are moving it with the mouse or the cursor keys.

Another way to extend the selection is with the Shift key. Regardless of whether the Ex code is on, you can extend the highlight with a Shift-arrow key or Shift in combination with the PgUp, PgDn, Home, or End keys.

Selecting columns

You can select a column of text with the Shift-F6 key combination. Place the cursor at one corner of the section you want to select. Press Shift-F6. As you move the cursor, either with the cursor keys or the mouse, the highlight changes, creating a rectangle of highlight with one corner on your first cursor location, and the opposite corner on your second cursor location. You can delete, copy, insert, or format any rectangle of text with this facility.

Deleting text

The process of deleting text has been glossed over earlier to treat the matter of selection (highlighting) of text in more detail. The Delete command is used many times while editing a document. You will find in later chapters that the Delete command is also essential for moving and copying blocks of text.

To delete text, you can either use the Delete command or the Del (delete) key. The Del key allows you to use the Delete command directly, without first pressing the Esc key.

Editing text

In the previous section, you deleted a sentence. The sentence, however, has not been lost. Instead, it has been stored in the *scrap*. The scrap is the location where Word stores the last deletion made from the text.

Look at the status line on the bottom of the screen (see Fig. 5-5). Between the braces, you can see the beginning and end of the deleted sentence: {With Wo . . . lized.} The deletions are stored in the scrap until another deletion takes its place. You will learn how to use the scrap to your advantage in the next section.

```
SPECIAL FEATURES OF WORD

Word processors used to be very complex and difficult to
learn. A new generation of word processors, however,
provides powerful functions without making them impossible
to use. Chief among this brave new world of word processors
is Microsoft Word. If you know how to use a typewriter, you
can quickly learn how to use Word.

Word is a state of the art word processor. It has many
features which previously were found only on dedicated word
processors costing upwards of six thousand dollars. One
notable feature is on-screen formatting. ■

In Microsoft Word, paragraph and page formats, such as
indentations and line spacing, are displayed on the monitor
as they would be in the final draft. Furthermore, Word does
not employ imbedded control characters to indicate character
formats. Microsoft Word can display character formats such
```

COMMAND: Copy Delete Format Gallery Help Insert Jump Library
        Options Print Quit Replace Search Transfer Undo Window
Edit document or press Esc to use menu
Pg1 Co43   {With·Wo...lized.}   Microsoft Word

                   Text moved to scrap

5-5 Deleted and copied text is placed in the scrap. Text in the scrap can be inserted anywhere in the document.

The Insert command

Once text has been placed into the scrap with the Del key, the text remains in the scrap until another deletion replaces it. While text is in the scrap, it can be inserted into the text of the document with the Ins (insert) key.

When the Ins key is pressed, it makes a copy of the contents of the scrap and places it into the document. The text is inserted in front of the cursor. As only a copy of the scrap is placed into the document, the contents of scrap itself are unchanged.

Suppose you wish to insert the sentence deleted in the last section at the end of the third paragraph. Move the cursor to the end of the third paragraph as shown in Fig. 5-6, employing the cursor movement commands that you studied in Chapter 4. Press the Ins key, and the sentence is appended to the end of the third paragraph (see Fig. 5-7).

```
Word processors used to be very complex and difficult to
learn. A new generation of word processors, however,
provides powerful functions without making them impossible
to use. Chief among this brave new world of word processors
is Microsoft Word. If you know how to use a typewriter, you
can quickly learn how to use Word.

Word is a state of the art word processor. It has many
features which previously were found only on dedicated word
processors costing upwards of six thousand dollars. One
notable feature is on-screen formatting.

In Microsoft Word, paragraph and page formats, such as
indentations and line spacing, are displayed on the monitor
as they would be in the final draft. Furthermore, Word does
not employ imbedded control characters to indicate character
formats. Microsoft Word can display character formats such       Move
as boldface, italics, and underlining on a monitor exactly    cursor with
as they will appear when printed (See figure 1-1).             arrow keys

COMMAND: Copy Delete Format Gallery Help Insert Jump Library
         Options Print Quit Replace Search Transfer Undo Window
Edit document or press Esc to use menu
Pg1 Co52        {With·Wo...lized.}                           Microsoft Word
```

5-6 Move cursor to the end of the document and follow the example.

Deleting and inserting with the mouse

The mouse can be used to delete and insert text. To delete text highlighted by the cursor point to the word "Delete" on the main menu and press the right mouse button. The text deleted is placed in the scrap.

To insert text from the scrap into the document, move the cursor to the point where you wish to insert the text. Then point to the word "Insert" on the main menu and press the right mouse button.

The Undo command

When writing a document, you might accidentally delete a paragraph from the document. On a typewriter, you would need to retype an entire page to correct the

```
provides powerful functions without making them impossible
to use. Chief among this brave new world of word processors
is Microsoft Word. If you know how to use a typewriter, you
can quickly learn how to use Word.

Microsoft Word is a state of the art word processor. It has
many features which previously were found only on dedicated
word processors costing upwards of six thousand dollars. One
notable feature is on-screen formatting.

In Microsoft Word, paragraph and page formats, such as
indentations and line spacing, are displayed on the monitor
as they would be in the final draft. Furthermore, Word does
not employ imbedded control characters to indicate character
formats. Microsoft Word can display character formats such
as boldface, italics, and underlining on a monitor exactly
as they will appear when printed (See figure 1-1). With
Word, the claim "what you see is what you get" is completely
realized.
```

Inserted text from scrap with the Ins key

```
COMMAND: Copy Delete Format Gallery Help Insert Jump Library
         Options Print Quit Replace Search Transfer Undo Window
Edit document or press Esc to use menu
Pg1 Co10        {With-Wo...lized.}                  Microsoft Word
```

5-7 Press Insert or select the Insert command to place a copy of the text in the scrap back into the document at the cursor position.

error. On Word, it takes you less than three seconds to correct the error with the Undo command.

The Undo command is used to "undo" your last editing change. Editing changes include typing in text, deleting text, inserting text, and formatting text (moving the cursor is not considered an editing change). Even if you accidentally delete your entire document with your last command, the Undo command can reverse your mistake. Undo can even act to reverse its own actions.

Suppose that you wished to have the sentence you inserted in the last section returned to the scrap. To do so, you need to use the Undo command. First press the Esc key, so Word will know you intend to give it a command. Now press U to execute the Undo command.

Word searches through its memory and undoes your last editing change. Everything is completely restored to its former state. In this case, the latest change carried out was the insertion of a sentence. Word thus puts the sentence back into the scrap.

An alternative to the Esc-U key sequence is using the mouse pointer to click on Undo in the main menu.

"Undoing" the Undo command

Another feature of the Undo command is that it cancels the previous command, even if the last command was another Undo command. Two Undo commands, thus, cancel one another.

There are both advantages and disadvantages to this aspect of the Undo command. One advantage is that you can reverse the effects of a Undo command. Another advantage is that you can switch back and forth between two versions of your text to find the best version.

For example, suppose you could not decide whether you wanted to have the sentence back in the document. Press the Esc-U key sequence once more. This Undo command will undo the previous Undo command. This puts the sentence back into the document. Study this version of the text, then use the Undo command again to remove the sentence. By using your Undo command to switch back and forth between the two versions of your document, you can easily decide which version you prefer.

The disadvantage in the Undo command's ability to reverse itself is that you cannot reverse commands given before the last command. You cannot use an Undo command to reverse a command given two commands ago. This is because the second Undo command reverses the first Undo command, not the editing change before that.

With the Undo command, you should not panic when you commit an editing error. If the error was the last editing change, you can easily correct your mistake by utilizing the Undo command. If you panic and start pressing keys at random, you can insert more editing changes into your document. As a result, you will be unable to use the Undo command to save your document.

Even if the Undo command is ineffective, you can always employ another Undo command to bring you back to your original state. You will then be no worse off than before.

Summary

In this chapter, you have learned the following:

- How to highlight blocks of text.
- How to delete blocks of text.
- How to insert blocks of text.
- How to undo the previous editing change.

CHAPTER 6

Word commands and menus

Until now, we have not discussed any method for producing printouts of your work. Nor have we discussed any method of storing the document for future editing. Printing and saving documents is so important that Microsoft shipped tens of thousands of demonstration copies of Word that were fully functional except that they would not save or print documents. Thus, the next step in learning how to use Word is to learn how to print and save documents.

Word has a list of commands that control printing and saving documents. These commands are arranged in menus. Before actually using either the Print or Transfer Save command, you must learn how to select commands from the Word menus. There are several ways to select commands.

Command selection

After entering Word, you are automatically placed in the text edit area. At this point, you are in "type-in" mode. This means everything typed on the keyboard is inserted into the document. You utilized the "type-in" mode earlier when you wrote the sample document. If you wish to do anything besides simply typing in text, you must use Word's commands. These commands are displayed at the bottom of the screen.

Selecting commands from type-in mode

The commands in the main menu can be selected from the type-in mode by pressing the Esc key. When the Esc key is pressed, Word cancels type-in mode. This permits selection of commands from the command menu. In Fig. 6-1, note how a cursor appears in the command menu, highlighting the Copy command.

```
                    Cursor moves to Edit menu

COMMAND: Copy Delete Format Gallery Help Insert Jump Library
              Options Print Quit Replace Search Transfer Undo Window
Copies selected text to scrap or to a named glossary entry
Pg1 Col       {}                                      Microsoft Word
```

6-1 Commands are selected by pressing Esc and then typing the first letter of the command. Also, commands can also be selected by pressing Esc, pressing Tab to highlight the appropriate command, and then pressing Return.

Choosing a command

After type-in mode has been canceled, a command can be selected by moving the cursor with either the Space or the Tab key. The cursor can also be moved backwards with the Shift–Tab and Backspace keys or with the arrow keys. Notice that the cursor highlights a command on the menu line. Once the command you wish to execute is highlighted, press Return. Word then processes that command.

Another method for selecting a command from a menu is to press Esc and then the first letter of the command. Pressing the first letter of the desired command, called the *command letter*, is fastest method for selecting commands. This method is faster than selecting commands by pressing Tab or Space. When the command you want to use is highlighted, press Return.

If you decide to employ command letters to invoke commands, be warned that it requires more skill than simply selecting commands with the cursor. When using command letters, you will be unable to use the on-screen help feature (described later) to examine the command. If you are unfamiliar with the effect of a command, it is safer to select commands using the cursor. After becoming more familiar with commands in Word, it is much faster to select commands by typing the command letter.

Selecting commands with the mouse

The mouse can also be used to select commands:

1. Point to the desired command.
2. Press and hold the left mouse button. One of the commands will be highlighted.
3. If the highlighted command is the command you wish to select, release the mouse button. If the highlighted command is not the desired command, move the mouse pointer until the desired command is highlighted and then release the mouse button.

Sub menus in Word

Not all commands perform actions in Word. A command might activate a second menu, called a *submenu*. In the submenu, other options or commands can be selected. Submenus themselves can contain more menus.

For example, select the Print command from the Edit menu by pressing Esc-P. You will be taken to the Print submenu instead of performing an immediate action. You take further actions from the Print menu (see Fig. 6-2).

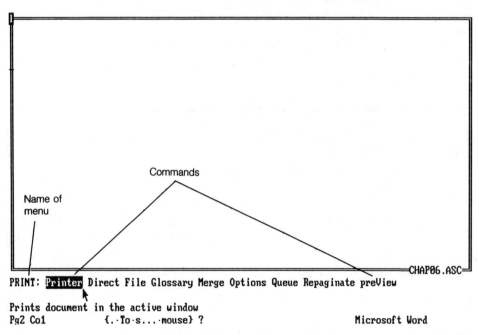

6-2 Selecting the Print command brings up the Print menu. The Print menu controls the printing of documents.

There are two ways to return to a menu after entering a submenu. The first method is to finish executing a command. After the command is executed, you are returned to the main menu and placed in the type-in mode. The second method is to cancel execution of the command with the Esc key. As a general rule, the Esc key returns you to the main menu. Pressing both mouse buttons simultaneously also cancels the current command.

Cancelling commands

Suppose that you wish to cancel execution of a command. To exit any menu except the Gallery menu, simply press the Esc key. This will cancel the command you are executing and bring you back to the main menu. By pressing Esc then P in the previous example, you entered the Print menu. To return to the document, press the Esc key. This places you in the Edit menu, where another command can be selected.

The Esc key is useful to exit from menus you entered accidentally. Once you press the Esc key, you are returned to the document.

The self help feature

Word is a professionally designed package with mnemonic command names. The mnemonic command names make Word easy to learn and use. In addition, the designers of Word have provided users with an on-screen help feature for immediate on-line help. This help feature serves two purposes, first to help you learn the function of new commands and, second, as a quick reference to remind you of the function and effects of commands.

One way to obtain help is to select the Help command. The Help command can be selected like any other command: press Esc then H. The screen will resemble Fig. 6-3.

```
                              Help
HELP     Screen 1 of 3
Every Help screen lists name of topic and number of screens related to
topic in upper-left corner.

To get Help on a      1. Use direction keys to move highlight to command
command or command       or field you want help on.
field                 2. Hold down Alt key while you press H (Alt+H).

To browse in Help     1. Press Escape key (Esc), then press H.
                      2. Press N (next) or P (previous) to view Help
                         information.

To view Help Index    1. Start Help (Press Esc, H, or Alt+H).
                      2. Press I to choose Index from Help menu.



                      ═ Tutorial: Getting Quick Help
                         Using: Ch. 6, "Getting Help"

HELP: Exit Next Previous Basics
      Index Tutorial Keyboard Mouse
Returns to location or menu where Help was requested
Pg4 Co1          {the·}            ?                        CHAP06.ASC
```

6-3 Word has an online help feature that supplies a summary of each command in Word. The help feature can be activated by pressing Alt-H or selecting the help command.

Specific help

Another method of obtaining on-screen help is to press Alt-H directly from the keyboard. Typing Alt-H takes you to the section of the help file most pertinent to your current situation. Alt-H is probably most useful when and if you need help on specific commands in Word.

Enter the command selection mode by pressing the Esc key. Use the Space and Shift-Tab key to move the cursor to the Print command. After the print command is highlighted, press Alt-H. The section of the help file describing the Print command appears on the screen as in Fig. 6-4.

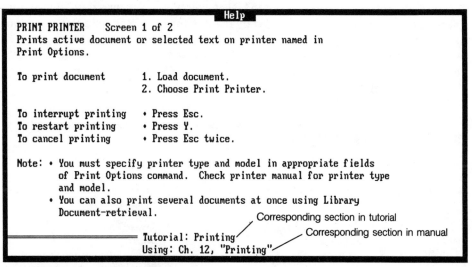

6-4 Help screens contain references to the Word manuals and Tutorial program for additional information on a help topic.

Commands in the Help menu

Notice that the Help command has a special menu. The menu contains three major commands, Exit, Next, and Previous, as well as several minor commands. These commands help you to leaf through the on-screen help file or to go straight to a given section.

Exit, Next, and Previous are the three main commands in the Help menu. The Exit command returns Word to the state before you called for help. The Next and Previous commands allow examination of the next and the previous page in the help file, respectively. You can also use the PgUp or PgDn keys to leaf through the help file.

52   Word commands and menus

Basics, Index, Tutorial, Keyboard, and Mouse represent various sections of the help file. To see information on a specific section, type the first letter of the corresponding command. You can also select the section by highlighting the command with the cursor and pressing Return.

Take this opportunity to look through the help file with the next command; type N to trigger the Next command. Word possesses very detailed on-screen help facilities. You might wish to take quick glances at the different sections in the help file with the help commands.

Employing the Help key

In Word, do not hesitate to press Alt–H whenever you are unsure about a function. Often your questions can be answered by reading the on-screen help feature. Word has comprehensive help facilities designed for your benefit. It would be advantageous to utilize this valuable resource. Together with the Undo command, the Help command provides a tremendous aid to the inexperienced Word user. Figure 6-5 shows the help index.

```
Align Left         Glossaries        Repaginate
Align Right        Graphics          Repeat
Annotations        Headers           Replace
ASCII file         Hidden text       Revision marks
Autosave           Hyphens           Ruler
Backup             Indent            Running heads
Block              Index             Save
Bold               Italics           Screen borders
Bookmarks          Jump              Search
Bulleted list      Justify           Select text
Calculate          Keyboard          Show layout
Center             Leader character  Side by side
Colors             Line break        Small caps
Columns            Line drawing      Sort
Commands           Line spacing      Speed keys
Copy               Load document     Spell
Cross referencing  Macros            Spreadsheet link
Delete             Mailing labels    Strikethrough
Division break     Margins           Style sheets

HELP INDEX: Align Left

Select Help topic; press PgDn for more topics
Pg6 Co30        {e}            ?                         CHAP06.ASC
```

6-5   The help index lists all the general help topics covered by the help command.

Running the Word tutorial

You can run the Word Tutorial from the Help menu. The tutorial is especially useful when you need more information than is provided by the regular Word help screen. Word automatically runs the tutorial lesson most closely pertaining to the current help screen. For example, if the current help screen explained the Transfer command, then selecting the tutorial command from the Help menu would bring up the lesson that explains how to use the Transfer command. First, you are given the choice between seeing the lesson itself or an index of the lessons available. Then you are given the option of seeing a lesson pertaining to keyboard use or mouse use, as shown in Fig. 6-6.

```
This disk contains both the mouse and the keyboard
versions of LEARNING WORD.  Which would you like to use?
```

[M] Press M to see the mouse
     version of LEARNING WORD.

[K] Press K to see the keyboard
     version of LEARNING WORD.

6-6 The opening screen of the tutorial program.

Press Space to continue the tutorial. Press Ctrl-Q to return to the Help menu. The tutorial lesson on printing has begin in Fig. 6-7.

Printing a document

Now that you know how to select commands, you are prepared to attempt the task of producing a paper copy of your document. Documents that have been printed on paper are called *printouts* or *hard copies* in computer jargon. They are so named to distinguish them from documents stored on magnetic media, sometimes called *copies*.

Documents written with Word are often printed for editing purposes as well as final copies. It is easier to edit a document on paper than on the computer because the paper copy is easier to read. In addition, letter, pamphlet, or manuscript masterpieces would be of little use to you if others could not read them. Thus, it is vital to learn how to print out documents.

```
┌─────────────────────────────────────────────────────────────┐
│ Printing                                         Overview   │
└─────────────────────────────────────────────────────────────┘

        ┌───────────────────────────────────────────┐
        │                 Printing                  │
        └───────────────────────────────────────────┘


        In this lesson you'll learn to:

          ■ print your document

          ■ indicate whether you're feeding the paper by hand,
            or the printer is feeding the paper continuously




        ┌───────────────────────────────────────────────────┐
        │ Estimated time to complete this lesson:  4 to 6 minutes │
        └───────────────────────────────────────────────────┘

┌─────────────────────────────────────────────────────────────┐
│ Press Control-Q to return to Quick Help      To go on: Spacebar │
└─────────────────────────────────────────────────────────────┘
```

6-7 The introductory screen for the Printing topic in the tutorial program.

Setting options for your printer

The first time you print a document, you must advise Word of three major parameters: the type of printer connected to the computer, the type of printer interface connected to the CPU, and the manner in which paper is fed to the printer. Only after Word has been informed of these three vital aspects of your printer should you attempt to print a document. In order to set up Word, you must use the Print Options command.

To set the Print options, you must enter the Print Options menu from the Edit menu, first press Esc to exit from the type-in mode. Press P to select the Print command, then press Q to select the Options command. You now face the Print Options menu (see Fig. 6-8).

First, you should to notify Word of the type of printer connected to the CPU. If the printer listed next to printer: on the Print Options menu is different from your printer, you must select a printer driver. (HP LaserJet is selected because the Star Laserprinter 8 printer can emulate the HP LaserJet (and other printers) and therefore the HP LaserJet driver was the best choice as driver for my printer.) To select the correct printer driver, press the Tab key until the cursor rests in the

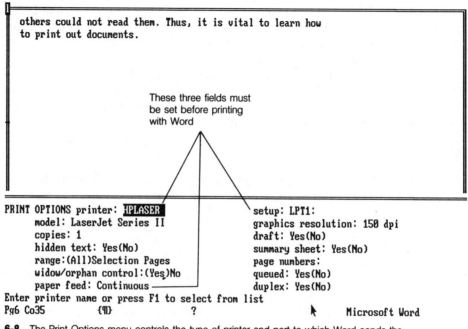

6-8 The Print Options menu controls the type of printer and port to which Word sends the output, the source of paper for the printer. These fields should be set before printing a document.

printer field. Press one of the arrow keys to see the list of printer settings stored on your disk. A list of printer drivers will appear on the screen.

Select a printer description by moving the cursor with the arrow keys to highlight the desired printer. Once the desired printer is illuminated, press Return.

Word operates with a variety of dot matrix and impact printers, as well as teletypes (TTY). If your printer is not listed on the screen, select TTY.

TTY is a general description that allows Word to use most printers. There might be minor difficulties caused by using the TTY description with your printer, because TTY is defined by a standard code. Many printers have their own unique codes that are incompatible with the TTY standard. For example, an Epson FX printer cannot create superscripts, subscripts, or italics when used with a TTY setting.

Once the proper printer description for Word is selected, you must tell Word how paper is fed to the printer. You can move between fields by pressing the Tab key. Move to the field labeled feed. Depending on the printer you are using, you might have various feed options. Use the spacebar or the mouse to select the correct option. If you are confused by the options, refer to your printer manual. Once the proper setting is highlighted, press the Tab key.

Finally, the last setting is the type of port the printer is connect to. Move the cursor to the field marked "setup" with the Tab key. Settings LPT1:, LPT2:, and LPT3: are for parallel printers. COM1: and COM2: are for serial printers.

You must know which port your printer is connected to before you can print your document. If you have a parallel printer, the printer is probably connected to LPT1:. A serial printer would probably connected to COM1:. If you do not know which type of printer you possess, try selecting LPT1: (use Space) and printing the document. LPT1: is the most common printer setting.

When you have finished selecting the settings, press Return to return to the Print menu. This also sets the Print options and stores them on disk. The next time you use Word, the settings will be set. Thus, you only need to set the printer settings once, unless you use Word on a different printer in the future.

Once the settings are correct, you are ready to print a document. To print a document:

1. If you are using fan-fold paper, adjust the paper, so the document does not print across the perforations separating pages. You can adjust the paper by moving the paper in the printer to the top of a new page. The printing mechanism should be at the same level as the perforations. Then, turn the printer off, wait three seconds, and turn the printer back on.
2. Make sure the printer is on-line. There should be a button on the printer that toggles the printer on-line and off (this is not the same as the power switch; a printer can be running but off-line).
3. Next, execute the Print command from the Print menu. If you are at the print menu, just press P to select Printer. If you are not at the print menu, hit Esc then P, and P.

If you encounter any difficulties while printing, press the Esc key twice to cancel the print job. Otherwise, just wait until the printer has finished. Barring accident or a faulty setting, you should have printed your first hard copy.

Saving text

At this point, some of your document is only in Word's temporary memory. If you exit from Word without saving the document on the disk, some of the document will be lost forever. Word can be set to store editing changes and additions to your document every few minutes. However, if you did not save the document, recent changes to the document would not be saved. It would be a waste to lose part of the document after all of that work. The Transfer Save command saves your document on a disk. In addition, the command can save any recent edits you have made.

There are many reasons why you should save your work. Suppose many small revisions are needed in the final copy. It would be a lot of work to retype the document to make a small change. If you save your document, it is much easier to edit an existing document than to retype one from scratch.

The Transfer Save command from the Transfer menu is used to save documents. To enter the Transfer menu, press Esc-T. The Transfer menu resembles Fig. 6-9. Select the Save command by pressing S. The Transfer Save menu looks like Fig. 6-10.

Word now asks for a filename under which to store the document. If you had saved an earlier version of this document, the document already has a name. If such a name is displayed, you can press Return to store the file or document under

```
TRANSFER: Load Save Clear Delete Merge Options Rename Glossary Allsave
Loads named document
Pg9 Co1          {S}              ?                    Microsoft Word
```

6-9 The Transfer menu controls the storing and retrieving of document.

```
TRANSFER SAVE filename: ▌
                format:(Word)Text-only Text-only-with-line-breaks RTF
Enter filename
Pg9 Co1          {S}              ?                    Microsoft WordCHAP06.ASC
```

6-10 Filenames can be one to eight characters long, followed by an optional period and three-character extension. If the optional period and extension are not included, Word attaches the extension .DOC for documents.

its original name. If you wish to change the name of a document that has already been named, simply type in another name to store the document.

If no name is displayed, as is the case now, you must enter a filename. The filename should be from one to eight characters (use letters or numbers) in length. Type a filename and press Return. If you don't specify an extension, Word automatically attaches the extension .DOC to your filename while storing the document. If the filename already exists, you are notified and given the option of overwriting the file on disk. If this document has been previously edited, the earlier version of the document will still be stored under the same name, but with the .BAK extension for your protection. If the document is new, then you are presented with the summary form shown in Fig. 6-11. You can fill in the blanks to provide a record of the revisions of the manuscript, or you can press Esc to skip it.

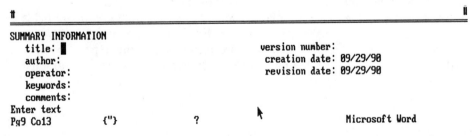

```
SUMMARY INFORMATION
    title: ▌                          version number:
    author:                            creation date: 09/29/90
    operator:                          revision date: 09/29/90
    keywords:
    comments:
Enter text
Pg9 Co13         {"}              ?                    Microsoft Word
```

6-11 The summary information sheet is displayed when you save a document for the first time. If you do not want to fill in the information, press Return.

Clearing a document from Word

After saving your document, you might be surprised that it's still in memory. After all, you just saved it in a document file. Word, however, does not actually place your document into a file. When you use the Transfer Save command, a copy of the file as it stands is saved, providing you the opportunity to continue editing the document.

The Transfer Clear command is used to erase the document displayed on the screen. Erasing the displayed document frees memory so you can begin editing other documents. Press Esc to escape type-in mode, then press T for Transfer, then C to select the Clear command.

The menu, shown in Fig. 6-12, has two options: All and Window. Select the Transfer Clear All option by pressing A. Word will obediently clear the screen, freeing the memory for other editing tasks.

```
‖                                                              ═LESSON.DOC═‖
TRANSFER CLEAR: All Window

Clears all documents, glossaries, style sheets
Pg10 Co33            {0}            ?            Microsoft Word
```

6-12 The Transfer Clear command can remove the document being edited so you may begin editing a new document.

Retrieving a document

In a preceding section, you saved a document on Word's data disk. Saving a document, however, would be totally useless unless it could be retrieved for additional editing in the future. In Word, documents are retrieved with the Transfer Load command.

With the Transfer Load command, you can move a copy of the document from permanent storage on disk to temporary storage in your computer. Once the document is in the computer, it can be edited with Word.

For the crash course, you will retrieve the document you saved in the previous session for an exercise. First, select the Transfer Load command. Press Esc to end type-in mode. Then, press T to select the Transfer command and enter the Transfer menu. Now, select the Load command by pressing L.

After entering the Load command, there are two different command fields in the Transfer Load options menu shown in Fig. 6-13. The first field, *filename:* requests the name of the document you are retrieving. In this type of command field, you can either type in the name of the file directly, or select it from a list of available files by pressing F1.

```
‖                                                                          ‖
‖                                                                          ‖
‖                                                                          ‖
TRANSFER LOAD filename: ■              read only: Yes(No)

Enter filename or press F1 to select from list
Pg1 Co1              {}                                       Microsoft Word
```

6-13 Exiting from Microsoft Word.

Word will display the document files on the disk. Use the arrow keys to highlight the name of the document you wish to load. Finally, press Return to execute the command. Word will load the document into memory for editing.

Exiting Word

Before concluding this crash course, you must acquire one last skill: exiting from Word. Fortunately, exiting from Word is not difficult. Use the Quit command from the Edit menu by pressing Esc to exit from type-in mode and then pressing Q for quit.

Once you select the Quit command, you are on your way out. However, before you exit from Word, Word checks to see if you have neglected to save any of your work. If you have saved all your work, Word ends and you return to the operating system. If you have not saved all your work, Word prompts you to press Y to save the work, N to quit without saving recent edits, or Esc to exit the Quit command and return to editing the document.

If you wish to save the latest edition of the document, press Y. If the document has a filename, Word saves the document and then returns you to the operating system. If the document is new and does not have a filename, Word returns to the Edit menu with the error message File may not be saved. You can now save the new document with the Transfer Save command.

On the other hand, if you are indifferent to losing the results of the latest editing session, press N. If you accidentally selected the Quit command, you can return to the document by pressing the Esc key.

Summary

In this chapter, you mastered the following skills:

- Selecting commands from the Edit menu with the Esc, Tab, Space, Backspace, Shift-Tab, and arrow keys.
- Selecting options from options menus with Space.
- Setting the print options.
- Printing documents with Print Printer.
- Saving documents with the Transfer Save command.
- Clearning Word with the Transfer Clear command.
- Retrieving documents with the Transfer Load command.
- Exiting Word with the Quit command.

CHAPTER 7

Formatting paragraphs

One of the traditional advantages of word processors is their ability to format paragraphs. Formatting paragraphs is the process of adjusting text qualities such as margins, indentions, and line spacing. With a word processor, not only is it easy for the writer to format documents, but it is also easy to change a paragraph's format. Formatted documents have a polished, organized appearance that makes these documents easier to read and comprehend. If the recipient of your business letter finds it easy to read and attractive in design, he or she might be a little more willing to purchase your services.

On-screen formatting

One important feature that simplifies paragraph formatting is "on-screen" formatting. On-screen formatting allows you to see how a document looks on the screen, before it is printed on paper. This preview allows you to see the current paragraph formatting effects and help you determine which formats need to be changed.

When you employ a formatting command, Word does not format the text a few seconds before printing it. Rather, Word formats your text immediately and displays it on the screen. For example, a double-spaced paragraph in Word is double-spaced on the screen and double-spaced on the printout.

On-screen formatting eliminates the need to show embedded characters and dot commands on the screen. You can see the text format on the screen, giving you a good idea of what the printed document will look like.

Selecting paragraphs

Before you can format a paragraph in your document, you must select it. When you move the cursor to a point in a paragraph, the paragraph format commands will affect the paragraph containing the cursor. If you wish to format a group of paragraphs, you must extend the cursor to highlight all the paragraphs you wish to format. After the paragraph(s) are selected, you can format the text with the direct format commands or with the Format Paragraph command.

You might wish to format a paragraph as you are writing it. To do so, select the paragraph by moving a cursor to any character within the paragraph (the cursor might already be within the paragraph). Then, select the appropriate formatting command. When the paragraph is completed, it will possess the formats assigned to it during its nascent stage.

The paragraph format assigned to the last paragraph in the text is applied to future paragraphs so that any new paragraphs following will have the same paragraph format as the previous paragraph.

Direct keyboard formatting

Formatting from the keyboard is a fast and simple method for formatting paragraphs. Word has special key codes that format paragraphs. The key codes are generated by holding down the Alt key and pressing certain formatting keys. The same paragraph formats can be set with the Format Paragraph command as with the formatting keys. The formatting keys can format paragraphs faster than the Format Paragraph command, but the Format Paragraph command offers options not supported by the formatting keys.

Using the direct format keys requires more expertise than using the Format Paragraph command, because the formatting keys do not have a menu. There are 12 paragraph format keys whose functions need to be memorized before they can be used properly. Should your memory fail, you can use the on-screen help facilities to recall the function of a direct format key.

Figure 7-1 shows a list of paragraph formatting commands. Test them on paragraphs in the document you created in the previous chapter. Note that when you format a paragraph, you do not need to select the entire paragraph with the cursor. Word knows that you wish to apply the format paragraph commands to the entire paragraph. If you wish to format several paragraphs, though, you must highlight each paragraph you want to format.

For practice, let us make the first paragraph double-spaced. Move to any character in the paragraph. Then, hold down the Alt key and press 2. The paragraph is reorganized and double-spaced. To return the paragraph to its normal

```
Paragraph Formatting Keys Used in Combination with the <Alt> Key

Alignment                              Miscellaneous

l    Flush left                        o    Open paragraph format
r    Flush right                            (One blank line placed
c    Centered                               between every paragraph)
j    Justified                         2    Double spaced
                                       p    Standard paragraph format
Indents

n    Left indent increase
m    Left indent decrease
f    First line indent
t    Increase hanging indent 1/2
q    Indent from left and right
```

7-1 The keys used in direct formatting paragraphs.

compact single-spaced state, press Alt-P. Alt-P returns the paragraph format to the normal paragraph format. Try using the other format paragraph keys.

The format keys were assigned letters that make it easy to remember their function. The letter of the format key is a mnemonic for the format keys function. Alt-C, for instance, stands for centered paragraph alignment. Another key, Alt-F, stands for first line indent.

Paragraph alignment

In Word, a line usually holds fewer characters than the maximum number possible. For example, a paragraph might allow 60 characters to a line. Suppose a line being typed in is 55 characters in length, and the next word entered is 10 characters long. The word wrap feature in Word moves the 10-character word to the next line as shown in Fig. 7-2. This move leaves 5 extra character spaces in the old line. The paragraph alignment determines what happens, if anything, to these extra spaces.

Word has four direct format keys to control alignment. Figure 7-2 shows how Alt-L, Alt-R, Alt-C, and Alt-J control the alignment of words in a line. Alt-L (left flush) pushes words to the left. Words are flush to the left margin, and spaces are placed at the end of the line. Left flush alignment results in a straight left margin and a ragged right margin. Alt-R (right flush) function is the opposite of left flush. With right flush alignment, spaces are placed at the left of the line. Thus, text is aligned along the straight right margin, leaving a ragged left margin.

The two other alignment format keys are Alt-C and Alt-J. Alt-C (center text) centers the text in the middle of the screen. Alt-C is used to format titles. Alt-J (justify text) straightens the left and right margins. Spaces are evenly distributed between words in the lines so that the first word of each line is flush against the left margin and the last word of each line is flush against the right margin.

LEFT ALIGNMENT

Word processors used to be poorly designed, being very complex and difficult to learn. A new generation of word processors, however, provide you with powerful functions without making them impossible to use. Chief among these quality word processors is Microsoft Word. If you know how to use a typewriter, you can quickly learn how to use Word.

RIGHT ALIGNMENT

Word processors used to be poorly designed, being very complex and difficult to learn. A new generation of word processors, however, provide you with powerful functions without making them impossible to use. Chief among these quality word processors is Microsoft Word. If you know how to use a typewriter, you can quickly learn how to use Word.

CENTER ALIGNMENT

Word processors used to be poorly designed, being very complex and difficult to learn. A new generation of word processors, however, provide you with powerful functions without making them impossible to use. Chief among these quality word processors is Microsoft Word. If you know how to use a typewriter, you can quickly learn how to use Word.

JUSTIFIED ALIGNMENT

Word processors used to be poorly designed, being very complex and difficult to learn. A new generation of word processors, however, provide you with powerful functions without making them impossible to use. Chief among these quality word processors is Microsoft Word. If you know how to use a typewriter, you can quickly learn how to use Word.

7-2 Examples of left aligned, right aligned, centered, and justified paragraphs. The centered format is often used for titles.

Indention

Indenting paragraphs is useful when designing tables, charts, and other documents in which layout is very important. When you want a paragraph to have a wider left or right margin, you indent the paragraph. Indenting widens the margins.

Placing a left indent on a paragraph is called *nesting* the paragraph. This term probably evolved because the paragraph appears nested in surrounding paragraphs. Alt-N (nesting) increases the left indent (nest) by one-half inch. Alt-M has just the opposite effect, decreasing the left margin by a half inch.

Word has other types of paragraph indention. Alt-F is first line indent. Alt-F indents the first line of the paragraph five spaces towards the right. First-line indent is used in letters, manuscripts, and other documents.

Another type of indent is called a *hanging* indent and is set by pressing Alt–T. A hanging indent is the inverse of first-line indent. In a hanging indent, all the lines except the first line are indented. This results in a paragraph that "hangs" from the first line.

The Alt–F (first-line indent) key indents the first line one-half inch. The Alt–T (hanging indent and tab) key, sets a one inch hanging indent. This is equivalent to adding an one inch tab to the each line in the paragraph except the first line. The Alt–F and Alt–T formats are shown in Fig. 7-3. Finally, the Alt–P

FIRST LINE INDENT
　Word processors used to be poorly designed, being very complex and difficult to learn. A new generation of word processors, however, provides you with powerful functions without making them impossible to use. Chief among these quality word processors is Microsoft Word. If you know how to use a typewriter, you can quickly learn how to use Word.

HANGING TAB
Word processors used to be poorly designed, being very complex and difficult to learn. A new generation of word processors, however, provides you with powerful functions without making them impossible

LEFT INDENT (NEST)
　Word processors used to be poorly designed, being very complex and difficult to learn. A new generation of word processors, however, provides you with powerful functions without making them impossible to use. Chief among these quality word processors

DECREASE LEFT INDENT
Word processors used to be poorly designed, being very complex and difficult to learn. A new generation of word processors, however, provides you with powerful functions without making them impossible to use. Chief among these quality word processors is Microsoft Word. If you know how to use a typewriter, you can quickly learn how to use Word.

7-3 Examples of first line indents, hanging indent, and left indents.

Formatting paragraphs

key combination allows you to restore the format of the paragraph to its default or normal state.

The final indention type is the indent from both left and right Alt-Q. This is the sort of indention scheme used when you lift a long quotation from another source. Each time you press Alt-Q, both margins creep inward one-half inch.

Combining paragraph formats

In Word, different paragraph formats can be combined to create new formats. Formatting keys can be combined to achieve formats that could not be created by a single key press. For example, by pressing the Alt-N (left indent or nest) key twice, you get a one-inch indent instead of the standard half-inch indent.

In some cases, the formatting keys complement each other. For example, Alt-F (first line indent) and Alt-N (left indent or nest) when combined produce a paragraph with both a left indent and a first line indent. Finally, there are cases where keys cancel; for example, Alt-N (left indent) and Alt-M (right indent) have the opposite effect, like taking two steps forward and taking two steps back. Your paragraph will be unaffected if you press each of these key combinations an equal number of times. Figure 7-4 shows the effects of various formats.

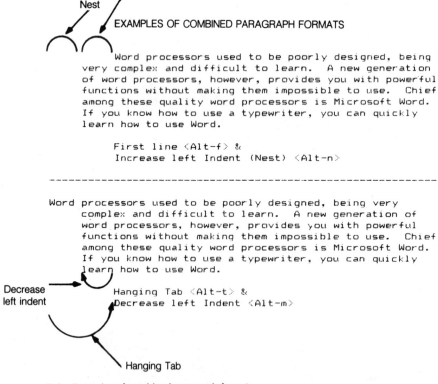

7-4 Examples of combined paragraph formats.

Double-spaced and open paragraphs

Word includes two miscellaneous paragraph formatting keys: Alt-2 and Alt-O. Alt-2 (double-space) double spaces lines in the paragraph. That is, it places blank lines between lines of text. Double-spacing makes pencil-editing hard copies of rough drafts much easier.

Alt-O (open paragraph) opens up paragraphs by placing blank lines between each paragraph. This is known as *open paragraph spacing*. You can also create a blank line between paragraphs by pressing Return twice. However, Alt-O is much easier to remove than a hundred Return characters, and therefore is the preferred method for opening paragraphs that might subsequently need to be closed up again.

The Format Paragraph command

The Format Paragraph command, as the name implies, can also be used to format paragraphs. Formatting paragraphs with the Format Paragraph command is a cumbersome but exact method of formatting text. When formatting text with the Format command, you can control the format of your text in much greater detail than you can with direct formatting commands. Unfortunately, the Format menu is large and it takes considerably longer to format paragraphs with the Format Paragraph menu than with the format keys.

To execute the Format Paragraph command, press Esc to end the type-in mode and enter the main menu. Now press F to select the Format command from the Edit menu, then press P to activate the Paragraph command from the Format menu. You should now be at the Format Paagraph menu as seen in Fig. 7-5.

```
         formatting. With Word, the claim "what you see is what you
         get" is completely realized.

         In Microsoft Word, paragraph and page formats, such as
         indentations and line spacing, are displayed on the monitor
FORMAT PARAGRAPH alignment: Left Centered Right Justified
   left indent: 0"          first line: 0"           right indent: 0"
   line spacing: 1 li       space before: 0 li       space after: 0 li
   keep together: Yes(No)   keep follow: Yes(No)     side by side: Yes(No)
Select option
Pg1 Col          {}                                         Microsoft Word
```

7-5 The Format Paragraph menu controls all possible paragraph formats.

From your experience with direct format keys, you should be familiar with many of the options fields in the Format Paragraph options menu. For example, the alignment field includes the options Left, Centered, Right, and Justified (these produce the same effects as Alt-L, Alt-C, Alt-R, and Alt-J respectively). If you are unsure about the function of any option field, you can use the Alt-H (Help) key. Alt-H produces a summary of the settings in the Format Paragraph menu.

By using the Format Paragraph command to format paragraphs, you can designate a more precise format than can be designated with the direct format keys alone. For example, utilizing Alt-N (nest a half inch), you can only increase the left indent by multiples of one-half inch. When employing the Format Paragraph command, you can nest the left indent by multiples of one-half inch.

Suppose you wanted the right margin for the paragraph to be 7/10 inch wide. You would enter .7 in the right indent field. Likewise, if you wanted to triple-space a report, then you would change the setting in the line spacing field to 3.

The left indent and right indent options control the indention from the left and right margins. The first line option controls the indention of the first line in the paragraph. Indentions can be set in 1/10-inch increments. The indentions are preset to zero. To change the indention, move to the appropriate field, and type the new setting. For example, if you want the right indent to be 1½ inches, move to the right indent field and type 1.5.

The line spacing option controls the number of spaces between lines in a document. The option is frequently changed to 2 or 3 for double or triple-spacing. The option can also be changed to auto, which sets the line spacing according to the size of the largest font on the line. Fractions of a line (such as 1.5) can be set, but might not work on all printers.

The space before and the space after options control whether lines are inserted before or after paragraphs. These features can be useful when putting together an enumerated list, such as a contract or a table. The options are preset to zero.

Initial paragraph format

Before you change any of the options listed, take a look at the initial format for the paragraph. This is the paragraph format that Word uses if you do not change the format yourself. This is also the format you assign to text when you employ the Alt-P command.

In the normal paragraph, lines are aligned flush left and are unjustified (alignment = left). There are no indentions from either the left or right margin (indents = 0). In the paragraph, all lines are single spaced (line spacing = 1). There are no blank spaces between paragraphs (lines after = 0), and Word splits paragraphs between pages (keep = no).

Joining and splitting paragraphs

At times you might want to splice two paragraphs or split one paragraph into two. Paragraphs can be split or spliced by inserting or deleting a Return character.

To start a new paragraph, all you need to do is move the cursor to the location where you wish the second paragraph to begin. Press Return, and the paragraph is split. The two new paragraphs share the same format as the parent paragraph.

Splicing two paragraphs is as simple as splitting one paragraph in two. Move the cursor to the first character in the beginning of the of the second paragraph as shown in Fig. 7-6. Press the Backspace key until the paragraph mark at the end of the first paragraph is erased and the two paragraphs are fused.

Without the Return, the first paragraph merges with the second to form a

> Move the cursor to beginning of the new paragraph and
> press Return to divide one paragraph into two paragraphs
>
> Word processors used to be very complex and difficult to learn. A new generation of word processors, however, provides powerful functions without making them impossible to use. Chief among this brave new world of word processors is Microsoft Word. If you know how to use a typewriter, you can quickly learn how to use Word. Word is a state of the art word processor. It has many features which previously were found only on dedicated word processors. One notable feature is on-screen formatting. With Word, the claim "what you see is what you get" is completely realized.
>
> Word processors used to be very complex and difficult to learn. A new generation of word processors, however, provides powerful functions without making them impossible to use. Chief among this brave new world of word processors is Microsoft Word. If you know how to use a typewriter, you can quickly learn how to use Word.
>
> Move cursor to the beginning of the second paragraph, then press Backspace to erase paragraph mark
>
> Word is a state of the art word processor. It has many features which previously were found only on dedicated word processors. One notable feature is on-screen formatting. With Word, the claim "what you see is what you get" is completely realized.

7-6 A paragraph can be split into two paragraphs by inserting a Return in the paragraph. The two new paragraphs have the same paragraph format as the original paragraph.

single paragraph. The new paragraph assumes the format of the second paragraph. The information controlling the format of paragraphs is stored in the paragraph mark at the end of the second paragraph.

Hyphens, spaces, and word wrap

Word wrap is a very useful feature, as has been discussed earlier. Word wrap enables you to write faster and more efficiently. Unfortunately, word wrap is also responsible for a host of minor annoyances. Word wrap automatically assumes that a Return character marks the end of a paragraph. Therefore, you must use the newline character to mark the end of a line that is not the end of a paragraph.

Likewise, word wrap automatically divides words separated by a space or a hyphen. Thus, World War II might be divided:

> One of the greatest human tragedies, World War
>
> II, should not be forgotten.

Likewise, the hyphens in Lotus 1-2-3 can result in havoc:

> The spreadsheet sensation, Lotus 1-2-

Formatting paragraphs

3, is sweeping the nation.

There are ways to correct these unfortunate divisions. The nonbreaking hyphen and nonbreaking space prevent these unsightly occurrences.

Newline key

While writing a document with Word 5.0, you might occasionally want to start a new line without starting a new paragraph. However, the Return key should not start the new line, because the Return character marks the beginning of a new paragraph. The Newline key is needed.

The Newline key cannot be found on the keyboard because Newline is a combination of two keys, Shift and Return. By pressing Shift-Return, you can start a new line without starting a new paragraph. Shift-Return is used to create tables and line breaks in poetry, among other tasks.

Nonbreaking space

Occasionally, you enter two or more words that must be on the same line. Unfortunately, word wrap might separate these words in an effort to place words within the right margin. Thus, if you were writing about the IBM PC, you might want to avoid situations like:

During the early 1980s, the IBM

PC was released.

To prevent this, you can utilize the nonbreaking space, which prevents words connected by a space from being separated. The nonbreaking space is created by holding down the Ctrl key and pressing Space. Word treats the nonbreaking space as if it were an indivisible character. Thus, words connected by a nonbreaking space are not separated to fit on different lines.

Hyphens

Word works with three types of hyphens: hyphens, nonrequired hyphens and nonbreaking hyphens. A *hyphen* is an ordinary dash. To enter it, simply press the hyphen key on the keyboard.

A *nonrequired* hyphen is used to divide long words into syllables. Dividing a long word enables Word to create a straighter right margin. If you wish to eliminate large gaps in the right margin caused by the word wrap juggling long words, you can insert nonrequired hyphens into big words in the document. Nonrequired hyphens are invisible hyphens that are only printed when the word with the hyphens falls at the end of the line. Word wrap will treat the nonrequired hyphen as a space and judge whethr the entire word fits at the end of the line. If the word does not fit, the word is divided at the point designated by the nonrequired hyphen. Thus, without nonrequired hyphens you might have margins that look like:

The Computer Works offers special

courses in word processing,

spreadsheet analysis, and

By inserting nonrequired hyphens, the text can assumed a polished look:

The Computer Works offers special

courses in word processing, spread-

sheet analysis, and programming.

A nonrequired hyphen can be entered by pressing Ctrl and the - (hyphen) key together. Nonrequired hyphens should only be placed in long words that might disfigure the right margin.

Nonbreaking hyphens

Hyphenated words can be divided by word wrap when the right margin is formed. In many cases, it does not matter whether state-of-the-art is printed like:

Microsoft Windows is a state-

of-the-art program.

However, some hyphenated words should not be separated. For example:

During the war years of

1861-1865 the United States

was nearly invaded by England.

Likewise, the hyphenated words should remain together in this example:

Capitalism can be summed up

in one statement:

income-expenses = profit.

If you want a hyphen in a word or words but want the word kept together on a line, you must use a nonbreaking hyphen. A nonbreaking hyphen is similar to a nonbreaking space in that both are handled like characters by Word. Thus, two words separated by a nonbreaking hyphen are regarded as a single word and are not split when the right margins are set by word wrap.

A nonbreaking hyphen is entered by holding down the Ctrl and Shift keys and pressing the hyphen key (Shift-Ctrl-Hyphen).

Finally, it is possible to enter a regular hyphen by simply pressing the Hyphen key. A regular hyphen is always displayed and used to break words at the right margin.

Advanced paragraph format options

The keep and side-by-side options cannot be set from the keyboard. These options can be ignored if you are just using Word to write letters, contracts, or plain reports. Nevertheless, the options are easy to learn, and especially useful in desktop publishing tasks.

Controlling page breaks in paragraphs with the Keep options

The Keep options in the Format Paragraph menu control where Word inserts page breaks in paragraphs. A page break designates where a new page in the printout begins. Ordinarily, a paragraph that begins at the bottom of the page starts on one page and is continued on the following page. The Keep options are especially useful in preventing tables from being split by a page break and printed on two pages, and preventing titles from being printed at the bottom of a page (see Fig. 7-7).

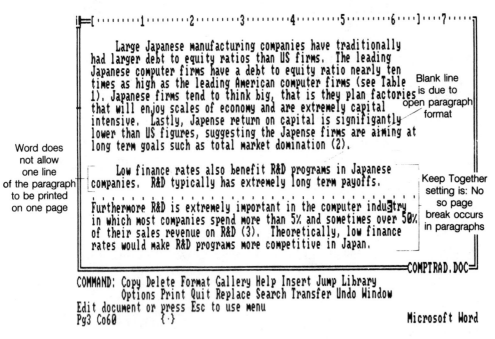

7-7 The keep together option controls page breaks where page breaks are inserted in paragraphs that are printed at the bottom of the page.

Controlling page breaks within a paragraph

If a paragraph is assigned the keep together option, Word does not place a page break in that paragraph and prints that entire paragraph on one page. Paragraphs that do not fit at the bottom of the current page are printed on the next page.

When the keep together option is on No, Word breaks the paragraph unless breaking the paragraph would cause a widow or orphan line. A widow line is the last line of a paragraph printed at the top of a page. An orphan line is the first line of a paragraph printed at the bottom of a page. The keep together option is ordinarily set to No.

If the keep together setting is No, the Print Options widow/orphan control determines whether widow or orphan lines are permitted. When the setting is No, Word allows widows and orphan lines. The standard widow/orphan setting is Yes, so that Word normally prevents widow and orphan lines.

Controlling page breaks between adjacent paragraphs

The keep follow paragraph format option is normally set to No. If two or more adjacent paragraphs are assigned the paragraph format keep follow: Yes and keep together: No, then Word makes sure that a page break does not occur between the paragraphs. If a page break would have fallen between two paragraphs, Word makes the page breaks fall before the last two lines of a paragraph and after the first two lines of a paragraph. Thus, keep follow: Yes prevents a paragraph from beginning at the top of the page (see Fig. 7-8).

```
⊫[·········1·········2·········3·········4·········5·········6····]····7·····⌐
  Marketing is especially important when considering microcomputers
  because there are many more firms producing personal computers
  than main frame computers and because main frames are not sold
  through retail outlets (10).

      Marketing is important because the computer industry unlike
  many other industries offers a complex, difficult to use, and      Page break occurs
  heterogeneous product.  Consumers are inclined to consider name    between two
  brands only when purchasing a computer.  Brand name are a signal   paragraphs when
  that there will be software, training, upgrades, and maintenance   Keep Follow
  available for the computer.  In addition, a brand name computer    setting is No
  like a brand name washer/dryer is a reliable product.█

  · · · · · · · · · · · · · · · · · · · · · · · · · · · · · · · · · · · · · ·
      The average consumer only recognizes a handful of brand
  names.  In addition, computer retail stores are constrained by
  display space and inventory requirements.  Thus, they are only
  able to stock a handful of different computers.  Japanese
  computer producers have tried to enter the US market on an OEM
                                                               ⌐COMPTRAD.DOC=
COMMAND: Copy Delete Format Gallery Help Insert Jump Library
         Options Print Quit Replace Search Transfer Undo Window
Edit document or press Esc to use menu
Pg4 Co54       { }                                             Microsoft Word
```

7-8 The keep follow option controls whether a page break can be placed between two paragraphs.

If you do not want a page break to occur anywhere within two or more adjacent paragraphs, then set keep together: Yes and keep follow: Yes. These setting are useful in preventing tables from being printed across two pages and in preventing titles from being printed at the bottom of a page.

Printing multiple columns with the side-by side option

The side-by-side option controls whether paragraphs are printed on one column as a letter or in multiple columns. The side-by-side option is normally off, causing paragraphs to be printed in a single column. When the side by side option is on, Word does not change the display of the paragraphs, but it prints the paragraphs in multiple columns.

74 *Formatting paragraphs*

The side-by-side option is best for printing two paragraphs that follow each other side-by-side, as in tables where paragraphs that follow each other are printed in different columns. Figure 7-9 shows a document in which the side-by-side is used. The Format Division Layout commands are best for printing text in columns, as in a newspaper, where paragraphs that follow each other are printed in the same column. Chapter 9 explains how to enter division markers, and Chapter 14 explains how to print multiple columns using the Format Division Layout command.

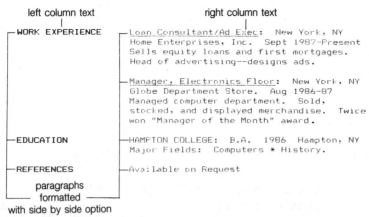

7-9 The side by side caption is useful when working with paragraphs that should be placed in two columns as in a table or resume.

To print paragraphs in multiple columns, you must first set the left and right margins for each paragraph. The margins define the position of the paragraphs when they are printed. The margins must allow a space between the two paragraphs, so that the paragraphs do not overlap. After the margins have been set, highlight the paragraphs to be printed in multiple columns and set the Format Paragraph side-by-side option to Yes. The position of the paragraphs on the screen does not change, but when the paragraphs are printed, they appear in columns.

If the multiple column option does not work, it is probably because your margins cause the paragraphs to overlap. Word will not print multiple columns if it would cause the paragraphs to overlap. If Word does not print multiple columns when the side-by-side option is on Yes, try redefining the margins and then reassign the side-by-side option to the paragraphs affected.

Summary

You have examined several paragraph formatting commands as well as several features that arrange text in the paragraph. Upon finishing this chapter, you should be able to:

- Select paragraphs for formatting.
- Format paragraphs using direct formatting keys.
- Format paragraphs with the Format Paragraph command.
- Create new lines by pressing Shift-Return.
- Create a nonbreaking space by pressing Ctrl-Space.
- Differentiate among hyphens, nonrequired hyphens, and nonbreaking hyphens.
- Create a nonrequired hyphen by pressing Ctrl-Hyphen.
- Make a nonbreaking hyphen by pressing Ctrl-Shift-Hyphen.
- Know about controlling page breaks in paragraphs with the keep options.
- Know about printing multiple columns by using the side-by-side option.

CHAPTER 8

Character format options

Word allows you to change the emphasis, style, and/or size of characters in a document. This process is called *character formatting.* The Format Character command or the direct formatting keys can be used to format characters. In Word, characters can be in boldface, italic, underline, and many other forms. In addition, the font name and font size of characters can be set.

Hardware capabilities

Although Word can format characters in many different styles, your monitor or printer might not display or print the nonstandard styles properly. Nongraphics monitors and letter quality printers cannot produce italics, subscripts, superscripts, double underlines, small capitals, and strikethrough character formats. Some dot matrix printers are also unable to produce all the character formats supported by Word.

If your printer behaves in an inexplicable manner when it encounters a specific character format, you might be using an incorrect printer driver. Chapter 2 covers printer driver installation, and Chapter 6 explains how to select a printer description prior to printing a document. Consult one of these chapters if your printer is misbehaving.

If your monitor cannot display a character format used in a document, a character format that can be shown is displayed. However, Word still uses the original character format with the hard copy. For example, nongraphics monitors cannot show italics. Characters formatted with italics are shown in underline format.

Likewise, if your printer cannot print a format used in the document, an alternate format is printed.

Even if a character format, like italics, cannot be displayed, Word stores the character format with the document. Thus, even though the correct format might not appear on the monitor, it still might appear on the printed copy, or on a graphics monitor, if you load the file into Word running on another machine.

Selection of text

Before formatting text, the cursor must be extended so that it highlights the characters to be formatted. Once the correct characters are highlighted, you can format the characters with either the Format Character command or the direct formatting keys.

Formatting with format keys

The character format keys, like the paragraph format keys, are combinations of the Alt key with the letter keys. Figure 8-1 shows the keys used to control character formats.

Alt-B and Alt-U are the direct format keys for boldface and underline. These two character formats can be reproduced on all monitors and most printers. Alt-Space is used to return a character to the normal format.

The Alt-I key is the format for italicized text. The Alt-S key is the format for strikethrough. Strikethrough is used to show text that you plan to delete in a later draft. A second reader might read the strikethrough text and decide whether or not the text should be deleted.

Format Keys	Graphics Monitor	Non-Graphics Monitor
<Alt-B>	**Boldface**	Boldface
<Alt-I>	*Italics*	Italics
<Alt-U>	Underline	Underline
<Alt-D>	Double Underline	Double Underline
<Alt-K>	SMALL CAPS	SMALL CAPS
<Alt-S>	~~Strikethrough~~	Strikethrough
<Alt-Plus>	Super^{script}	Superscript
<Alt-Minus>	Sub$_{script}$	Subscript
<Alt-E>	Hidden Text	Hidden Text
<Alt-Space>	Normal	Normal

8-1 The character formats controlled by direct formatting keys.

The Alt–D (double underline) and Alt–K (small capitals) format keys complete the list of character emphasis keys. As you have seen in Fig. 8-1, these formats are displayed as underlined text on nongraphics monitors.

Combining character formats

As with the paragraph format keys, the effects of the character format keys are cumulative. Formats can be combined to the produce special formats. Alt–K (small caps) and Alt–B (boldface), for example, combine to form bold small caps.

Other formats, however, cancel or nullify one another. Selecting Alt–u (underline) followed by Alt–D (double underline), reduces to a double underline format. Do not be afraid to experiment with combinations of character formats. Remember that you can return the text to normal format by using the Alt–space key combination.

Combination Formats

Alt–B	**Boldface**
Alt–K	SMALL CAPS
Alt–B Alt–K	**BOLD SMALL CAPS**
Alt–I	*Italics*
Alt–U	Underline
Alt–I Alt–U	*Underline Italics*
Alt–D	Double Underline
Alt–U	Underline
Alt–D Alt–U	Double Underline

8-2 Some character formats can be combined to create new character formats. The double underline character format cancels the underline character format.

Superscripts and subscripts

Word can also create superscripts and subscripts with the Alt–Plus (superscript) and Alt–Minus (subscript) keys. Note that the case of the keys is irrelevant. Alt–Equal has the same effect as Alt–Plus. Likewise, Alt–Underscore has the same effect as Alt–Minus. Superscripts and subscripts are portrayed in Fig. 8-1.

Superscripts are often used in footnote references, trademarks, and mathematical and scientific formulas. Subscripts are often used in chemical formulas and mathematical equations. The subscript and superscript formats can be triggered to combine with other formats. The Alt–Space combination returns all character formats to normal.

The Format Character command

The Format Character command is also used to format characters. The Format Character menu is reached by selecting the Format command from the Edit menu, and then the Character command from the Format menu (when in the type-in mode, type Esc, F, C). The Format Character menu has several option fields. You already know how to control character formats like boldface and underline with the direct formats keys, so this section is devoted to font type and size.

```
‖ This text is BOLDFACED & UNDERLINED ──── Highlighted text                    ‖
═══════════════════════════════════════════════════════════════════════════════
FORMAT CHARACTER bold: Yes No        italic: Yes(No)        underline:(Yes)No
               strikethrough: Yes(No)  uppercase: Yes(No)      small caps: Yes(No)
               double underline: Yes(No) position:(Normal)Superscript Subscript
               font name: Courier      font size: 12          font color: Black
               hidden: Yes(No)
Select option
Pg4 Co35            {&······...re·8-4} ?                 OT    Microsoft Word
```

8-3 The Format Character menu controls all possible character formats, including different font sizes and font types.

Font type

A character's appearance is controlled by many attributes. These attributes can have a dramatic effect on text presentation, as shown in Fig. 8-4. The character font is an important factor controlling the appearance of a character. Fonts control the type style of printed characters, but do not affect the monitor's display of characters. The popular font styles include Modern, Roman, and Script.

The fonts usable by Word are limited by the printer in use. Most printers do not offer all possible fonts. Pica (Modern a), the font offered by all letter quality and dot matrix printers, is shown in Fig. 8-4. Pica (Modern a) is also used on most typewriters.

```
PICA (Modern a)
The quick brown fox jumped over
the lazy dog.

ELITE (Modern c)
The quick brown fox jumped over the lazy dog.

PS (Roman a)
The quick brown fox jumped over the lazy dog.

PICA D (Modern b)
The quick brown fox jumped over the lazy dog.

ELITE D (Modern d)
The quick brown fox jumped over the lazy dog.
```

8-4 An example of different font types produced with an Epson printer.

To see what fonts are supported by the printer, move to the font: options field of the Format Character menu. Press F1 and a list of fonts supported by the printer appears on the screen. To select a font, highlight the font desired with the arrow keys and press Tab. Pressing Tab returns you to the Format Character menu, allowing you to set other formatting options. Once the settings on the Format Character menu meet your requirements, press Return to change the font of the highlighted text in the document. (Note that "PS" means *proportionally spaced*.)

Font size

The font name: field controls the style of the printed character, but it is the font size: field that determines the size of the printed character. The available font sizes are determined by the printer connected to the computer. Font sizes for Pica (Modern a) range from 8 through 16 points. The normal font size for characters is 12.

The same process used to select the font style is used to select the font size. To assign a font size to a selection, first highlight the text, then, enter the Format Character command menu (type Esc, F, C), move the cursor to the font size: field, press F1 to list the available sizes, and select a font size with the arrow keys. Finally, press Tab to return to the Format Character menu. Finally, press Return when the settings on the Format Character menu are appropriately set.

Some font sizes cannot be used with the bold character format. For example, the Epson MX printer supports bold format with font sizes 12 and 16, but not with font sizes 8 and 14. If you set bold text to a font size of 8 or 14, Word will use a different font size. Examples of different font sizes appear in Fig. 8-5.

Font Size 8

The quick brown fox jumped over the lazy dog.

Font Size 12

The quick brown fox jumped over the lazy dog.

Font Size 14

The quick brown fox jumped over the lazy dog.

Font Size 16

The quick brown fox jumped over the lazy dog.

8-5 An example of different font sizes produced with an Epson printer.

Hidden character format

Assigning the Hidden Character format to text causes that text not to be displayed on the screen or printed. This command is easy to use, but only applicable to power users. If you had a document that included confidential information and you worked in a crowded office, you could assign the hidden text format to the confidential phrases. The confidential material would not be displayed on the screen or printed on a printout as long as the hidden character format was assigned to the phrases. Once the hidden text format was removed, the text would be displayed on the screen again, and could be printed.

For example, if you were typing a letter to a partner regarding a deal to sell a multimillion dollar building, you might use hidden text on important figures, including the lowest price at which you would accept a deal. This precaution would prevent people walking by your machine from seeing the secret figures.

Normally, Word does not show even the position of hidden text. If you set the Options show hidden text setting to Yes, then all hidden text is shown and underlined with a dotted line on the screen (see Fig. 8-6). Thus, if you forget the position of the hidden text in the document, set the Options show hidden text setting to Yes and visually search for any underlined text. Note that information in hidden text is

```
 lowest price at which you would accept a deal. This
 precaution would prevent people walking by your machine from
 seeing the secret figures.
```

Text that would normally be hidden

Option to show hidden text

```
WINDOW OPTIONS for window number: 1        show hidden text: Yes No
        show ruler: Yes(No)       show non-printing symbols:(None)Partial All
        show layout: Yes(No)           show line breaks: Yes(No)
        show outline: Yes(No)           show style bar: Yes(No)

GENERAL OPTIONS mute: Yes(No)              summary sheet:(Yes)No
        measure:(In)Cm P10 P12 Pt           display mode: 1
        paginate:(Auto)Manual                     colors:
        autosave: 4                      autosave confirm: Yes(No)
        show menu:(Yes)No                  show borders:(Yes)No
        date format:(MDY)DMY             decimal character:(.),
        time format:(12)24              default tab width: 0.5"
        line numbers: Yes(No)            count blank space: Yes(No)
        cursor speed: 3                   linedraw character: (|)
        speller path: C:\X\BOOKS\WORD\PROGRAM\SPELL-AM.LEX
Select option
Pg5 Co18              {2}                ?                  Microsoft Word
```

8-6 Hidden text format can be used when editing sensitive documents. More commonly, hidden text format is used when generating tables, indexes, and when importing data.

not very secure, and therefore, you should never trust hidden text to protect important secrets.

Near letter-quality fonts and font names

Medium- and high-priced dot-matrix printers can emulate letter-quality printers by printing with near letter-quality fonts. To use near letter-quality fonts on a dot-matrix printer, highlight the portion of the document to be printed in near letter-quality. If you want the entire document to be printed with near letter-quality characters using just one font type, press Shift-F10 to highlight the entire document. Then select the Format Character command and set the font name field to an appropriate near letter-quality font.

For example, if you were using an IBM Proprinter, you would assign the PICAD font to text to print in near letter quality. Word places certain characters at the end of a font name to indicate special font qualities (see Fig. 8-7).

The endings, unfortunately, do not always correspond with these meanings, so you have to experiment with the fonts.

C— Correspondence quality
D— Double-strike
NLQ— Near letter-quality
PD— Proportional space double-strike
PS— Proportional spacing

8-7 Font endings sometimes give clues to appearance of font.

Downloadable fonts

Many companies such as VS Software and Bitstream Fontware provide downloadable fonts to be used with laser printers and other printers. If you are not satisfied with the fonts available, you should look into these fonts for your printer. they can add to the capabilities of your printer and the quality of your printout.

Font color

The final option in the Format Character menu is the font color option. This option only applies if you are using a color printer. Use F1 to show the available colors. Use the arrow keys to highlight the color you wish to use and then press Tab to return to the menu.

Summary

You should know how to do the following:
- Select text to be formatted by extending the cursor.
- Employ the direct formatting keys to change character formats.
- Use the Format Character command to set the font and font size.

Character format options

- Underline text and display text in boldface (these are the two most frequently used character formats in word processing).
- Return formatted characters to normal characters with the Alt–Space key.
- Combine character formats.
- Understand the use of hidden text and the show hidden text option on the Options menu.
- Understand the fonts available for your printer according to their suffix.

CHAPTER 9

Setting tabs, margins, and page numbers

This chapter covers document margins, tabs, and automatic page numbering. The Format Division command controls margins and page numbering for the entire document. Setting the document margins is very important when preparing Word to print on different sizes of paper, assigning margins for an entire document, or designing margins for a large section of a document. Margins for a single paragraph or group of paragraphs are best set with the Format Paragraph command covered in Chapter 7. The Format Tabs command controls tabs. Changing tab stops is especially useful when working on tables.

Default page settings

Word's tabs, margins, ruler line, and automatic page numbering system are preset to work with 8.5 by 11 inch paper. The margins of a document determine the distance between the edges of the page and the text. The left and right margins are each set to 1.25 inches (on an Epson FX80 printer) while the top and bottom margins are one inch each.

Tab stops are used to mark locations for tab characters. They can be used to arrange items in a table in columns. In Word, the default tab stops are set every half inch. Page numbers are used to mark locations in the document. Word normally does not provide page numbers. If page numbers were provided, they would be placed in the upper right corner of the page by default.

Changing default settings

Microsoft considered these default settings to be the most practical they could install. In fact, on most occasions you will probably get along just fine with these settings. With these defaults, your document is ready to be printed on normal-sized sheets of paper, on normally set-up printers. At times, however, you might need to change these default settings.

For example, you will find that realigning tab stops is convenient when constructing tables, outlines, and other similar documents. Word's tab stops provide a number of different features that allow you to align columns automatically along the decimal point, the leftmost character, or the rightmost character. You also have the option of centering the column and using *leader characters* between tab stops (like the dots that separate the names and numbers in the telephone book).

Modifying margins is also useful when designing the layout of a document. If you are writing a brief letter and would like the text to appear longer, you can increase the left and right margins. Likewise, if you are planning to add charts to a report, you might wish to decrease the left or right margin temporarily to accommodate the charts. (Word can do this automatically; see Chapter 34.)

Page numbering, another Word feature, comes in handy when you are working with long documents. Page numbering has several benefits. It enables you to quickly jump from one page to another, estimate the length of a passage, or approximate the layout of the printed document. Of course, page numbering is also helpful in numbering the pages of your finished work. You can even choose the position and style of the page numbers on the printout.

Entering and deleting divisions

When you change the division settings with the Format Division command, the new settings are applied to all text that occurs before the first division mark that follows the cursor and the last division mark that precedes the cursor. That is, the previous and next division marks define the bounds of the current division, and therefore the bounds of all text affected by the Format Division command. The beginning and end of the document also define the bounds of divisions.

Because a Format Division command affects all text between the previous and next division mark, it is important to be able to enter and delete division marks. To enter a division mark, move the cursor to the location where you wish to start a new division. Press Ctrl-Return (division break). Do not confuse this command with Shift-Return (newline).

The division mark appears on the screen as a line of colons. The formats for the entire division are stored in the division mark. A newly created division assumes the same format as the succeeding division. Later, the new division format can be redefined.

Division marks are deleted like regular characters. To delete a division mark, move the cursor to the mark, highlight it, then press Del.

The ruler line

When you first run Word, the top line of the screen contains two parallel lines. These lines form the top border of the window. If you intend prolonged work with margins and tabs, you need to replace these lines with a more informative *ruler line*. With the ruler line, you can clearly see the position and type of all margins and tab stops.

The ruler line is automatically activated when you employ the Format Paragraph or Format Tabs commands, but it remains on only for the duration of the command. To turn on the ruler for longer durations, use the Options show ruler command.

To employ the Options show ruler command, first press Esc to retreat from type-in mode. Now press O to select the Options command. This shows the Options menu as in Fig. 9-1. Move the cursor to the show ruler: command field with the Tab key, then set the option to Yes by pressing Y.

```
WINDOW OPTIONS for window number: 1        show hidden text:(Yes)No
            show ruler: Yes No        show non-printing symbols:(None)Partial All
           show layout: Yes(No)              show line breaks: Yes(No)
          show outline: Yes(No)               show style bar: Yes(No)

GENERAL OPTIONS mute: Yes(No)                 summary sheet:(Yes)No
              measure:(In)Cm P10 P12 Pt        display mode: 1
             paginate:(Auto)Manual                   colors:
             autosave: 4                    autosave confirm: Yes(No)
            show menu:(Yes)No                 show borders:(Yes)No
          date format:(MDY)DMY              decimal character:(.),
          time format:(12)24             default tab width: 0.5"
         line numbers: Yes(No)             count blank space: Yes(No)
         cursor speed: 3                  linedraw character: (|)
          speller path: C:\X\BOOKS\WORD\PROGRAM\SPELL-AM.LEX
Select option
Pg3 Co46          {Window·}         ?                        Microsoft Word
```

9-1 The Options menu controls the display of documents and the layout of the Word screen.

88 *Setting tabs, margins, and page numbers*

Now press Return to carry out the command. the ruler line appears immediately, as in Fig. 9-2. On the ruler line, you see two square brackets ([ ]). These brackets mark the current position of the margins. Tab stops are indicated on the ruler line by the letters L, C, R, and D. Since there are currently no tab stops (other than the default tab stops, which are not displayed) on the ruler line, you do not see any tab characters.

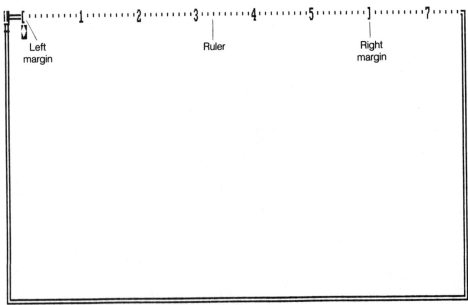

9-2 The rule liner displays the position of the left and right margins and the tab stops.

The Format Division command

Now that you have turned on the ruler, you can confidently change the margins of your document. The margins are controlled by the Format Division command. Select the command in the same fashion as you selected the other Format commands. First press Esc, then F to select the Format command from the Edit menu, then D to select the Division command from the Format menu. The Format Division menu appears on the screen as in Fig. 9-3.

Changing the margins

Move the cursor to the appropriate margin command field with the Tab key, then enter the new margins from the keyboard. The left and right margins are preset to

```
┌─────────────────────────────────────────────────┐
│                                                 │
│                                                 │
│                                                 │
│                                                 │
└─────────────────────────────────────────────────┘
```

FORMAT DIVISION: **Margins** Page-numbers Layout line-Numbers

Sets margins, page length, and running head position for current division
Pg1 Co1   {}   Microsoft Word

9-3   Format Division menu.

1.25" each, but they can be set to some other measurement such as 1". The left and right margin must be set independently.

Just for practice, try changing the right margin to 1.4 inches and the bottom margin to .7 inch. Bring up the Format Division Margins menu. Tab to the bottom margin entry and type .7, tab to the right margin entry and type 1.4. The menu should show the new margin settings and match Fig. 9-5. Finally, press Return to record the changes. For additional practice, return the margins to their original settings as shown in Fig. 9-4.

FORMAT DIVISION MARGINS
    top: **1"**   bottom: 1"
    left: 1.25"   right: 1.25"
    page length: 11"   width: 8.5"   gutter margin: 0"
    running-head position from top: 0.5"   from bottom: 0.5"
    mirror margins: Yes(No)   use as default: Yes(No)
Enter measurement
Pg4 Co34   {press·}   ?   Microsoft Word

9-4   The Format Division Margins menu controls the margins of all paragraphs within a division.

FORMAT DIVISION MARGINS
    top: 1"   bottom: .7
    left: 1.25"   right: **1.4**
    page length: 11"   width: 8.5"   gutter margin: 0"
    running-head position from top: 0.5"   from bottom: 0.5"
    mirror margins: Yes(No)   use as default: Yes(No)
Enter measurement
Pg4 Co34   {press·}   ?   Microsoft Word

9-5   Margins are normally calculated in tenths of an inch, although other measurements can be used.

90 *Setting tabs, margins, and page numbers*

Note that you can use centimeters and points when specifying measurements. For example, you could type 5 cm in the top margin field to indicate a five-centimeter top margin. Type 10 pt to indicate 10 points. Word automatically converts all measurements to the default measurement (the default unit of measure can be changed in the Options menu).

Redefining the margins has several affects. The new margins are indicated on the ruler line by square brackets ([]); they apply throughout the division. The paragraphs that have already been typed in are automatically expanded or condensed to fit the new margins. Future paragraphs typed in the division will also reflect the modified specifications.

As a side effect of your use of the Format Division command, a division mark has been created that holds these formats. The division mark appears as a row of colons (:::) stretching across the page (see Fig. 9-6). Selecting the Format Division command creates a new division mark at the end of the document whenever no division mark follows the cursor.

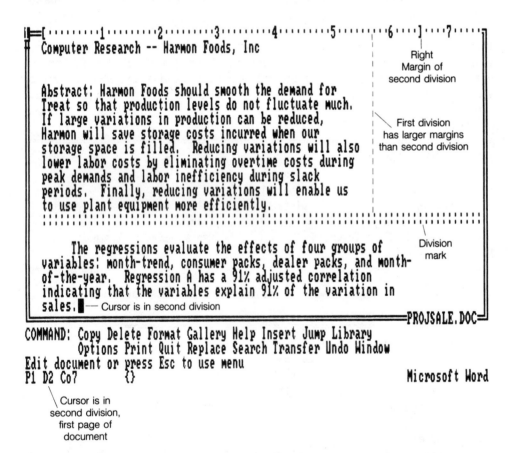

9-6 Pressing Ctrl-Return inserts a division mark within a document. The bottom left corner of the screen displays the number of the division containing the cursor.

Dividing the document

When you work with lengthy documents, you might wish to use different margins in different sections throughout the document. For example, you might wish to reduce the margins in the first section of the document because the document contains a long quotation. In the next section, however, you need enlarged margins to accommodate graphs and tables.

Using the Format Division command, you can change the margins of the document to any one measurement. To create different margins in the same document, however, you need to separate your document into sections called *divisions*. You may then use the Format Division command to define different margins for each division in the document (you can also format paragraphs as discussed in Chapter 8).

For an explanation of the purpose of a division, think back to Chapter 7 when you were working with paragraph formats. Paragraph formats included attributes such as indention, alignment, and spacing. When you needed to change the paragraph format of the text, you would start a new paragraph by pressing Return. You could then use the Format Paragraph command to reformat the resulting paragraph.

The same solution exists for division formats. Any time you wish to provide a section of text with a different page layout, simply start a new division. By starting a new division, you allow the new division to possess its own division formats. Because division formats control page layout, you can then regulate attributes such as margins, footnotes, number of columns, and page breaks.

Tabs

When Word is initially activated, tabs are automatically set every half inch. If you need to set your own tabs, you can insert them with the Format Tab command. Selecting your own tab stops becomes very useful when you are designing tables; however, tab stops are slightly difficult to learn.

To set your own tabs, you must first familiarize yourself with the Format Tab command. The Format Tab command contains all the various commands you need to create and edit tabs. Your first step is to get to the Format Tab menu, which resembles Fig. 9-5. Press Esc to get out of type-in mode, then press F for format and T for tab.

There are three commands in the Format Tab menu: Set, Clear, and Reset-all. The Format Tab Set command allows you to designate your own tabs and locations. The Format Tab Clear command is used to eliminate specific tabs. The Format Tab Reset-all command resets all tabs to their original positions, spaced at by half-inch intervals.

Tabs are assigned to paragraphs. Therefore, if you want to assign a new set of tabs to the entire document, press Shift–F10 to select the entire document before selecting the Format Tab command. To change tabs for several paragraphs, highlight just those paragraphs before selecting the Format Tab command. To change the tabs for all new paragraphs, change the tab settings for the end of document

92 *Setting tabs, margins, and page numbers*

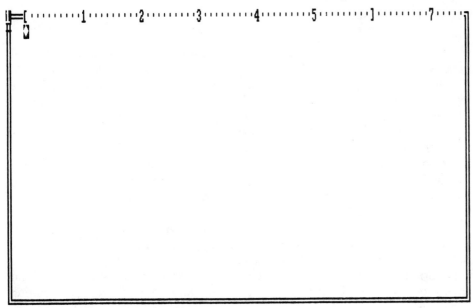

9-7 The Format Tab menu governs the addition and removal of tab stops.

marker (or endmark), and then insert new paragraphs at the character before the end of the document marker.

Note that when you change the tab settings in a paragraph, Word adjusts any existing tabs so they fit the new tab settings. Thus, if a table uses different tab stops from the remainder of the document and the tab stops for the entire document are changed, the tab stops in the table are changed and Word rearranges the table.

Setting tabs

To set a tab, choose the division you wish to be affected, then select the Format Tab Set command. The Format Tab Set menu, seen in Fig. 9-8, defines the position, alignment and leader character of tabs. When you are in the position field, enter the position (in the default unit of measurement) of the tabs you want to create.

Another method for entering tabs is to use the arrow keys. Click on the ruler line with the mouse pointer or press F1 while the Format Tab Set menu is visible (or press Alt–F1 at any time). A cursor appears on the ruler. When you press the right arrow key, a cursor appears on the ruler line. The cursor can be moved along the ruler line with the left and right arrow keys. Furthermore, if the ruler contains a number of tabs, the up and down arrows move the cursor to the next tab left or right, respectively. Press Return or L where you want a left tab, R where you want a right tab, and so on. More than one tab may be entered while in the Format Tab Set command.

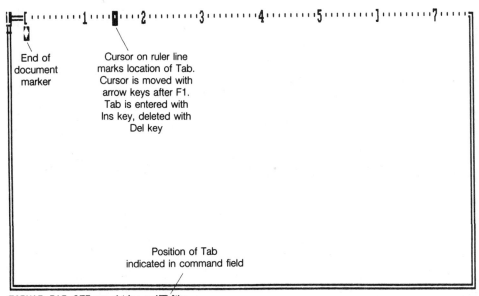

9-8 The Format Tab Set command inserts tab stops.

Use the PgUp and PgDn keys to move the tab marker at one-inch intervals. The Home and End keys move the marker to the left and right margins, respectively.

Once you have designated a tab position and before you press Ins to create the tab, you can determine the type of tab. Word offrs a variety of alignments and leading characters by which you can designate tabs. There are five alignments to select from: Left, Center, Right, Decimal, and Vertical. Figure 9-9 illustrates four of the types of entries.

The left alignment is the common tab alignment typewriters use. When you press the Tab key, the cursor is moved to the tab. The text you enter is then aligned so that it begins at the tab stop.

A right tab aligns text on the right at the tab. Pressing the Tab key moves the cursor to the right tab mark, but once there, the text entered ends instead of begins, at the tab mark. The cursor moves away when another Tab or a Return key is pressed.

The center tab centers text on the tab. When the Tab key is pressed, the cursor jumps to the center tab. Any text entered then aligns itself so that the center of the text remains at the tab stop. The end of the text is marked by pressing Tab or Return.

The decimal tab aligns text so that the decimal place is at the tab mark. This makes the decimal tab very useful in aligning numbers. Note, however, that even

```
|=[····C··1·······2···R···3···D···4···L····5·········6······]··7·····

                    TABS ALIGNMENTS    Codes for
                                       tabs on
                                       ruler line

      CENTER         RIGHT    DECI.MAL    LEFT
    -----------------------------------------------

      Company        Brand    Unit.Price  Comments


       IBM            IBM      $3.15      DSDD, plastic case
      Maxell          MD-1     $2.10      SSDD, 95% reliable
      Maxell          MD-2     $2.85      DSDD, 95% reliable
      Verbatim      Datalife   $2.80      DSDD, cardboard jacket
```

```
COMMAND: Copy Delete Format Gallery Help Insert Jump Library
         Options Print Quit Replace Search Transfer Undo Window
Edit document or press Esc to use menu
Pg1 Co1         {¶}                                   Microsoft Word
```

9-9 A demonstration of center, right, decimal, and left tab stops. Left tab stops are similar to the tab stops on typewriters and are the most common.

words with a period can be aligned at the period employing the decimal tab. If there is no decimal place or period in the text, the Decimal tab behaves as if it were a right tab.

Concluding a tab stop entry

The Right tab and the Center tab are tricky to employ. There are only two keys you can press following a tab entry: Return or Tab. If the entry is not followed by a Tab or Return, Word does not realize that the entry has ended. The cursor thus remains at the tab until you enter either a Tab or Return key.

This aspect of tabs can cause problems if you do not conclude your tab entry properly. Once at a right tab stop, for instance, any text you type is pushed to the left, keeping the cursor at the tab. This can continue until there is no space between the tab and the left margin, at which point Word releases the cursor.

If you enter the ruler by clicking on it with the mouse, the default tab type appears at the extreme left end of the ruler. You can click or press Ins along the ruler and the indicated tab type will be inserted. Click on the default type with either mouse button to change it. The default leader type appears to the left of the tab type. Click on it to change it.

Tab alignments

If you enter a tab at the same location as another tab, the original tab is erased and the new tab takes its place. When you have designated all the tabs that you desire in their appropriate locations, press the Return key, and you will return to the main menu.

Remove a tab by placing the cursor on it and pressing Del or clicking on it with both mouse buttons at once.

Tab leader characters

Another feature of tabs in Word is that you can set their leader characters. Leader characters are characters that fill the spaces created by the use of tabs. There are four different leader characters you can choose from: Blank, Period, Hyphen, or Underscore. The symbol for the leading character is placed in front of the symbol for the tab (except for blank leader characters).

These characters fill in the spaces between tabs as shown in Fig. 9-10. The blank character is automatically chosen by Word as a default leader character. You might wish to select different leader characters for each tab. To do so, simply choose a different option in the leader character field of the Format Tab Set command.

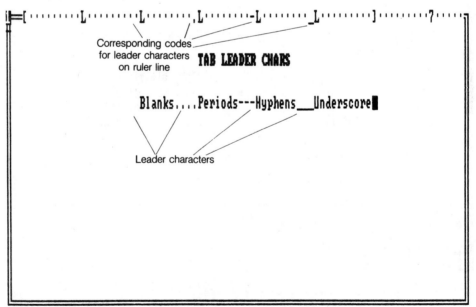

9-10 Different leader characters can be specified for tab stops. The most common leader character is blank, which prints blank spaces.

96 *Setting tabs, margins, and page numbers*

Erasing or resetting tabs

There are four methods to eradicate unwanted tab stops. If you are still in the Format Tab Set command, highlight the tab stop you wish to remove and press the Del key. The tab stop is promptly deleted. You are then free to reset the tab in some other location, or insert and delete other tabs.

The second method of erasing tab stops is to select the Format Tab Clear command. Once you have done so, you are asked to enter the position of the tab stop or stops you wish to delete. You can enter the location or use the arrow keys or mouse to highlight the tab stop to be removed from the ruler line.

If you then wish to delete another tab stop, type comma and select another tab stop. If you wish to continue erasing tab stops, keep entering commas and entering tab locations (see Fig. 9-11). After you have listed all the unwanted tabs, press the Return key to finish them off. Word removes the tabs you have marked and returns you to the Edit menu.

```
=[······C··1·········2···R···3····))····4··L·····5·········6······]··7·····

                    TABS ALIGNMENTS        Cursor may be
                                           moved with arrow keys

        CENTER         RIGHT        DECI.MAL       LEFT
        -----------------------------------------------------

        Company        Brand        Unit.Price     Comments

        IBM            IBM          $3.15          DSDD, plastic case
        Maxell         MD-1         $2.10          SSDD, 95% reliable
        Maxell         MD-2         $2.85          DSDD, 95% reliable
        Verbatim       Datalife     $2.80          DSDD, cardboard jacket

                       Several tabs may be erased
                       at once by separating positions   Position of cursor
                              with commas                on ruler line

FORMAT TAB CLEAR position: 0.7",2.5",3.5"

Enter list of measurements
Pg1 Co1         {¶}                                      Microsoft Word
```

9-11 The Format Tab Clear command removes one or more tab stops.

The third method of erasing tab stops is to use the Format Tab Reset-all command. This command provides a quick method to erase all the special tabs in Word. By using the Format Tab Reset-all command, you return Word to its default state, reinstating the normal half-inch-spaced tabs.

A fourth method to remove tabs is to click on them with both mouse buttons on the ruler line.

Using vertical lines in tables

Word offers a special tab alignment that creates vertical lines in the paragraphs highlighted. The vertical tab alignment is set like any other tab alignment, but it creates vertical lines that can be extremely attractive and effective in tables (see Figure 9-12). The vertical lines do not delete any text and partially obscure any text covered by the line.

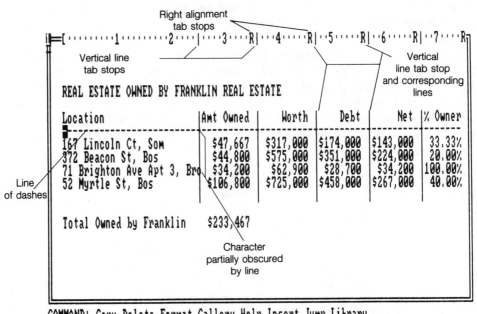

9-12 Tab stops are ideal for creating tables. The vertical tab is designed specifically for creating vertical lines in a table.

Vertical line tab stops are entered and removed in the same manner as regular tab stops. To create or delete vertical lines easily, select the Format Tab Set command, set the alignment to Vertical, move to the position field and enter the new vertical tab stops. You can press F1 and use the arrow keys and Ins and Del to enter and delete the vertical tab stops. Press Return after the appropriate tab stops have been entered. Use the Format Tab Clear or Format Tab Reset-all commands to remove the vertical line tab stops. You can also use the mouse. Click on the tab type at the left end of the ruler until the vertical bar appears, then click wherever the vertical lines should be printed. Or you can use the cursor keys to place the tab and type the vertical bar character (usually Shift–Backslash).

Activating page numbering

Word allows you to number pages in a document automatically. Short documents, such as letters and memos, customarily do not need to have page numbers. On the other hand, lengthy documents such as term papers, theses, and books do require page numbers.

Page numbers can be placed in a document with the Format Division Page-numbers command or with the Page glossary buffer (discussed in Chapter 10). The page glossary buffer can be placed in a running head (covered in Chapter 14), achieving the same effect as the Page-numbers command. This method is more complex, however.

In Word, automatic page numbering is controlled by a command field in the Format Division command. To switch page numbering on or off, call up the Format Division Page-numbers command by pressing Esc, F, D, P.

Once in the Format Division Page-numbers menu, move the command cursor to the Page-numbers option field (see Fig. 9-13). Select the Yes setting, and the page numbering option will be on. You do not see these page numbers on the screen, but they appear on the printout.

```
FORMAT DIVISION PAGE-NUMBERS: Yes (No)    from top: 0.5"    from left: 7.25"
        numbering:(Continuous)Start       at:               number format:(1)I i A a
Select option
Pg1 Co1              {}                                              Microsoft Word
```

9-13 The Format Division Page-numbers menu controls whether or not page numbers are printed.

Setting page number options

If you are using page numbering, a collection of commands under the Format Division Page-numbers menu allows you to control the position, sequence, and style of the page numbers. By default, Word places arabic numerals in the upper right corner of the page. To change these attributes, you need to change the following options in the Format Division menu

Location The command field from top: controls the vertical position of the page number. A small value places the page number at the top of the page, while a large number places the page number at the bottom of the page. Page numbers are placed half an inch from the top of the page by default.

The from left: field, on the other hand, controls the horizontal position of the page number. A small number would place the page number close to the left edge of the page, while a large measurement would place the page number close to the right edge of the page. The default value for the field is 7.25 inches, placing the page number at the right side of the page. By specifying the measurements from the top and left edges of the paper, you can position the page number anywhere on the page.

Numbering The numbering: field determines whether page numbers of the division continue from the page number of the previous division, or start at some new page number. If the Cont setting is chosen, the first page of the division begins with a number one greater than the page number of the last page in the previous division. If this is the first division, page numbers begin at 1.

If the Start setting is chosen, you can assign a page number to the first page of the division. Later pages are numbered according to this page number. To enter the page number at which you wish the division to begin, type the number in the at: command field. Note that the at: command field has no effect if the Start setting is not selected in the numbering: field.

If you are working on a thesis divided into three parts, you might print one part independently of another. If the first part ends on page 34, you want to start printing the second part at page 35. Therefore, chose the Start setting in the numbering: field and type 35 in the at: field.

Style Finally, the field format selects the type of numerals used by Word in printing the page numbers. The list includes:

(1) Arabic numerals
(I) Roman numeral uppercase
(i) Roman numeral lowercase
(A) Alphabetic numeral uppercase
(a) Alphabetic numeral lowercase

Page numbers are printed in arabic numerals by default.

Summary

Upon completing Chapter 9, you should be familiar with:

- Setting up the ruler line through the Options command.
- Redefining the margins for the entire document with the Format Division command.
- Creating and deleting tab stops with the Format Tab command.
- Selecting the alignment of the tab stops.
- Switching page numbering on and off with the Format Division Page-numbers command.
- Defining the style and position of the page numbers.

CHAPTER 10

Manipulating blocks of text

This chapter examines Word's ability to move text. Moving, copying, and replacing text are specialties of word processors. Word provides a set of simple yet efficient commands for moving text.

Moving text

In Word, moving blocks of text is very straightforward. To move a block of text:

1. Highlight the block of text you want to move.
2. Press the Del key. This deletes the text and places it into the scrap.
3. Move the cursor to the spot where you want to move the block.
4. Press Ins. This inserts the block into the document.

To select the text you wish to move, highlight it with the cursor. To remove the text from the document and place it into the scrap for temporary storage, press the Del key. The text seems to disappear.

Your text has not been lost. The text has been stored in the scrap. Observe the status line. The deleted text is now within the braces {}. The braces enclose the contents of the scrap. If the entire block of text cannot be shown in the scrap, you only see the first and last few characters of the block.

As you have just seen, the scrap offers temporary storage for blocks of text. With the Delete command, you can remove a block of text from the document and save it in the scrap for later use. You can store a block of text of any size in the scrap, but only one block of text can be stored at one time. If another block of text is deleted and placed in the scrap, the original contents of the scrap is lost.

The text in the scrap can be inserted in a new location with the Ins key. The contents are inserted just in front of the cursor. Move the cursor to where you wish the text to be moved. Press the Ins key, and the text is placed in the new location. The contents of the scrap remain unchanged by the insertion process, so you can use the Ins key to insert the scrap text wherever you want.

Copying text

In Word, you can copy a block of text and insert the block into the document. Copying text is as simple as moving text. To copy text:

1. Highlight the block of text to be copied.
2. Select the copy command by pressing Esc then C. This places a copy of the highlighted text into the scrap and leaves the highlighted block intact.
3. Move to the destination of the block of text.
4. Press Ins.

The Copy command places a copy of the highlighted text into the scrap without affecting the highlighted text itself. Once the block of text is in the scrap, it can be inserted in another location with the Ins key. The scrap remains unchanged by the insertion. Thus, after the text has been copied into the scrap, the text can be inserted many times in different places in the document. Such repetition is common when writing computer programs.

Managing the scrap

One drawback of the system for moving text in Word is the transient nature of the contents of the scrap. The content of the scrap is determined by the last Delete or Copy command executed. If the Del key is accidentally pressed while important text is stored in the scrap, the text being stored is lost. The text in the scrap is lost even if you delete one character with Del. Text is lost because the scrap is intended for temporary storage during editing.

If you catch the mistake in time, selecting the Undo command will reverse the last deletion and save the day. Once you execute any other command, not even the powerful Undo command can save you. Therefore, it is good practice to perform the entire move text operation before resuming editing. Later, you will learn how to store blocks of text in Word's glossary.

For now, Word offers the Shift-Del combination to protect the contents of the scrap. To avoid losing the contents of scrap while deleting text, type Shift-Del. Pressing Shift-Del deletes text like the Del key, except that the text deleted is not placed in scrap. The Shift-Del combination is useful when you must preserve the contents of scrap.

Replacing blocks of text

Word provides you with a command that is useful for replacing one block of text with another block: the Shift-Ins combination. Shift-Ins replaces the highlighted text with the contents of the scrap. Before you press Shift-Ins, you must place the text you want in the document in the scrap. Next, highlight the block of text that you want to replace.

You cannot simply use the Del key to delete the highlighted block of text, because the highlighted text would replace the contents of scrap. You could use the Shift-Del combination to delete the highlighted block (this would preserve the contents of the scrap). You could then enter the replacement text with the Ins key.

The most efficient method for replacing highlighted text with text from the scrap uses the Shift-Ins command. Shift-Ins erases the highlighted text, and inserts the current contents of the scrap at the location of the cursor. Shift-Ins is very useful when you wish to replace a sentence or paragraph with a second sentence or paragraph. Figure 10-1 shows the keys for moving text in and out of the scrap.

Key	Function
Del	Deletes highlighted text from document. Text is placed into scrap.
Shift-Del	Deletes highlighted text. Scrap is unaffected.
Ins	Inserts a copy of the text located in scrap in front of the cursor. Scrap is unaffected.
Shift-Ins	Replaces highlighted text with text located in scrap. Scrap is unaffected. Equivalent to Shift-Del followed by Ins.

10-1 Keys used to delete and insert blocks of text using the scrap.

Fast mouse commands

Word provides a series of copy and delete commands available through the mouse. First, you can delete to the scrap by highlighting the text and clicking the right mouse button on the Delete command. Similarly, you can insert from the scrap by clicking with the mouse pointer on the place to insert text and then clicking the right mouse button on the Insert command. You can copy text to the scrap by highlighting it and clicking the right mouse button on the Copy command.

To speed copying text without using the scrap, highlight the text to copy, move to the new location, hold down the Shift key and press the left mouse button.

A similar speed move action is available. Highlight the text to move, move to the new location, hold down the Ctrl key and press the left mouse button.

The overtype option

Normally whenever you type in text, the text is inserted in the document before the character marked by the cursor. The overtype option allows you to type over existing text. When overtype is on, text entered replaces text in the document.

104 *Manipulating blocks of text*

The overtype option is turned on by the F5 (overtype) key. Turn on the overtype option by pressing the F5 key. The overtype key is a toggle key, meaning that once F5 is switched on, F5 remains on until switched off. Like all toggle keys in Word, if the overtype option is in operation, an appropriate status code is displayed on the status line. The status code for the overtype option is OT. If you see the characters OT on the status line, overtype is on.

When the overtype option is on, characters you type replace the characters highlighted by the cursor. Overtype thus allows you to replace text by typing over it with new text.

The overtype option can be used in conjunction with the Del key to replace blocks of text. First, highlight the block of text that you wish to replace. Switch on the overtype option by hitting the F5 (overtype) key, then, type in the replacement text. As you type in the new text, notice that the highlighted region shrinks after the cursor, so that only the text to be replaced remains highlighted.

If the new text is shorter in length than the original text, leftover text is in the highlighted region. You can delete this surplus by employing the Del (delete) key. The Del key deletes the leftover text, but leaves the replacement text alone (see Fig. 10-2).

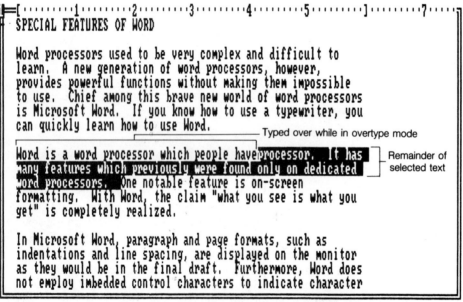

10-2 The F5 key toggles the overtype mode on and off. When the overtype mode is on, Word does not insert new text into the document but places the new text into the document over existing text.

If the replacement text is longer than the original text, turn off the overtype option by pressing the F5 key when you reach the end of the highlighted text. Then, you can continue to enter text. In overtype mode, the Backspace key only deletes text entered while in overtype mode.

The glossary

The scrap provides only temporary storage for blocks of text. To store blocks of text for later recall, you must use the *glossary*. The glossary is similar to the scrap in that text of any size can be stored in the glossary. The glossary, however, is superior to the scrap in that it can store many text fragments at one time.

The glossary can store phrases, sentences, and paragraphs that are used often. Text placed into the glossary can be reused without retyping the text. Text destined for the glossary might include addresses, parts of form letters, and long names. The glossary can even store blocks of text permanently on disk for use from session to session and document to document.

Placing text in a glossary buffer

When a fragment of text is stored in the glossary, it is placed into a *glossary buffer*. The glossary buffer is a temporary storage location in Word similar to the scrap. You must then provide a name for the glossary buffer. The name identifies the glossary buffer for storage and retrieval. Any number of glossary buffers can be created in a session with Word.

A block of text can be placed in a glossary buffer with the Delete or Copy commands. The Del key is no longer a substitute for the Delete command, because the Del key only deletes to the scrap. To place text in a glossary buffer:

1. Highlight the text that to be placed in the glossary.
2. Select the Delete or Copy command. Use Delete, if you want to delete the highlighted text from the document; use Copy, if you want to preserve the highlighted text.
3. Enter the name under which you want the text to be stored in the glossary buffer. Word then places the text in the glossary buffer under that name.

For practice, store the phrase Microsoft Word in a glossary buffer. Type out Microsoft Word and then highlight it with the cursor. Now select either the Delete or Copy command. Enter the glossary name MW (see Fig. 10-3). Press Return to delete or copy Microsoft Word into the glossary buffer.

As stated before, once a piece of text is placed in a glossary buffer, it can be retrieved by referring to the text by that name when using the insert command or the F3 key. If the name assigned to the new text has been used, Word warns you of the error and gives you the opportunity to overwrite the other glossary entry or back out of the command.

Retrieving text from a glossary buffer

There are two methods for retrieving text from a glossary buffer, just as there are two methods to save text in a glossary buffer. One method is for you to employ the

106 *Manipulating blocks of text*

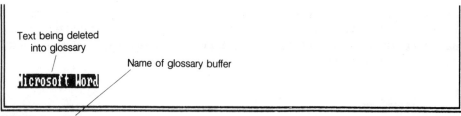

10-3 The Delete and Copy commands can place phrases and macro commands into the glossary.

Insert command from the Edit menu. For practice, retrieve the glossary buffer that you created in the previous section with these steps:

1. Press Esc then I for the Insert command.
2. Enter the name of the text in the glossary buffer, or use F1 to retrieve a list of all the text in the glossary buffer. Use the arrow keys to highlight the glossary to insert and press Return to insert the glossary text.

In the Insert menu (see Fig. 10-4), Word prompts you to enter the name of the text in the glossary buffer to be inserted. If, at the Insert menu, a name is not entered and just the Return key is hit, the default option is to insert text from the scrap. On this occasion, however, you want to insert text from the glossary.

10-4 The Insert command and the F3 key can place phrases stored in the glossary into a document.

Enter MW or highlight it in the list and press Return. It will be inserted into text at the current cursor location. Seven glossary names are provided by Microsoft as shown in Fig. 10-5:

page
nextpage
date

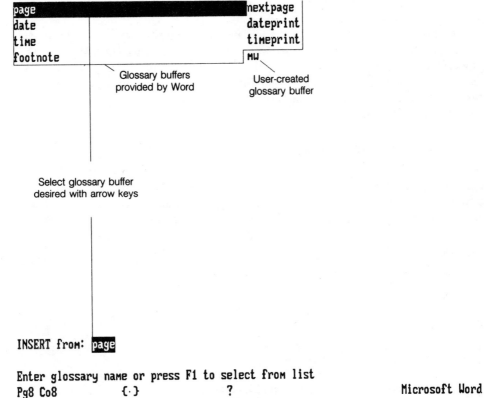

10-5 Selecting the Insert command and pressing F1 lists the contents of the glossary. You can highlight any buffer and press Return to insert it in the document.

    dateprint
    time
    timeprint
    footnote

These will be explained later.

The F3 (glossary reference) key

The F3 (glossary reference) key can also be used to insert text from the glossary. To employ the F3 key, first type the name of the text stored in the glossary buffer. The name must be separated from the preceding text for the F3 key to function. A space, a newline, and a tab character can be used to separate the name from the preceding text.

    Immediately after entering the name of the text stored in the glossary buffer, press F3. The name of the glossary buffer disappears, replaced by the the text inserted from the glossary buffer. F3 retrieves text from a glossary buffer faster than the Insert command, but to use F3 you must know the glossary name of the text you want to retrieve.

Practice with the F3 key with the text placed in the glossary earlier. Type MW, being careful to keep the name separated from surrounding text. Hit F3. The glossary name MW disappears, and the contents of the glossary buffer MW, Microsoft Word, appears in its place. As with the Insert command, you can retrieve text from the glossary buffer as many times as you please without erasing the text stored in the glossary buffer.

Inserting page numbers and footnote marks from the glossary

Earlier, you discovered that Word provides seven glossary names: page, nextpage, date, dateprint, time, timeprint, and footnote. These glossary entries do not represent text in the glossary as other names do. Instead, these entries insert numbers according to the current page, or footnote reference, and so on (see Fig. 10-6).

```
L[·········1·········2·········3·········4·········5·········]·········7····
Microsoft Word


  Page glossary buffer          (page)

  Footnote glossary buffer      1

  Date glossary buffer          July 14, 1991

  Dateprint glossary buffer     (dateprint)

  Time glossary buffer          4:15 PM

  Timeprint glossary buffer     (timeprint)

  Nextpage glossary buffer      (nextpage)



▮
COMMAND: Copy Delete Format Gallery Help Insert Jump Library
         Options Print Quit Replace Search Transfer Undo Window
Edit document or press Esc to use menu
Pg1 Co1          {·}                 ?                       Microsoft Word
```

10-6 There are seven special glossary buffers that can insert the current page number, upcoming page number, footnote number, date, or time in a document or printout.

When the page glossary entry is inserted, page appears in the document. When the document is printed, however, the glossary reference text page is transformed into the number of the page the mark is in. Thus, if page falls on the fifth page of the document, a 5 appears on the printout.

Similarly, when the footnote reference mark is placed in a document, Word inserts the special character it uses for footnote reference marks. The character is then transformed into the current footnote number. It is probably better for you to use the Format Footnote command described in Chapter 14 to create footnote references.

Suppose you want to insert the current page number in your document. Move the cursor to where you want the page number to appear. Then, select the Insert command and type Page and hit Return. Remember that the Format Division Page-numbers command is used to paginate a document.

Glossary nextpage, date, dateprint, time, timeprint

The date and time glossary entries insert the current date and time respectively in the document. Similarly, the dateprint and timeprint glossary entries insert the date and time the document is printed. Word uses two different date and time formats. The default is the American month-day-year (October 15, 1991). The alternative is the European day-month-year (15 October 1991). Likewise, the time format can be either a 12-hour clock (the default) or a 24-hour clock. The date and time entries can be changed using the Options menu.

Nextpage inserts the page number of the next page at the time of printing. If it is inserted on page 4, it will print out 5. This is important on some legal documents. You can insert it into the footer, for instance, along with some text, such as Continued on page newpage.

Glossary files

A glossary file in Word is a file that contains selections of text stored in a glossary. Glossary files are saved on the disk in the same fashion as document files. They have the extension .GLY (for glossary) instead of the extension .DOC (for document).

Word provides you with a standard glossary file named NORMAL.GLY. This glossary file is automatically loaded with your document. Only glossary buffers in this glossary file can be used with the document. When you wish to work with a different glossary file, you use the Transfer Glossary Merge command to merge a different glossary file temporarily with the NORMAL.GLY glossary file. Glossary buffers can be used immediately after they are created, because these glossary buffers are automatically placed into the current glossary file.

During a session with Word, any blocks of text you store in the glossary become a glossary buffer in the glossary file NORMAL.GLY. These glossary buffers, however, are not stored permanently. If you exit Word or employ the Transfer Clear All command, only the original buffers in the glossary file NORMAL.GLY remain.

Saving glossary files

The Transfer Glossary command is used to save permanently additions to the glossary file on a disk (see Fig. 10-7). The three commands in the Transfer Glossary command menu are Clear, Merge, and Save. The Transfer Glossary Save command stores glossary items on the disk.

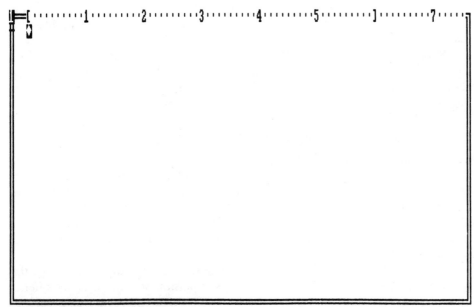

10-7 The Transfer Glossary menu can store and retrieve glossary files.

Choose the Save command from the Transfer Glossary menu. Word asks you to enter a name for the glossary file. The default name is listed in the options field. The default name is the name of the glossary file currently loaded in Word. Provide a name one to eight characters in length and press Return to enter your choice. Word stores a version of the glossary file on the disk.

Merging (retrieving) glossary files

To use a glossary buffer saved in a file, you must merge the glossary buffer into the active or current glossary file. You can merge the buffers with the Transfer Glossary Merge command. When executing the Transfer Glossary Merge command, you are asked which glossary file you wish to merge into the current glossary file. As before, you can obtain a list of the glossary files stored by pressing F1.

When the Transfer Glossary Merge command is executed, the glossary file being merged is not changed at all. A copy of the file has been made and glossary buffers within it have been added to the current glossary file. A situation to avoid is having two glossary buffers with the same name. If this occurs, the glossary buffer in the old glossary file is replaced by the glossary buffer with the same name in the new glossary file.

Printing glossary buffers

The Print Glossary command prints the contents of the glossary loaded in memory. If you do not load a glossary, the glossary in use is NORMAL.GLY. The printer, setup, and feed options must be correct in the Printer Options menu before you can print a glossary. To print the glossary in memory, simply select the Print Glossary command.

Clearing glossary buffers

The Transfer Glossary Clear command has two functions. First, it can be employed to remove specific glossary buffers from the active glossary file. To remove a specific glossary buffer, select the Transfer Glossary Clear command. Then, enter the name of the glossary buffer in the name: field of the Transfer Glossary Clear command. More than one name can be entered if the names are separated with commas.

If you need to see a list of the glossary buffers in the glossary file, press F1 in the command field. The screen is replaced by a list of the buffers in the current glossary file. You can then select the buffer(s) that you wish to delete. If there are several you want to delete, use the arrow keys to select the first, press the comma key, highlight the second, press the comma and so forth, until all are selected. Press Return. Word pauses to give you a chance to back out of the procedure. If you want to continue, press Y for Yes, and the buffers will be removed from the buffer.

The Transfer Glossary Clear command can also be used to clear all the glossary buffers in the glossary file. To delete all the glossary buffers, select the Transfer Glossary Clear command. Leave the name: field of the Transfer Glossary Clear command blank and press Return. Word erases all of the glossary buffers in the glossary file.

Deleting glossary buffers from a glossary file with the Transfer Glossary Clear command does not delete the buffers from the disk. If you wish to delete buffers permanently from the glossary file on the disk, you must save the modified glossary file with the Transfer Glossary Save command. When you save the modified glossary file with the same filename as the original glossary file, the modified glossary replaces the old glossary file.

Summary

You should be conversant with the following after reading this chapter:
- Moving blocks of text with the Del and Ins keys.
- Copying blocks of text with the Copy command and Ins key.
- Using the overtype F5 option to replace text.
- Placing blocks of text in the glossary with the Delete and Copy commands.

- Adding text to the document from the glossary with the Insert command and the F3 key.
- Editing glossary files with the Transfer Glossary Clear command.
- Saving and retrieving glossary files with the Transfer Glossary Save and Transfer Glossary Merge commands.

CHAPTER 11

Searching and replacing text

Word takes full advantage of the PC and PS/2's ability to perform mundane tasks at the speed of light. So far, Word has used the PC's capabilities to move text around in a document, to store paragraph formats and character formats, and to provide an on-line help feature. A computer's speed, however, is most impressive when used to search for and replace text.

The Search and Replace commands search for and replace text. If you have written a forty-page report on personal computers and want to replace the term microcomputer with personal computer throughout the document, you need the Replace command. If you have written a twenty-page report and have spelled Malaysia incorrectly several times in the document, you can find and correct each incorrect spelling with the Replace command (or use the Spell program to correct such errors). The Replace command can perform these and other find-and-replace missions with unbeatable accuracy.

The Search command

The Search command is used to search for a phrase in the document. The Search command can search a selected area or the entire document. You can specify whether you wish Word to ignore the case of the text fragment, or to search for whole words only. Wildcards can be employed to enable Word to search for special text fragments.

When the Search command is selected, Word searches from the position of the cursor to the beginning or end of the document, depending on the direction you specify. To search the whole document from beginning to end, press Ctrl-PgUp to move to the beginning of the text and then select the Search command. Word continues searching until it either finds the search text or reaches the end of the document.

Regardless of the search method selected, if Word finds the selected pattern, it moves the cursor to where the pattern was found. The cursor highlights the text pattern. If the text pattern is not found, Word beeps and prints a message informing you that the search text could not be found.

Selecting the text pattern

Select the Search command from the Edit menu. The menu will resemble Fig. 11-1. The four fields in the Search menu are: text:, direction:, case:, and whole word:. Enter in the text: field the text you wish to find. With the Search command, you can look for text fragments up to 40 characters long.

```
SEARCH text:
       direction: Up(Down) case: Yes(No) whole word: Yes(No)
Enter text
Pg1 Col           {}                                    Microsoft Word
```

11-1 The Search command can rapidly find a phrase in the document.

Wildcards

The text pattern entered in the text field can be composed of letters, numbers, and punctuation marks. Word also provides a special question mark (?) called a *wildcard*. By using wildcards, you can instruct Word to search for unspecified text.

When a wildcard is entered in the text, Word allows it to match any single character during the search. For example, searching for c?t lets Word find a match with cat, cot, or cut. Word does not, however, find matches to words like cart, because the wildcard can only match a single character. You can, however, employ as many wildcards as you wish in a phrase.

Special symbols

In addition to wildcards, Word has a group of symbols that allow it to search for special characters within the text. These symbols must be inserted in the text pattern being searched for. These symbols possess no special qualities when used as replacement text. All symbols in this group must be preceded by the caret mark (^) symbol (Shift-6). The special characters are listed in Fig. 11-2.

```
?     Matches any single character.
^?    Matches question mark.
^^    Matches caret.

^-    Nonrequired hyphen.
^d    Division mark <Ctrl-Shift> or
      Page break <Ctrl-Shift-Return>.
^n    Newline character <Shift-Return>.
^p    Paragraph mark <Return>.
^s    Nonbreaking space.
^t    Tab character.
^w    White space. Word expands this into any mix of
      spaces, tab characters, paragraph marks <Return>,
      newline characters <Shift-Return>, division breaks
      <Ctrl-Return>, and page breaks <Ctrl-Shift-Return>.
```

11-2 Word enables you to search or replace hyphens, division marks, paragraph marks, tabs, and other special characters by using the special codes listed.

These symbols are invaluable in allowing you to search for complicated fragments of text. Without these symbols, it would be impossible to search for text patterns with paragraph marks or tab characters. For instance, if you tried to enter Tab directly into the text field, the cursor would be propelled into the next field. You have to enter the code ^t instead, as in the pattern month ^t.

The caret mark (^) serves another function in addition to marking special symbols. The caret mark (^) tells Word to take the next character at its face value. For example, entering ^? causes Word to search for a question mark (?) instead of a wildcard. The caret mark (^) inhibits the special nature of the question mark.

The caret mark (^) can even affect itself, as searching for ^^ would result searching for a caret mark (^) in the text. This effect occurs because the first caret mark cancels the special nature of the second caret mark.

Searching and hyphens

Note that nonrequired hyphens (Ctrl-Hyphen) are not regarded as characters by Word, while hyphens and nonbreaking hyphens are. This results in nonrequired hyphens being ignored during the matching process.

If, however, the text pattern being searched for includes a nonrequired hyphen, Word looks for the nonrequired hyphen in the text pattern. The nonrequired hyphen in the pattern, shown as ^— must exactly match the location of the nonrequired hyphen in the text. In other words, the nonrequired hyphen in the pattern is treated as a character which must be matched by a nonrequired hyphen in the text.

For example, suppose that you were searching for an occurrence of the word photo-typesetter (with a nonrequired hyphen). Word will not accept phototype-setter or phototypeset-ter in its search. Only if Word finds photo-typesetter does Word conclude its search. If you were searching for phototypesetter, Word will find phototypesetter, photo-typesetter, phototype-setter, and all other occurrences of phototypesetter regardless of the position of the nonrequired hyphen.

Direction of search

The three other fields of the Search command, direction:, case:, and whole word:, set up conditions Word follows when searching for text. The direction field is significant when searching to either the beginning or the end of the document. If the search is made in a highlighted region, the direction: field has no effect.

The two settings offered in the direction field, Up and Down, determine the direction the search takes. Word uses the Down setting by default. When the Down setting is selected, Word searches from the location of the cursor to the end of the document for the text pattern. When the Up setting has been selected, the opposite action results: Word searches towards the beginning of the document.

Case

The case: field of the Search menu determines whether Word considers whether the characters in the search text are upper- or lowercase. If you do not enter a response, the default setting for the case field is No. In this situation, Word only checks whether the characters in the search text match those found in the document. The casing of the letters is ignored.

When the setting chosen for the case field is Yes, Word compares the case of the text pattern to the text in the document. Only when the text in the document has precisely the same upper- and lowercase letters does Word decide that it has located the given text pattern. Of course, this option is significant only to letters. Numbers, punctuation, and other characters that have no case are unaffected.

Whole word

The whole word option informs Word whether to search for the text as an entire word. If the Yes setting is selected, Word concludes the search only if the text found has word breaks, such as spaces or punctuation, before and after the pattern. That is, Word only looks for complete words, not patterns that might be part of other words.

If the No setting is chosen, Word ends the search at the first occurrence of the specified pattern in the text. Word stops even if the pattern is embedded in other words.

For example, suppose that the pattern being searched for is cat. With the whole word option on, Word concludes the search only if the word cat is found. With the whole word option off, any words that contain the word cat signify the end of the search. Word could stop the search after locating such words as caterpillar, bobcat, or advocate.

The whole word option allows you to search for single words without having to worry about finding parts of other words instead. It is more exact to employ the whole word option rather than place spaces on either side of the search text, because the whole word option also considers punctuation as marking the end of a word.

The whole word option is set to No by default. Upon occasion, when you are searching for single words, it can be very useful to select Yes. The whole word option is even more useful in the next section when you use the Replace command.

Extending the cursor with the Search command

A recently added feature of the Search command is its ability to extend the cursor. To use the Search command to extend the cursor, first press the F6 (extend) key to toggle on the extend feature. Now execute the Search command.

When Word locates the text pattern in the document, it usually moves the cursor to the first occurrence of the text pattern in the document. With the extend feature on, the cursor stretches to highlight the text between the cursor location at the beginning of the search and the location of the first occurrence of the text pattern.

You might want to use the extend feature if you need to select a large amount of text. For example, you can place the cursor in the middle of a division, turn on the extend feature, and search down to the next division mark by placing ^d in the text field.

The Replace command

The Replace command is similar to the Search command, but it goes a step further in that it both finds and replaces text. One application of the Replace command is in making changes to the text throughout a document. Another application is in correcting errors on a document-wide basis.

As an example of the power of the Replace command, suppose you have written a 20-page report on the bicycle industry in China. You discover later that Peking is now spelled Beijing. You want to correct your report to avoid offending the Chinese officials with whom you are working. Going through the document correcting the misspelling by hand would be a long and tiresome task. With the Replace command, Word can go through the document and replace all instances of the word Peking with the word Beijing in a few seconds.

Select the Replace command. The screen appears as in Fig. 11-3. The five option fields are text:, with text:, confirm:, case:, and whole word:. You have encountered three of these fields (text, case, and whole word) with the Search command. These three command fields can be considered the Search portion of the Replace command.

118 Searching and replacing text

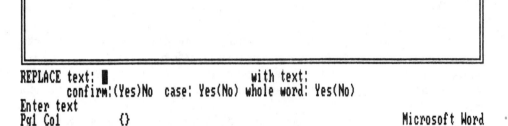

11-3 The Replace command can replace a single or multiple occurrences of a phrase with another phrase.

Region to be replaced

As with the Search command, the Replace command can be restricted to act within a limited region. To restrict the Replace command to a given area, highlight the area with the cursor. To search through the entire document, do not extend the cursor. The Replace command then affects only text from the cursor to the end of the document.

Entering the text pattern to be replaced

As in the Search menu, the text pattern you wish to replace is entered under the text field. Wildcards and symbols from Fig. 11-2 can be used in the Replace text field. The other two fields, case: and whole word:, operate in exactly the same fashion as they did under the Search command. These three options specify how the text to be replaced is found when the Replace command is executed.

You might have noticed that the direction: field is not present in the Replace command menu. This is because Word only searches from the cursor position to the end of the document or in the highlighted text when executing the Replace command. Word maintains a permanent "Down" setting in the direction field.

With text

The other two option fields, with text: and confirm:, are exclusive to the Replace command. The replacement text to be entered by the Replace command is placed in the with text: field. The replacement text can be up to 40 characters long. It might contain any of the special caret mark (^) codes listed in Fig. 11-2. Wildcards, however, have no effect when placed in the with text: field.

As an example, suppose that the text cat?^p was placed in the with text: field of the Replace command. The question mark (?) wildcard has no special effect; it shows up as a literal question mark (?) in the replacement text. The special symbol ^p, however, represents a paragraph mark (see Fig. 11-2), so a paragraph mark is inserted in the replacement text.

Confirm

The confirm: field determines whether Word pauses to ask you to verify each replacement. If you choose the No setting, Word replaces all occurrences of the pattern with the replacement text without pausing to ask you for verification. You would only use the No setting if you had no question in your mind that the substitution must be carried out everywhere in the document, and that there is no possibility that important text will accidentally be replaced.

If you are not sure that you wish to replace every occurrence of the text in the document, choose the Yes setting in the confirm field. Word then pauses after locating each instance of the text pattern. After pausing, Word prompts you to enter Y to replace, N to ignore, or cancel the replacement by pressing Esc. Enter Y if you wish to replace the occurrence with the text. If you do not wish to replace this particular occurrence, press N and Word skips to the next occurrence. If you want to abandon the Replace command altogether, press Esc. You are then returned to the document.

After the Replace command has been executed, the cursor returns to its original location. In addition, the total number of occurrences found and replaced by Word is printed on the message line.

Default values of Search and Repeat commands

If you have been experimenting with the Search and Replace commands, notice that Word remembers the last Search or Replace that was carried out. The next time the Search or Replace command is executed, the parameters from the last execution are listed as default options. This feature saves you work if you wish to execute a similar Search or Replace command.

You might also have noticed that changing the options in the Search command affects the default selections in the Replace command. Changing options in the Replace command also has an effect on the default options in the Search command. As discussed earlier, you can consider part of the Replace command to be the Search command. An event that affects one of the two commands is sure to affect the other.

The repeat search key

A function key you will find very useful with Search commands is the Shift-F4 (Repeat search) key. Word has included this function key to allow searches for a specific text pattern to be conducted easily. When Shift-F4 is pressed, Word conducts a search according to the default settings in the Search command.

If the Replace command has not been used since the last Search command, then the default options are those of the last Search command. Pressing Shift-F4 key thus has the effect of repeating the last Search command.

If a Replace command was executed recently, the default options of the Search menu are reset to that of the Replace command as mentioned earlier. Shift-F4 would then not repeat the last Search command, but the search portion of the latest Replace command.

The Redo key

The Shift-F4 (Repeat search) key is one specific aspect of the F4 (Repeat last edit) key. The F4 key, instead of just repeating the last Search command, repeats the last editing change in the document. F4 can be considered the antithesis of the Undo command that cancels the last editing command. The F4 key is very useful for performing repetitive editing.

Editing changes in Word include entering text, deleting text with the Del key, inserting text with the Ins key, or inserting text from the glossary with the F3 (Expand glossary name) key. Another category of editing changes is use of the Copy, Delete, Format, Insert, or Undo commands. Any of these actions can be repeated as many times as you desire with the F4 key.

Searching and replacing formats and styles

The ability to search and replace is not limited to text and formatting characters. Word features a complete format and styles search and replace facility, under the Format command. Select Format sEarch, and you will see the screen shown in Fig. 11-4.

```
IL====================================================CHAP11.ASC=J

FORMAT SEARCH: Character Paragraph Style


Searches for character formats
Pg10 Col          {}              ?                      Microsoft Word
```

11-4 The Format Search menu.

You can select Character, Paragraph, or Style. (Styles refer to formats imposed by a stylesheet. Stylesheets are covered in Chapter 16.) This search can include the entire document or only a selected part of the text.

Begin by selecting character. You will see the screen shown in Fig. 11-5.

```
FORMAT SEARCH CHARACTER direction: Up Down
        bold: Yes No              italic: Yes No          underline: Yes No
        strikethrough: Yes No     uppercase: Yes No       small caps: Yes No
        double underline: Yes No  position: Normal Superscript Subscript
        font name:                font size:              font color:
        hidden: Yes No
Select option
Pg10 Col          {}              ?                      Microsoft Word
```

11-5 The Format Search Character menu allows you to search for specific character formatting.

Say, for example, that you have used boldface characters to indicate the questions in a Q-and-A interview, and you want to make sure you didn't use italics instead. You can use this facility to search for italic text.

Paragraph formats can also be searched. Simply select Format Paragraph, and you will see the screen in Fig. 11-6.

```
FORMAT SEARCH PARAGRAPH direction: Up Down
     alignment: Left Centered Right Justified
     left indent:              first line:              right indent:
     line spacing:    ▌        space before:            space after:
     keep together: Yes No     keep follow: Yes No      side by side: Yes No
Select option
Pg10 Co1              {}                  ?                        Microsoft Word
```

11-6 The Format Search Paragraph menu searches for specific paragraph formatting.

Word only searches for the specified formats. Some styles are not applied through the menus, but as a result of stylesheets. If you are searching for a style imposed by a stylesheet, you must select Format sEarch Style. You are prompted for the keycode that corresponds to the style you are searching for (see Fig. 11-7).

```
╚══════════════════════════════════════════════════════════CHAP11.ASC╝
FORMAT SEARCH STYLE key code: ▌         direction: Up(Down)

Enter one or two letter key code for style
Pg10 Co1              {}                  ?                        Microsoft Word
```

11-7 The Format sEarch Style menu searches for specific style codes.

The Replace facility is only a little more complicated. Select Format repLace Character, and you will see the screen in Fig. 11-8.

```
║                                                                              ║
FORMAT REPLACE CHARACTER confirm: Yes No
     bold: Yes No                italic: Yes No              underline: Yes No
     strikethrough: Yes No       uppercase: Yes No           small caps: Yes No
     double underline: Yes No    position: Normal Superscript Subscript
     font name:                  font size:                  font color:
     hidden: Yes No
Select option
Pg1 Li1 Co1           {}                  ?                        Microsoft Word
```

11-8 The Format repLace Character menu.

Fill in the appropriate formats to search for, then press Return. You will see another screen just like Fig. 11-8, only with a prompt to enter the replacement format. When you select the replacement format from that menu and press Return, Word searches out the first incidence of the specified format and replaces it with the replacement format. You can select whether the search and replace pause to ask permission before making a change. The Format repLace Paragraph and Format repLace Style options work in the same manner.

Summary

In this chapter, you explored the Search and Replace commands. You should be able to:

- Select area of the document to be searched.
- Set the case:, whole word:, and direction: options that control searching.
- Use the confirm: option controlling replacement.
- Enter the text to be searched for and the text to be inserted in the document.
- Repeat the latest Search command with the Shift–F4 (Repeat search) key.
- Repeat the latest editing change with the F4 (Repeat last edit) key.
- Perform a search or search and replace with format of characters, paragraphs, or styles.

CHAPTER 12

Window operations

When you first run Word, the screen is divided into two areas: the window area and the command area. The text that is being edited is displayed in the window area. This window area can be divided into eight windows. Word can display eight different documents on the screen at the same time or show eight parts of the same document.

Being able to open different windows grants you several advantages. You can compare two or more documents at once without having to load and unload documents constantly. Moreover, copying and moving text between two documents is vastly simplified when using windows.

Editing large documents is also facilitated with multiple windows. You can open several windows on a large document so that different sections can be examined simultaneously. By using several windows you can avoid laboriously scrolling your document to move text from one section of the document to another.

Opening windows

Word has a number of commands for controlling windows. These window commands are found in the Window command menu. Select the Window command. The Window command menu is shown in Fig. 12-1.

The Window Split command opens new windows. Select the Window Split command. The Window Split menu is shown in Fig. 12-2 and should be on your monitor. Word offers three ways to split the present window. You can split the window horizontally, split it vertically, or create a lower section for a footnote window.

```
|· · · · · · · · · · · · · · · · · · · · · · · · · · · · · · · · · · · · · · · · · · · · · · · |
|                                                                        =CHAP12.ASC=|
WINDOW: Split Close Move

Divides current window; opens footnote window
Pg1 Co61          {·}              ?                        Microsoft Word
```

12-1 The Window menu manipulates multiple windows. You can use up to eight windows in Word. Windows can be used to view different documents or different parts of a single document.

```
|                                                                                    |
|                                                                                    |
|                                                                                    |
|                                                                                    |
|                                                                                    |
|                                                                                    |
WINDOW SPLIT: Horizontal Vertical Footnote

Divides current window horizontally at specified line
Pg1 Col           {}                                         Microsoft Word
```

12-2 The Window Split menu splits the current window into two windows.

    A horizontal split divides the original window into an upper and lower section. A vertical split divides the window into a left and right section. The footnote window option is used in Chapter 14 which discusses footnotes.

    Once the type of window split has been selected, you must mark where the active window will be divided. One way to select the location of the split is to enter the line or column number of the current window where the split is to occur. The keyboard is used to enter the line or column numbers. This method is risky as the split might not occur where you expect it to (it is difficult to think in terms of lines and columns).

    The second method of selecting the location of the window split uses the arrow keys or mouse. If you press F1 and then an arrow key when the Window Split menu is displayed, a cursor appears on the screen (see Fig. 12-3). The cursor can be moved with the arrow keys to point where you want to split the window and press Return. Notice that the command field displays the column or line number the cursor is in.

    A third method is to use the mouse. If the ruler isn't visible, you can simply click on the top border or the left border where a split should occur. When the ruler is visible, clicking on the top window border sets a tab stop, so another method had to be used to make a vertical split. Hold down Alt, and click on the ruler to make a vertical split with the ruler visible.

    Regardless of which method you select, note that Word allows window splits only between certain ranges. Horizontal splits are allowed between the third line

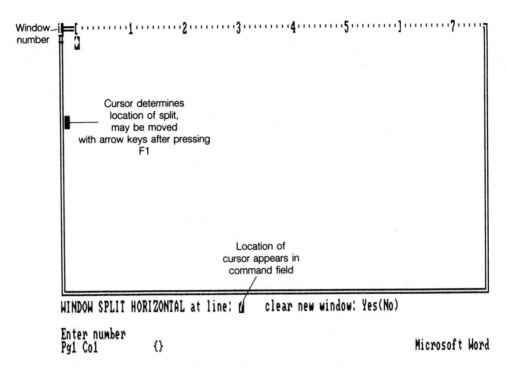

12-3 The cursor can be used to select the position of a window split. Pressing Return at this point splits the window horizontally at line 7.

from the top and one line from the bottom of a window. Vertical window divisions are possible between the fourth column from the left and four columns from the right of the window. These restrictions set a minimum size for windows.

If you are setting the location of the split with the cursor, you can use the Home and End keys to outline the possible locations for the window split. Pressing the Home or End key moves the cursor to the limits of possible splits. For a valid window split, choose a point between the two boundaries. If you try to enter a window split outside these boundaries, Word cancels the command and displays a message informing you that you are trying to create an invalid window.

Word handles a maximum of eight windows. If execution of a Window Split command will create a ninth window, Word cancels the command. Moreover, Word only supports two vertical window splits. If you attempt to add a third vertical window split, Word displays an error message.

The clear new window setting

The Window Split Horizontal and Window Split Vertical menus have a setting to clear the new window. When this is set to No, the new window contains the same document as the window from which it was split. If this option is set to Yes, the new window is cleared as it is created.

126 *Window operations*

Practice opening a new window

For practice, split the current window. Select the Window Split Horizontal command. Then, press F1. Use the arrow keys to move the cursor to line 7 so the screen matches Fig. 12-3. Leave the clear new window option set to No. Finally, press Return to split the window. The screen should match Fig. 12-4.

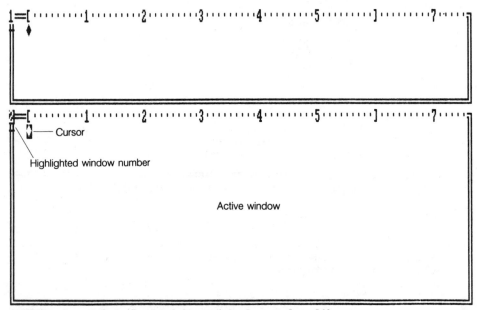

12-4 The screen after being split horizontally at line 7.

Moving between windows

You can only work with one window at a time. The window in use is called the *active* window. Word marks the active window by highlighting the window number in the upper left corner of the window (see Fig. 12-4). The active window contains the cursor.

When you split a window in two, the second of the two windows always becomes the active window. Unless you change the active window (described later), any editing commands executed affect the second window. Any text entered is placed in the active window.

You can change the active window by clicking in it with the mouse, or by pressing the F1 (Next window) key. Pressing F1 moves you to next window, making that the active window. The window that becomes active is the window with the next greater number. If you press F1 when the active window is the one with the greatest number, window 1 becomes active. Remember the F1 key. If you are not using the mouse, it provides the only method for changing the active window.

Changing window dimensions

Windows are flexible. A window's dimensions can be enlarged or reduced to provide a better view of a document. When you change the dimensions of a window, Word modifies the dimensions of the surrounding windows to accommodate your change. The Window Move command is used to change the size of windows.

The Window Move menu is shown in Fig. 12-5. There are three option fields in the menu. The first option field, window #:, determines the window that the command affects. The Window move command changes the location of the lower right corner of a window. Thus, it might be necessary to use the Window Move command on a neighboring window to give your window the dimensions you require.

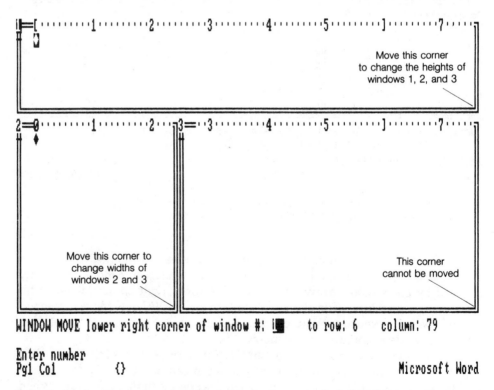

12-5 The Window Move command adjusts window sizes by moving the bottom right corner of the window.

128 *Window operations*

Consider, as an example, the three windows in Fig. 12-6. Suppose you want to increase the height of window 2 by four lines. You cannot lower the lower right corner of window 2 by four lines, because window 2 is at the bottom of the screen. Instead, you must move the lower right corner of window 1 up four lines. The Window Move can also be used to change the width of window 2.

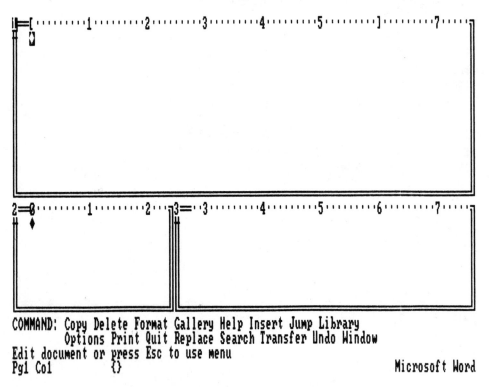

12-6 The screen after the bottom right corner of window number 1 (the top window) has been moved down. This made the top window larger at the expense of the bottom windows.

Because of this system of changing the dimensions of windows, it should be clear that the window at the lower right corner of the screen cannot be directly changed by the Window Move command. The lower right corner of the entire screen cannot be moved. If an attempt is made to use the Window Move command on the lower right window, Word cancels the command. For example, employing the Window Move command on window 3 in Fig. 12-6 has no effect.

The two options, to row: and column:, set the new location of the lower right corner of the window. As before, the new location can be entered by typing in a number or by positioning the cursor at the new location with the arrow keys. When using the cursor, the line or column that the cursor is in is shown in the command field at the bottom of the screen. The restrictions on window dimensions apply to the new dimensions.

Options

The Options menu provides a number of options that apply to the active window (shown in Fig. 12-7).

The next few paragraphs cover the options that apply to the window. The window number allows you to select the window the Window Options command affects. The window affected by default is the active window.

```
WINDOW OPTIONS for window number: 1        show hidden text:(Yes)No
            show ruler:(Yes)No         show non-printing symbols:(None)Partial All
            show layout: Yes(No)              show line breaks: Yes(No)
            show outline: Yes(No)             show style bar: Yes(No)

GENERAL OPTIONS mute: Yes(No)                 summary sheet:(Yes)No
            measure:(In)Cm P10 P12 Pt         display mode: 1
            paginate:(Auto)Manual             colors:
            autosave: 4                       autosave confirm: Yes(No)
            show menu:(Yes)No                 show borders:(Yes)No
            date format:(MDY)DMY              decimal character:(.),
            time format:(12)24                default tab width: 0.5"
            line numbers: Yes(No)             count blank space: Yes(No)
            cursor speed: 3                   linedraw character: (|)
            speller path: C:\X\BOOKS\WORD\PROGRAM\SPELL-AM.LEX
Enter number
Pg5 Co6              {resemb...ler:..} ?                      Microsoft Word
```

12-7 The Options menu contains many options that pertain to the appearance and utility of a window.

You've already seen the show ruler line option. The show layout option changes the display to include frames and graphics (these will be covered later in the book). Show outline refers to Word's powerful outlining capability. Sometimes it is useful to have the outline visible on the page while writing.

Show hidden text allows hidden text to be displayed on the screen (underlined). The show non printing symbols option allows you to see normally hidden characters that mark the end of the paragraph, tab marks, spaces, and vertical tabs. The show line breaks & option allows you to see how the lines appear if you are using a differently sized font. Smaller fonts squeeze more characters in a line than larger fonts. With this option off, this difference is not visible.

The style bar option activates and deactivates the style bar. When the style bar is activated, two columns are reserved on the left window border for the style bar. These two columns are used to display the format of text in the document. A few common codes are shown and listed in Fig. 12-8 and 12-9.

To turn off any options, you must employ the Options command to reset manually the window to its original options. Window options are maintained even

Window operations

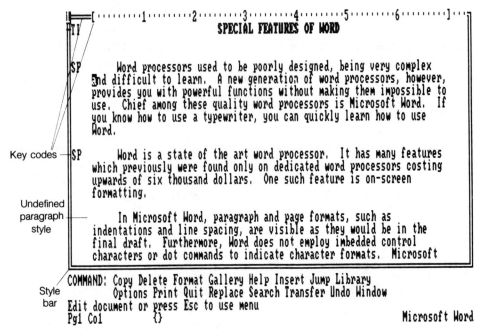

12-8 The style bar shows the different styles assigned to paragraphs. The codes displayed are equivalent to the style key codes on the attached style sheet. This feature is useful when a style sheet is attached.

Blank	Paragraph style not defined on current style sheet or a paragraph with no style assigned to it.
* (asterisk)	Paragraph style not defined on current style sheet.
1-2 characters	The key code used with Alt to assign the style.
b	Running head appearing at bottom of all pages
be	appearing at bottom of even numbered pages
bo	appearing at bottom of odd numbered pages
bf	appearing on first page
t	Running head appearing at top of all pages
te	appearing at top of even numbered pages
to	appearing at top of odd numbered pages
tf	appearing at top of first page

12-9 The codes shown in the style bar and what they represent.

when the window is split. When you split a window in two, both windows have the same options as the original window, though the options of each can then be changed independently.

Closing windows

The third command in the Window menu is the Window Close command, which is employed to unify two windows. Before closing a window, you should move the cursor to the window you wish to close. The active window is closed by default.

You can also select the window you wish to close by typing in its window number from the keyboard.

If the window is but one of a number that displays a document, nothing is lost when the window is closed. If the window is the only window displaying a certain document, any editing changes to that document is lost if the window is closed. To save hours of hard work, first make the window containing the document the active window and then use the Transfer Save command to save the editing changes.

If Word detects unsaved editing changes about to be lost with execution of the Window Close command, the window is not closed until Word confirms whether you want to lose the edits in the document in that window. At this point you can type Y to ignore the loss or press the Esc key to cancel the command.

Working with windows

Windows can be considered miniature versions of the original window. Each window is numbered in the top left corner. As stated previously, Word can accommodate up to eight windows at once. All of Word's editing commands function in the same manner in each window.

Each window displays a document. If more than one window is present, they might show either the same or different documents. If you have more than one window showing a document, any editing is shown in all the windows displaying the same document.

When you split a window, the two resulting windows look upon the document shown in the original window. To display a different document, use the Transfer Load command. The Transfer Load command loads a document into the active window (Fig. 12-10).

Having a number of windows lends an additional dimension to the Transfer Clear command (see Fig. 12-11 on the next page). The Transfer Clear command offers two options: Clear Window and Clear All. Previously with only one window open, the Transfer Clear All and Transfer Clear Window commands seemed to be identical. When a number of windows are open, the Transfer Clear Window command only clears the active window.

The Transfer Clear All command, on the other hand, clears and closes all the windows. If there are any unsaved editing changes in any of the windows, you are prompted either to save or discard the edits. For each unsaved document Word asks you to enter Y to confirm loss of edits. After you tell Word whether or not to save your editing changes, only an empty window remains. The screen looks as if Word has just been started up.

Scrolling

One disadvantage of multiple windows is that they are smaller than the original window. Therefore, to view a document, it is necessary to scroll the document more often.

All the scrolling keys perform in exactly the same fashion whether one window or many windows are open. The scrolling keys can be utilized to scroll the active window. The PgUp and PgDn keys scroll the document in the active window up

Window operations

```
1=[········1·········2·········3·········4·········5·········6···]·····7·····
  Outline  Comparison of Riverside-DEC and Salty Dog Negotiations

  Strategy
    Suspected that DEC had different prices for ,,,
    Suspected DEC would want to test Technoclean.
    Stated Position, threat of lawsuits, possible closing, law
       did not require us to purchase the Technoclean only Rotoblue
    DEC insisted that a scrubber was necessary, response was to

2=[········1·········2·········3·········4·········5·········]·····7·····
  ▯
```
Active window — File being loaded into active window

```
TRANSFER LOAD filename: tariffs█          read only: Yes(No)

Enter filename or press F1 to select from list
Pg1 Co1       {}                                        Microsoft Word
```

12-10 Windows can be used to view more than one document on the screen at a time. This is especially advantageous when transferring data from one document to another.

```
1=[········1·········2·········3·········4·········5·········6···]·····7·····
  Outline  Comparison of Riverside-DEC and Salty Dog Negotiations

  Strategy
    Suspected that DEC had different prices for ,,,
    Suspected DEC would want to test Technoclean.
    Stated Position, threat of lawsuits, possible closing, law
       did not require us to purchase the Technoclean only Rotoblue
    DEC insisted that a scrubber was necessary, response was to

2=[········1·········2·········3·········4·········5·········6···]·····7·····
  █    "The International Negotiation Game: Some Evidence from the
  Tokyo Round," by Kenneth S. Chan analyzes several models that
  attempt to explain the outcome of the Tokyo Round of tariff
  reduction negotiations.  If the correct model can be found, then
  it could be used to predict outcomes of future negotiations,
  judge the acceptability of other proposals on tariff reductions,
  and explain to what extent efficiency and fairness are important
                                                       ═TARIFFS.DOC═
```
Note that different documents can be in different windows

```
TRANSFER CLEAR WINDOW:                      Clears active window

Enter Y to save, N to lose edits, or Esc to cancel █
Pg1 Co1       {}                                        Microsoft Word
```

12-11 The Transfer Clear Window command clears the document in the current window. Word gives you one warning if clearing the window will cause a loss of new data.

and down one window. The Ctrl-PgUp and Ctrl-PgDn keys scroll to the beginning or end of the document.

The left and right scroll commands have barely been mentioned. Windows formed with the Window Split Vertical command must be scrolled left or right because the text is almost certainly wider than the window. Set the Scroll Lock toggle and use the left and right arrow keys to move the text under the window (see Fig. 12-12).

Scrolling Keys	Scrolls
Left, Right	Moves cursor left or right one character, scrolls document if necessary.
F7, F8	Moves cursor left or right one word, scrolls document if necessary.
PgUp	Up one page
PgDn	Down one page
Ctrl-PgUp	Jump to beginning of document
Ctrl-PgDn	Jump to end of document
Ctrl-Right	Right one word
Ctrl-Left	Left one word
Scroll Lock + Right	Right 1/3 window
Scroll Lock + Left	Left 1/3 window
Scroll Lock + Up	Up one line
Scroll Lock + Down	Down one line

12-12 Keys used to scroll documents. Scrolling documents left and right is important when working with narrow windows.

Zooming windows

Word includes a Zoom command that increases the size of a window to the maximum window size. Pressing Ctrl-F1 (Zoom window on/off) activates the Zoom command. Thus, if you are using a window that is too small to easily edit a document, press Ctrl-F1 to make the window full size and then edit the document. When you no longer want to work with that window, press Ctrl-F1 a second time to return the window to its original size. When a window has been blown up, ZM is displayed on the status line at the bottom of the screen.

Practice with one of the windows on the screen now by pressing Ctrl-F1. The window is blown up. Press Ctrl-F1 a second time to return the window to its original size.

Press F1 to zoom the next window. Click on the window number with the mouse to return the window to its normal size.

Cut and paste windows

Windows simplify copying and moving text from one section of a document to another, or among documents (see Fig. 12-13). Use the Window Split command to divide the original window in two with the Window Split command. Load the first document into one window with the Transfer Load command. Now, activate the other window with the F1 key and load the other document.

With the two documents in memory, you are ready to copy and move blocks

134 *Window operations*

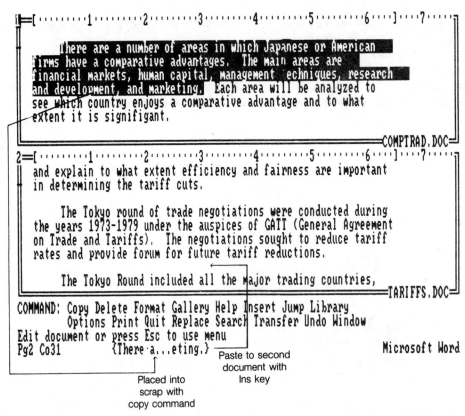

12-13 You can copy or delete text from one document and insert into another document when using multiple windows.

of text between the two documents. Use F1 to activate the window from which you plan to copy or move text. Highlight the block of text you want to copy or move. Place the block in the scrap with the Copy command or Del key. Activate the second window. The cursor moves to the other window. Place the cursor where you wish the text to be inserted and use the Ins key. The text is transferred into the document.

You can use the same procedure for cut and paste in the same document. If a document is so long that scrolling between parts becomes tedious, you can consider opening up a second window to keep track of different parts of your document.

Other uses for multiple windows

Another application of multiple windows is simultaneously editing two or more documents. You might decide to open a second window to examine another document while editing the first document. Frequently, you might open a second window to view an outline while writing a document. The second window can also be used as a notebook where you place your scratch work. Feel free to experiment with various uses for multiple windows.

Controlling windows with the mouse

The mouse can be used to open, close, and activate windows. In addition, the ruler line can be turned on and off with the mouse. Using the mouse to control windows is not easy. There are a number of combinations that must be memorized to use the mouse fully. When you use the keyboard, Word always offers a menu that helps you select commands and set options, but when you use a mouse, you must know the various mouse movements and buttons to press to adjust the windowing environment.

To activate a window, point the mouse at the center of the window. Individual characters or words in the window can be selected by pointing to them.

Turning the ruler line on and off

To turn the ruler line on or off, move the mouse pointer to the upper right corner of the window. When the mouse is in position, the mouse pointer resembles three vertical lines (in each of these exercises, the mouse pointer looks like a vertical box on a monochrome text monitor). When the mouse is in position, press the left mouse button to turn on the ruler line. Press the both buttons to turn off the ruler line.

Opening and closing windows

As mentioned earlier, the mouse pointer must be moved to the right border of a window to open or close a horizontal window or the top border to open a vertical window (if the ruler is visible, close it before trying to open a window). When the mouse is in position, the pointer looks like an empty box. When the mouse is in position, press the left button to open a new horizontal window. Press the Shift key and either mouse button to open a footnote and annotation window. Press both buttons on the right or top window border to close a window.

The mouse pointer can be moved to the upper border of a window to open or close a vertical window. When the mouse is on the window border, the pointer again resembles an empty box. At this position, the left button can be pressed to open a vertical window. Both buttons can be pushed to close a vertical window. When you tell Word to close the last window on a given document, if there have been any editing changes in the document, Word gives you the opportunity to save the changes before closing the window.

If you want to close and save all the windows, use the Transfer All-save command.

Moving windows

Windows can be moved with the mouse. To move a window, the mouse pointer should be on the lower right corner of the window. Once the mouse pointer is in place, the mouse resembles a cross. To move the window, press and hold the left or right button. Then, move the mouse to a new point and release the button. The window size is adjusted. The window with its lower right corner in the lower right corner of the screen cannot be changed in size.

Summary

You have examined the following in this chapter:

- Opening windows with the Window Split command and the mouse.
- Moving from window to window with the F1 key and the mouse.
- Changing the dimensions of windows with the Window Move command and the mouse.
- Setting window options with the Window Options command.
- Closing windows with the Window Close command and the mouse.
- Scrolling windows.
- Some uses for windows.
- The Zoom command.

CHAPTER 13

The Jump and Option commands

This chapter examines the Jump and Option commands. The Jump command allows you to move quickly to any page or to the next footnote in the document. The Options command changes a number of Word features. Combined, these two commands offer a view into Word's fascinating and versatile nature.

The Jump command

The Jump command allows quick movement between different locations in the document. Select the Jump command from the Edit menu. The Jump menu resembles Fig. 13-1. The four commands in the Jump menu are Page, Footnote, Annotation, and bookmarK. They represent the variety of jumps you can make with the Jump command.

Jumping to pages

The Jump Page command is used to jump between pages of the document. Press Esc, J, P. The resulting menu resembles Fig. 13-2. The number of the current page

138 *The Jump and Option commands*

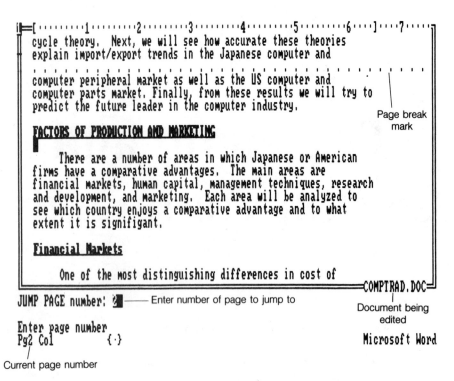

13-1 The Jump Page command can instantaneously move the cursor to any page. The Jump Footnote command moves the cursor between a footnote reference and the corresponding footnote text. The Annotation command is similar to the Footnote command. Finally, the bookmarK command takes you to a previously placed bookmark in the text.

13-2 A document must be paginated before the Jump Page command works.

is listed in the number: field. Place the number of the page to which you wish to jump in the number field. If you enter a page number past the end of the document, Word jumps to the last page.

Page breaks in a document mark the beginning of a new page. Word numbers pages in a document based on the page breaks it assigns during printing or repaginating a document. The position of page breaks is determined by conditions such as the size of the paper, the margins of the page, and the line spacing. Page breaks are represented by a dotted line across the page. You can set the pagination process as automatic with the Options menu (the default), or set Word to repaginate only when printed, or when Repaginate is selected from the Print menu.

Editing changes made in a document do not immediately change the page breaks in the document unless Auto is selected in the paginate option in the Options menu. Otherwise, Word assigns page breaks to a document only before printing the document or when executing the Print Repaginate command. Therefore, page breaks in a document might not reflect the actual page breaks that appear on the printed copy.

Because page breaks in a document might not be updated until printing or repagination, the latest printout of a document is a good guide to the page numbering of the document. For example, if a paragraph appears in page 6 of the printout, it will be on page 6 in the document until the document is repaginated or printed. This is true even if the paragraph is printed on page 4 after the page breaks have been updated. Generally, it is more convenient simply to leave automatic repagination turned on. It doesn't slow the program to any appreciable degree.

The Jump Footnote command

The next Jump command is the Jump Footnote command. More is covered about footnotes in Chapter 15. For now it is enough to say that a footnote is composed of two parts: the footnote reference and the footnote text. The footnote reference, commonly a number, is part of the text of the document. The reference mark indicates the location of the reference. For each footmark reference, some footnote text explains the reference.

In Word, footnote references are located in the text area. Footnote text is located at the end of the division containing the footnotes. The footnote text, however, only appears there on the screen. In the printed copy, the footnote reference is located either at the end of the division or at the end of the page.

To the reference mark The Jump Footnote command has three uses. First, it can be used to locate the next footnote reference in the text. Word searches from the location of the cursor to the end of the document for a footnote reference mark. If none are found, Word gives a beep of disapproval. If a reference mark is found, the cursor moves there and highlight the mark.

To the footnote text If the cursor is already highlighting a footnote reference mark when the Jump Footnote command is selected, a different action occurs. Instead of moving down to the next reference mark, Word jumps to the end of the division, to where the corresponding footnote text is located. The Jump Footnote command thus provides a quick method of selecting the appropriate footnote text for the reference mark.

Back to the text The third function of the Jump Footnote command is performed when the command is executed while the cursor is highlighting some footnote text. When this occurs, the cursor jumps back to the footnote reference mark that corresponds to the text. The Jump Footnote command provides two-way transportation between the two parts of a footnote, the reference mark and the footnote text.

The Jump Footnote command is not the only method that can be used to move back and forth between a footnote reference mark and the accompanying footnote text. As the footnote text is located at the end of the division, the window can simply be scrolled until the footnote text comes into view. Using the Jump

Footnote command is the recommended method for finding footnotes. Not only is employing the command a simple process, but the same method applies when jumping to the footnote window.

The Jump Annotation command

Annotations are special footnotes covered in Chapter 14. The Jump Annotation command works in a similar manner to the Jump Footnote command.

The Jump bookmarK command

Bookmarks are markers you can leave in text to allow you to return to a specified location after you have moved somewhere else. Often a writer works on several sections of a manuscript at the same time, making progress in one spot as he or she awaits additional material (or, inspiration) for another spot. Word also allows you to use bookmarks as cross-references. This is covered in Chapter 14.

The Jump bookmarK command prompts you for the name of a bookmark. If you would like to see a list of bookmarks, press F1 and then select from the list, pressing Return to jump to the bookmark. When you arrive at the bookmark, the text that makes up the bookmark is selected.

Rapid cursor movement with the mouse

The mouse may also be used to move rapidly from one section of a document to another section. The mouse uses the left window border, called the "scroll bar," to move to any point in the document. This is one of the most attractive features of the mouse.

The scroll bar has a short line across it. This line, called the *thumb*, marks the relative position of the window in the document. If the window shows text near the beginning of the document, the thumb line are near the top of the scroll bar. If the window shows text near the end of the document, the thumb line is near the bottom of the scroll bar. Likewise when the window shows text at the middle of the document, the thumb line is near the middle of the scroll bar.

The mouse can be used to move the cursor to any position in the document. To move the cursor thus, move the mouse pointer to the scroll bar. When the mouse is on the scroll bar, the mouse pointer resembles a double arrow (see Fig. 4-13). Move the mouse pointer to a position on the scroll bar relative to the position you want to move to in the document. Thus, if you wish to move to a page in the middle of the document, move the mouse pointer until it is in the middle of the scroll bar. Likewise, if you wish to move to a page that is near the end of the document, move the mouse pointer near the end of the scroll bar.

Once the mouse pointer is in position on the scroll bar, press both mouse buttons. After a short pause, the appropriate text appears on the screen. The cursor does not move, however. To place the cursor in the text that is visible, click in the text. If you simply start typing, the window jumps back to the cursor position.

Word options

The Options command allows you to look at and set many of Word's different options. Options set with the Options command are saved at the end of the editing session, as are the options set with the Print Options. When Word is subsequently started up in later sessions, these options are automatically set.

Select the Options command from the Edit menu. The Options menu should match Fig. 13-3. Some of these options were covered in Chapter 12. The remaining command fields listed are mute:, measure:, paginate:, autosave:, show menu:, date format:, time format:, line number:, cursor speed:, speller path:, summary sheet:, display mode:, colors:, autosave confirm:, show borders:, decimal character:, default tab width:, count blank space:, and linedraw character. These are options that affect the general operation of Word, so they are found in the Word Options command. Each option is examined in the upcoming section.

```
WINDOW OPTIONS for window number: 1         show hidden text: Yes(No)
             show ruler: Yes(No)     show non-printing symbols: None Partial All
            show layout: Yes(No)             show line breaks: Yes(No)
           show outline: Yes(No)              show style bar: Yes(No)

GENERAL OPTIONS mute: Yes(No)                  summary sheet: Yes(No)
             measure:(In)Cm P10 P12 Pt         display mode: 1
            paginate:(Auto)Manual                    colors:
            autosave: 4                    autosave confirm: Yes(No)
           show menu:(Yes)No                  show borders:(Yes)No
         date format:(MDY)DMY             decimal character:(.),
         time format:(12)24              default tab width: 0.5"
        line numbers: Yes(No)            count blank space: Yes(No)
        cursor speed: 3                  linedraw character: (|)
        speller path: C:\X\BOOKS\WORD\PROGRAM\SPELL-AM.LEX
Select option
Pg4 Co18             {·and·W...mmands} ?                    Microsoft Word
```

13-3 The Options menu controls many different features in Word.

The mute option

The mute option is aptly named. It controls the audible alarm incorporated in Word. With the alarm on, Word utters a beep to call for attention when a command or operation cannot be completed. Trying to enter an invalid option, attempting to examine an empty list, or forcing an invalid window split are all common causes for Word to sound the alarm.

The default setting for the mute: field is No. This choice leaves the audible alarm on. If the Yes setting is selected in the mute: field, Word turns off or "mutes" the audible alarm. Word still continues to employ other warning methods, such as flashing the screen and placing error warnings on the message line. You might or might not want the computer to beep at you. You might have a headache and wish to turn off Word's beeping, or you might be working in an office environment where Word's beeping is disturbing your coworkers.

The measure option

The measure: field sets the unit of measure utilized in Word. This unit is the default unit in almost all of the commands fields that require a measurement. Margins, indents, and distances are all be measured in this unit. It is therefore prudent to select a unit of measure you can use comfortably. The default measure Microsoft selects is inches.

Word supports five different gauges in the measure: field: In, Cm, P10, P12, and Pt. These are the abbreviations for units of measure. In and Cm stand for inches and centimeters. P10 stands for 10-pitch (10 characters per inch). P10 measures a unit of distance that is equal to $1/10$ inch. P12 stands for 12-pitch. A P12 unit of distance would measure $1/12$ inch. Finally, Pt is an abbreviation for points. There are 72 points in an inch, so a point measures $1/72$ inch.

Paginate

Paginate was covered briefly earlier in this chapter. If this option is set to Auto, Word paginates each time a change is made to the manuscript, with virtually no loss of processing speed. Set to Manual, Word repaginates only when it is printing out a document, or when specifically told to repaginate by the Print Repaginate command.

Autosave

Autosave is a very handy feature for creative writers. Loss of a document in electronic memory is always a hazard. Setting autosave to a value greater than zero causes Word to save your current document at regular intervals. If your Autosave is set to 4, your manuscript is saved every four minutes. Experiment with this value to find an interval that matches your personal rhythms. Saving a backup of the document takes only a couple of seconds. While the save is going on, Word is fairly good about storing your mouse and keyboard input for use as soon as the autosave is finished.

Show menu

Once you have used Word for a few months, you will know the main menu intimately. You won't need to refer to it anymore. Set show menu to No and you won't have to waste screen space on it anymore. That will give you three more lines of text on-screen.

Date and time format

Date and time format were discussed earlier in the book. Basically, there are American and European styles of dates and civilian and military styles of time. MDY (Month-Day-Year) is the American style of representing dates (October 3,

1991). DMY (Day-Month-Year) is the European style (3 October 1991). It should be noted that the latter style is the one preferred by the bible of the publishing industry, the *Chicago Manual of Style*. The 12 (12-hour clock) is the civilian style of representing time. The other option, 24, is the military 24-hour clock.

Line number

On the bottom line of the screen, the page number and column number are displayed, sometimes along with the division number. Selecting line numbers provides the current line number as well. To print the line numbers on the page, you will want to select the Format Division line-Numbers command.

Cursor speed

Whenever you press a cursor key, Word moves the cursor one space, hesitates about half a second and then moves the cursor in the indicated direction until the key is released. The speed of the movement after the hesitation is controlled by cursor speed in the Options menu. A high value produces a faster cursor. If the movement is too fast, you will have trouble placing the cursor accurately.

Speller path

The speller path entry represents the path to the speller. It is set by the setup program when you install Word.

Summary sheet

When you use the Transfer Save command, you are prompted to enter information on a summary sheet that tells information about the document like the last time it was altered, the first time it was entered, the name of the writer, and so on. If summary sheet is left on, you are prompted for the summary information. If not, the summary sheet won't appear. Summary sheets are most useful when a number of people have access to a document at the same time.

Display mode

If your display is capable of different configurations, select the display mode option and press F1 to see how many different ways you can view your work. On the Hercules display, for instance, you have the choice of text mode (80 by 25 display), graphic mode (80 by 25) or graphic mode (80 by 43). This last option uses a smaller typeface that the standard PC character set in order to place larger sections of windows on-screen at the same time, nearly doubling the amount of text without severely compromising the readability of the text.

Colors

If you have a color monitor, you can use the colors option to adjust the colors used on screen.

Autosave confirm

Autosave is generally a useful thing, but sometimes you make changes you want to think about before you make them permanent. In that situation, select autosave confirm to make the computer check with you before saving the current text in memory to disk.

Show borders

The borders around the windows take up space that might better be filled with text. Turn off show borders to get a couple of extra characters and lines on screen. This option only works when you have a single window showing. As soon as you try to split a window (only with the Window Split command; the mouse-on-border options don't work when the border is hidden), the borders reappear.

Decimal character

In Europe, the comma is used as a decimal separator. You can specify either the period or the comma in the decimal character option. The principle action of this option is the alignment on decimal tabs.

Default tab width

The default decimal tabs are set at half inch intervals. You can enter any value in the default tab width option. Default tabs are set at that interval.

Count blank space

If you want the line count reading at the bottom of the screen to include blank lines as well as lines filled with text, set the count blank space option to Yes. If you don't want the blank lines included, set this option to No.

Linedraw

The linedraw option allows you to select the characters you will use when drawing lines. Select this option and press F1 to see the options available.

Summary

By the end of the chapter, you should be familiar with using:
- The Jump Page command to move to specific pages in a long document.
- The Jump Footnote command to find footnote reference marks, and to move between the reference marks and footnote text.
- The Jump Annotation command and the Jump bookmarK command.
- The scroll bar and the mouse to rapidly move to any point in the document.
- The Options command to set the mute, measure, paginate, autosave, show menu, date format, time format, line number, cursor speed, speller path, summary sheet, display mode, colors, autosave confirm, show borders, decimal character, default tab width, count blank space, and linedraw character.

14
CHAPTER

Advanced page formatting

Text in a document is arranged in pages. The manner in which text is displayed on a page is called *page layout*. Page layout is determined by several elements, including margins, page dimensions, footnotes, and running heads. Another element, graphics, is covered in a separate chapter (see Chapter 34).

Some of these powerful page formatting elements are controlled by the division. Others have become so important that they now demand their own formatting commands under the Format menu.

A *division* in Word is a unit used to group together text with the same page layout. You encountered the Format Division command earlier when you set a few basic division formats in Chapter 9. You will examine the other division format options in this chapter, as well as the process of setting up footnotes, running heads, bookmarks and annotations.

Starting a new division

Whenever you wish to create a section of text with a new page layout, you must start a new division. To begin a new division, move the cursor to the location where you want the new division to begin. Then, press Ctrl–Return (division break), and Word places a division mark at that location.

The division mark shows up on the screen as a line of colons running across the screen. The division mark can be selected, deleted, or moved just as any other character. The format of the entire division is stored in the division mark.

Page break

A new division starts a new page. If you want to begin a new page without starting a new division, you should insert a page break. To insert a page break in your document, move to point where you want the page to start. Then hit Ctrl–Shift–Return (page break). Because starting a new division has several ramifications, it is wise to employ the Ctrl–Shift–Return (page break) key instead of starting a new division to begin a new page.

Establishing a new division

The Format Division commands largely control the attributes of page layout in a document. As with formatting paragraphs, you might decide to format an existing division or a division you are in the process of creating. To format an existing division, simply move the cursor and select a character in the division. If you must format more than one division, it is necessary to highlight all the divisions that must be formatted.

To format an incomplete division, enter a division break by pressing Ctrl–Return. The new division has the same format as the previous division. Type a few characters in the new division, then employ the Format Division command to set the desired format.

The Format Division Layout command

You should now examine the Format Division Layout menu. Press Esc, F, L. The Format Division Layout menu resembles Fig. 14-1. The division break field controls the manner in which the attributes of the division begin. The settings listed are Page, Continuous, Column, Even, and Odd. The meanings of most of these settings is obvious. The Continuous setting specifies no particular boundaries between divisions.

A division created with the Continuous setting does not start a new page. Rather, the Continuous setting assigns the attributes of the new division to the first page composed entirely of the new division. If there are different numbers of columns above and below the division mark, then the old division's number of columns appear above the division mark and the new division's number of columns appear below.

The Page setting causes the new division to begin a new page. The layout of the page then depends on the format or attributes of the new division. The column setting is similar to the page setting. The Column setting causes a new column to be started. If the division format specifies only one column to a page, this is equivalent to starting a new page.

14-1 The Format Division Layout menu controls the placement of footnotes, columns, and division breaks.

The Odd and Even settings are employed only when the document is being printed on both sides of the page. In such cases, a distinction exists between the pages with odd page numbers and pages with even page numbers. When pages are double-sided, as in a book, odd-numbered (recto) pages are on the right. And even-numbered pages (verso) is on the left. The Odd and Even options start a new division on either an odd- or even-numbered page, skipping a page if necessary.

Document dimensions

Many fields in the Format Division commands ask you to enter a measurement. Some of these fields list the unit of measurement used. If no unit of measurement is listed, the default measurement specified in the Options menu is used. The process of setting the default measure was examined in Chapter 13. If the Options command has not been used to change the unit of measure, the default measurement used by Word is inches.

If you desire to enter values in other units of measurement, enter the appropriate unit of measurement after the response as in 1cm or 12pt. The abbreviations for units of measurement recognized by Word are listed in Fig. 14-2.

The page length: and width: fields specify the dimensions of the page. The default values are set for 8.5 by 11-inch pages. The margin top:, bottom:, left:, and right: fields set the margins of the page. Margins measurements refer to the distance between the text and the edges of the paper.

Gutter margins for bound documents

Gutter margins are set with the gutter margin: field on the Format Division Margins menu. The gutter margins are utilized when the document is printed on both sides of a sheet and undergoes binding. When a document is bound, space from the left margins of odd-numbered pages and from the right margins of even-numbered pages is consumed by the binding process (see Fig. 14-3). The white

Advanced page formatting

Measurement	Abbreviations
in	Inches
cm	Centimeters
P10	10-pitch (10 characters per inch). Each p10 unit is one-tenth of an inch long. If 10-pitch font is the font size selected for characters in the document, the number of P10 measures would equal the number of character positions.
P12	12-pitch (12 characters per inch). Each p12 unit is one-twelfth of an inch long. If 12-pitch font is the font size selected for characters in the document, the number of P12 measures would equal the number of character positions.
Pt	Typesetters' points. There are 72 points to the inch.
li	Lines (12 vertical points). Lines are used for vertical measures only.

14-2 The measurements that can be used to define positions and margins.

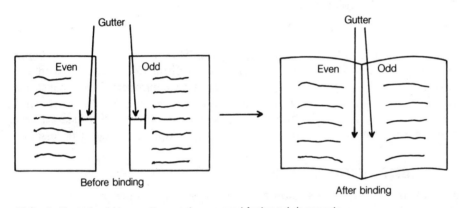

14-3 An illustration of how gutter margins are used for bound documents.

space between the right margin of a verso page and the left margin of the next recto page, which is gathered into the binding, is called the *gutter*. To prevent uneven margins, Word places wider margins on the appropriate pages. Word refers to this extra margin as the gutter width.

If the document is being printed only on one side of a sheet, only space on the left margin is taken up by the binding process. In such cases, the gutter margins would be zero. You should augment the left margin. If you are not binding the document, then the gutter margin should be zero.

Columns

Word possesses the ability to separate text into columns. Normally there is only one column of text, but the number of cols: field of the Format Division command allows you to specify a greater number of columns (see Fig. 14-4).

When there are two or more of columns of text, Word does not show all the columns on the screen. Instead, the column shown decreases in width to show the correct line breaks. The printed document, however, possesses the correct number of columns per page.

14-4 The Format Division Layout command determines whether a document is printed in single or multiple columns.

After stating the number of columns on a page, you must set the space between the columns with the space between columns: field. The space placed between columns decreases the amount of text that can be displayed on the screen. Therefore, the left and right margins should be reduced so that more text can be displayed on the monitor. Do not specify too many columns of text. Otherwise, your columns become too narrow. Note that justifying columns of text can make narrow columns of text difficult to read.

Footnotes

Word has special commands for footnotes, annotations, bookmarks, and running heads. Footnotes are composed of two parts: the footnote reference mark and the footnote text. The reference mark is placed in the document to mark a footnote. The footnote text contains the comment. Word stores footnote text in the footnote area at the end of the document. You can review footnote text by scrolling to the end of the document. You can open a footnote window with the Window Split Footnote command so that the footnotes and document are displayed simultaneously. The Jump Footnote command offers a fast way to skip ahead to the footnote text from the reference or to skip back to the reference from the footnote text.

Creating a footnote

Footnotes are constructed while editing a document. To insert a footnote reference mark, move the cursor one character to the point where you want the footnote reference mark. Now select the Format Footnote command. The menu resembles Fig. 14-5.

```
SPECIAL FEATURES OF WORD ▋ ─── Footnote reference mark to be inserted here

Word processors used to be poorly designed, being very complex
and difficult to learn.  A new generation of word processors,
however, provide you with powerful functions without making them
impossible to use.  Chief among these quality word processors is
Microsoft Word.  If you know how to use a typewriter, you can
quickly learn how to use Word.

Word is a state of the art word processor.  It has many features
which previously were found only on dedicated word processors.
One such feature is the on-screen formatting offered by Word.
With Word, the claim that "what you see is what you get" is
completely realized.

In Microsoft Word, paragraph and page formats, such as
indentations and line spacing, are visible as they would be in
the final draft.  Furthermore, Word does not employ imbedded
control characters or dot commands to indicate character formats.
                                                        ═LESSON2.DOC═
FORMAT FOOTNOTE reference mark: ▋ ─── Leave blank for automatic numbering
Enter text
Pg1 Co26        {}                                      Microsoft Word
```

14-5 The Format Footnote command enters a footnote reference into the document at the cursor's position and then allows you to enter the corresponding footnote text. The footnote number is automatically assigned so that it is in sequence with all preceding and succeeding footnotes.

    Word prompts you to enter a symbol in the command field reference mark:. This symbol marks the location of the comment. Reference marks are normally numbered consecutively. If you want Word to number the footnote automatically, leave the field blank. Otherwise, enter the character or characters to be used for the reference mark.

Finally, press Return to execute the command. The reference mark selected is inserted at the cursor. Word jumps to the footnote area at the end of the document. The footnote area stores the footnote text. Enter the text for the footnote. The footnote text can be of any length and can encompass any number of paragraphs. When the footnote text is completed, you can return to editing the document by scrolling up the document or using the Jump Footnote command (see Fig. 14-6).

```
┌[·········1·········2·········3·········4·········5·········]·········7····┐
│ formats such as boldface, italics, and underlining exactly                │
│ as they would appear in print (See Figure I-1). ♦                         │
│ 1. Johnathan J. Jones, Facts of Word Pr█                                  │
│ ♦                                                                         │
│     \                                                                     │
│      Jumped to end of division                                            │
│                                                                           │
│                                                                           │
│                                                                           │
│                                                                           │
│                                                                           │
│                                                                           │
│                                                                           │
│                                                                           │
│                                                                  FIG14-7.DOC│
COMMAND: Copy Delete Format Gallery Help Insert Jump Library
         Options Print Quit Replace Search Transfer Undo Window
Edit document or press Esc to use menu
Co41                {}                                         Microsoft Word
```

14-6 Footnote text is placed at the end of the document, although footnotes can either be printed at the bottoms of pages or at the end of the document.

The Jump Footnote command

To move back and forth between the reference mark and the footnote text, you can either scroll the document or employ the Jump Footnote command. Chapter 13 examined this method while discussing the Jump command. The Jump Footnote command offers the quickest way to reach the footnote text from the reference mark and back.

The function of the Jump Footnote command depends on the location of the cursor. If the cursor is in the text of the document, the Jump Footnote command takes the cursor to the next footnote reference mark. If the cursor is on a footnote reference mark when the Jump Footnote command is selected, the cursor travels to the corresponding footnote text. If the Jump Footnote command is selected while the cursor is on footnote text, the cursor moves to the corresponding reference mark in the text.

Opening a footnote window

The third and final method of moving between the text area and the footnote area is to open a footnote window. The footnote window is opened with the Window Split Footnote command discussed in Chapter 11.

When the Window Split Footnote command is executed, a horizontal window is opened below the main window. The top window displays the document while the bottom window displays footnote text. Once the footnote window has been created, you can move between the reference mark and corresponding footnote text by pressing the F1 (next window) key.

The footnote window is not needed to create or edit footnotes. A footnote window provides easy movement between footnote text and footnote reference marks by pressing the F1 (next window) key. A footnote window eliminates the need to scroll the screen or to use the Jump Footnote command. More importantly, the footnote window also provides a view of the document itself while the footnote text is being created (see Fig. 14-7).

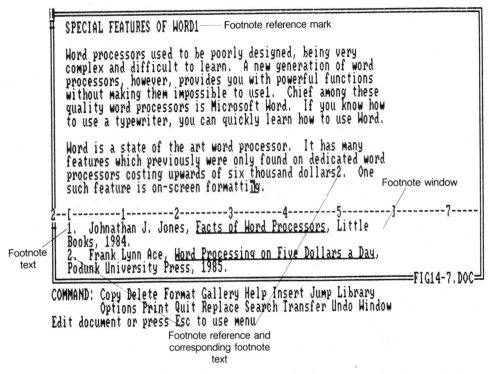

14-7 A footnote can be opened to display a document and the accompanying footnote text simultaneously.

Placement of footnotes

When the document is printed, the footnote can be placed on the same page as the the reference mark, or at the end of the division. The footnotes: option in the

Format Division command controls the placement of footnotes. The two settings offered are Same-page and End.

If you decide to place the footnote text on the same page as the reference mark, select the Same-page option. If you select the End option, all the footnote text for the division is printed together at the end of the division as in Fig. 14-8.

```
                                              Footnote reference marks
    SPECIAL FEATURES OF WORD

    Word processors used to be poorly designed, being very
    complex and difficult to learn.  A new generation of word
    processors, however, provides you with powerful functions
    without making them impossible to use¹.  Chief among these
    quality word processors is Microsoft Word.  If you know how
    to use a typewriter, you can quickly learn how to use Word.

    Word is a state of the art word processor.  It has many
    features which previously were only found on dedicated word
    processors costing upwards of six thousand dollars².  One
    such feature is on-screen formatting.

    In Microsoft Word, paragraph and page formats, such as
    indentations and line spacing, are visible as they would be
    in the final draft.  Furthermore, Word does not employ
    imbedded control characters or dot commands to indicate
    character formats.  Microsoft Word displays character
    formats such as boldface, italics, and underlining exactly
    as they would appear in print (See Figure I-1).


Footnote reference marks
                                       Footnote text

    1.   Johnathan J. Jones, Facts of Word Processors, Little
    Books, 1984.
    2.   Frank Lynn Ace, Word Processing on Five Dollars a Day,
    Podunk University Press, 1985.
```

14-8 Footnote text can be printed at the bottoms of pages that contain footnote references.

Editing footnotes

To edit footnote text, first select the appropriate footnote reference mark. Then, use the Jump Footnote command to bring the cursor to the footnote text. The footnote text can then be edited in the same manner as text in the document. The footnote text can also be reached by scrolling down the document or, if there is a footnote window, by moving to the footnote window with the F1 (next window) key.

Entire footnotes can be deleted or moved by deleting the reference mark. By highlighting the reference mark and pressing the Del key, the entire footnote, including the footnote text, is placed in the scrap. The footnote can then be moved to a new location and inserted with the Ins (insert) key.

You might have chosen earlier to let Word number your footnote reference marks for you. If a footnote is destroyed or moved, Word automatically renumbers all the affected footnotes.

Annotations

Word provides a special form of footnote called an annotation. Creating and formatting an annotation is very similar to creating and formatting a footnote. The Format Annotation menu is shown in Fig. 14-9. Type in your initials and select whether the annotation should be date- and time-stamped. The annotation is numbered consecutively as if it were a footnote.

```
                                                            CHAP14.ASC
FORMAT ANNOTATION mark:
         insert date: Yes(No)         insert time: Yes(No)
Enter text
Pg7 Li20 Co20     {OOTNOTES}     ?                 Microsoft Word
```

14-9 The Format Annotation menu.

Bookmarks

Another Word innovation is the *bookmark*. Bookmarks are called citations by other word processor publishers. The bookmark can be a section of text or a head, such as a chapter or section head or a table or figure head.

Creating a bookmark

A bookmark is created by selecting a section of text, and then issuing the Format bookmarK command. When you issue this command, you see the menu in Fig. 14-10.

```
                                                            CHAP14.ASC
FORMAT BOOKMARK name:

Enter bookmark name or press F1 to select from list
Pg7 Li46 Co1      {When y...text.} ?               Microsoft Word
```

14-10 The Format bookmarK menu.

Enter a name for the bookmarK. Use something logical, because this is the name you will know the bookmark when you use it in cross references and Jump bookmarK commands later. The bookmark name can be up to 31 characters in length, and can contain underscores, hyphens, and periods (though it cannot begin or end with these characters) and it cannot contain colons or spaces. When you set up a bookmark, Word establishes and remembers the location of the first and last characters in the bookmark. It calls these locations *anchors*. Press Return to establish the bookmark. You can assign two or more names to the same bookmark simply by going through the Format bookmarK process again.

To remove the bookmark, select the bookmark and issue the Format bookmarK command. Press Return with the name field blank and the bookmark is removed.

To move a bookmark, select the new text, issue the Format bookmarK command and enter the name of the bookmark you want to move. Word warns you that this is a duplicate and asks if you want to move the bookmark. Answer Yes to move the bookmark.

As mentioned, a bookmark is a very useful tool for making crossreferences and citations. Select a section of text and assign it a bookmark name. To refer to the page on which the bookmark appears when printed, type page: followed by the bookmark name. Press F3 and the text you just typed is placed in parentheses. When the manuscript is printed, this parenthetical section is replaced with a page reference to the page of the bookmark. To refer to a paragraph number rather than a page number, enter para-num: in place of page:. To cross-reference a footnote, select some text immediately following the footnote reference and establish it as the bookmark. Then, refer to this bookmark with the code footnote: followed by the bookmark name. Press F3 and the reference is set up to be inserted at the time of printing.

Many manuscripts have series of tables and figures (usually independently numbered as Figure 1, Figure 2, Table 1, Table 2, and so on). To set up an item as a member of a series, type the text that precedes the series number, such as Figure, remembering to leave a space after the word. Then type the series code name, such as figure: Press F3. This enters the series code in parentheses, which means that at the time of printout, the series codes are changed into consecutive numbers. The figure number would be followed by the caption or cutline that describes the figure. Your final entry might be Figure (figure:): The Mona Lisa.

Finally, you probably want to place a reference to the figure or table in the text (failure to refer to figures and tables at appropriate points makes a report look disconnected, and, if the figures and tables are separated from the text by a page or two, it can look surrealistic). To refer to this figure, select the name Mona Lisa and establish it as a bookmark. Then, at the reference point, type See Figure, leave a space, and type figure:Mona Lisa and press F3. When the manuscript is printed, the reference in text will say See Figure 1.

Running heads

Another page layout feature in Word is the running head. The term *running head* in Word refers to text that appears at either the top or bottom of each printed page. Running heads can include page numbers, dates, titles, and headings. Running heads can be of any length and can be placed in different locations on the page.

Creating running heads

Like footnotes, running heads are constructed while creating or editing the document. Running heads in Word are built using the Format Running-head com-

156 *Advanced page formatting*

mand. The Format Running-head command can transform any paragraph in the document into a running head. Running heads are only in force within the current division.

When a paragraph is transformed into a running head, it is marked with carets (^) at the left of the paragraph (see Fig. 14-11). Once a paragraph is formatted as a running head, it is no longer printed as part of the document. Instead, the paragraph is printed as a running head at the top or bottom of the page.

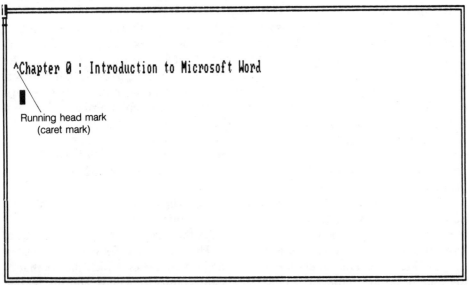

14-11 Running heads can print a line at the top of selected pages or at the bottom of selected pages. Running heads are especially useful when printing reports and manuscripts. A caret in front of a line indicates that the line is a running head.

A running head appears in the printout starting on the page containing the running head. The running head appears on every page from that point to the end of the division. Thus, if a running head is contained on page 8, the running head appears on page 9 (unless the running head is the very first text on the page) and each subsequent page until the end of the division. Likewise, if you place the running head at the beginning of page 3 in the division, running heads appear on page 4 and any succeeding pages within the division.

To place the running head on every page of the division, the running head must be created on the first page of the division. Type the paragraph or paragraphs that you wish to be the running head at the beginning of the division. Remember to select first page: and place the running head immediately after the division mark, with no intervening text or paragraph marks. This places the running head on the first page of the division.

To change a paragraph into a running head, highlight the paragraph with the cursor. If the running head includes more than one paragraph, highlight all the paragraphs at once. Then execute the Format Running-head command.

Specifying the position of running heads

The Format Running-head command menu resembles Fig. 14-12. After the menu appears at the command area, you must select the type of running head to be created. Running heads can appear at the top and bottom of pages, on odd pages, even pages, or both pages and can also appear on the first page of the division. The default running head is located at the top of the page and is on all pages of the division except the first page.

```
FORMAT RUNNING-HEAD position: Top Bottom None
         odd pages:(Yes)No  even pages:(Yes)No  first page: Yes(No)
         alignment: Left-margin(Edge-of-paper)
Select option
Pg10 Li22 Co23    {.SPECI...·HEADS} ?                    Microsoft Word
```

14-12 The Format Running-head menu controls the inclusion and position of running heads in a document.

Choose one of the options, Top or Bottom, from the position: field. This specifies whether the running head appears on the top or bottom of the page. Next, specify whether the running head appears on odd numbered pages, even numbered pages, or both. Select whether the running head should appear at the left margin or at the edge of the paper.

If you wish the running head to appear on odd-numbered pages, select the Yes setting offered in the odd pages: field. If you want the running head to appear on even-numbered pages, select the Yes setting in the even pages: field. By setting both the even pages: field and the odd pages: field to Yes, running heads can appear on all pages. If you want the running head to appear on the first page, select the Yes setting from the first page: field. Press Return to enter these settings.

The Format Division Margins command is used to specify the exact location of the running head. The position of the running head on the printout is determined by its distance from the top and from the bottom of the page.

The from top: and from bottom: fields are located at the bottom of the Format Division Margins menu (Fig. 14-13).

Note that is possible to have two or more running heads.

Page numbers in running heads

Frequently you might want to have the page number of the document incorporated in the running head itself. To do so, you need to employ the page glossary buffer, mentioned in Chapter 11. The page glossary buffer can be entered by typing page and pressing the F3 (glossary reference) key, or by typing Esc, I, page, and hitting Return to use the insert command to add text from the scrap.

158 *Advanced page formatting*

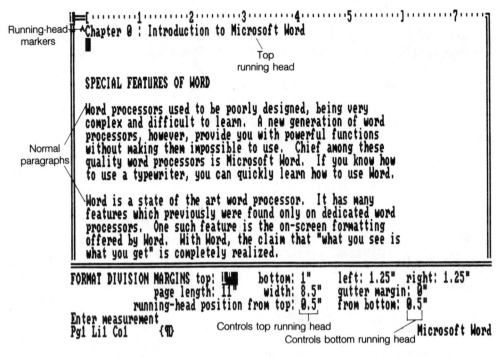

14-13 The Format Division Margins menu controls the position of running heads in a printout. A caret at the beginning of a line denotes that the line is a running head.

When the page glossary buffer is activated, it appears as (page) on your screen as shown in Fig. 14-14. When printing out the hard copy, however, Word replaces the glossary buffer with the current page number. You will probably wish to turn off the automatic page numbering option in the Format Division Page-numbers command if you incorporate page numbers in your running heads (see Fig. 14-15).

Deleting running heads

Word places a caret (^) in the left margin of a paragraph defined as a running head. These paragraphs are not printed with the remainder of the text. To delete a running head, you must change the running head back to a normal paragraph. The Format Running-head command is used to change the status of paragraphs. To change a running head into a normal paragraph, highlight the paragraph with the cursor. Then, select the setting None in the position: field. Word then transforms the running head into a normal paragraph.

Summary

You have practiced the following skills in this chapter:

- Starting a new division with the Ctrl–Return keys.
- Setting page length and width with the Format Division Margins command.

```
┌═[······1······2······3······4······5······6······7·····┐
│ ^Chapter 0 : Introduction to Microsoft Word    (page)  │
│  │                                              │      │
│  Running head                            Page glossary │
│    mark                                      buffer    │
│                                                        │
│ SPECIAL FEATURES OF WORD                               │
│ Word processors used to be poorly designed, being very │
│ complex and difficult to learn. A new generation of    │
│ word processors, however, provide you with powerful    │
│ functions without making them impossible to use. Chief │
│ among these quality word processors is Microsoft Word. │
│ If you know how to use a typewriter, you can quickly   │
│ learn how to use Word.                                 │
│                                                        │
│ Word is a state of the art word processor. It has many │
│ features which previously were found only on dedicated │
│ word processors. One such feature is the on-screen     │
│ formatting offered by Word. With Word, the claim that  │
│ "what you see is what you get" is completely realized. │
│                                                        │
└════════════════════════════════════════════LESSON2.DOC═┘
COMMAND: Copy Delete Format Gallery Help Insert Jump Library
         Options Print Quit Replace Search Transfer Undo Window
Edit document or press Esc to use menu
Pg1 Li1 Col       {¶}                              Microsoft Word
```

14-14 A demonstration of what a running head looks like when on the screen and when printed. The (page) buffer from the glossary has been placed in the running head so page numbers will be printed at the top of the page.

Printed running head
│
Chapter 0 : Introduction to Microsoft Word   1 — Page number from glossary buffer

        SPECIAL FEATURES OF WORD

        Word processors used to be poorly designed, being very
        complex and difficult to learn. A new generation of word
        processors, however, provide you with powerful functions
        without making them impossible to use. Chief among these
        quality word processors is Microsoft Word. If you know how
        to use a typewriter, you can quickly learn how to use Word.

        Word is a state of the art word processor. It has many
        features which previously were found only on dedicated word
        processors. One such feature is the on-screen formatting
        offered by Word. With Word, the claim that "what you see is
        what you get" is completely realized.

        In Microsoft Word, paragraph and page formats, such as
        indentations and line spacing, are visible as they would be
        in the final draft. Furthermore, Word does not employ
        imbedded control characters or dot commands to indicate
        character formats. Microsoft Word can display character
        formats such as boldface, italics, and underlining on a
        monitor exactly as they will appear when printed (See figure
        I-1).

14-15 The printed running head with page number.

- Setting the top, bottom, left, and right page margins with the Format Division Margins command.
- Creating gutter widths and columns with the Format Division Margins Command.
- Creating and editing footnotes with the Format Footnote command.
- Creating a footnote window with the Window Split Footnote command.
- Moving between the footnote text area and footnote reference marks with the Jump Footnote command.
- Using Annotations.
- Using bookmarks for reference and as citations in text.
- Building and deleting running heads with the Format Running-head command.

15
CHAPTER

Advanced Transfer and Print commands

The Transfer command is used to manipulate Word data files on disks. The Transfer Merge command is used to merge two data files into one file. Merging files is very useful when you plan to cut and paste passages from two documents. The advanced Transfer commands also include commands that organize data files on the disk. These Transfer commands are similar to many operating system commands.

The advanced Print commands provide greater control over printer settings. With the advanced Print commands, you can print several documents at once, use the computer like a typewriter, select draft quality printouts, and create multiple copies of a document.

The default drive

Transfer commands in Word deal with files and file operations. Unless you work with a hard disk drive, you must use a number of floppy disk drives and floppy disks. As a result, you must keep track of your files, disks, and disk drives when you use Word.

When you use a Transfer command, Word asks you to enter the name of a file. If you enter a drive specification if front of a filename, Word searches for that file in the drive specified. For example, if you wanted to load a file from the B drive, the drive specification would be B:. If you wanted to save a file onto the E disk drive, the drive specification would be E:. Thus, if you wanted to save a file called SMITH on a disk in drive B, you would enter B:SMITH when the Transfer Save command asks for name of the file.

You can enter the path of a file when asked for a filename. For example, if your office owned a hard disk, and everyone had his or her own directory, you might want to save a copy of the annual budget in your own personal directory. To save the file in your own directory, you would use the filename ANNE\BUDGET85\SECTION1. Likewise, a coworker might wish to load the file MARK\MAINTREP\NYCBOS. Word can handle these path names, but you should be familiar with the operating system before attempting to decipher such complex file specifications.

Changing the default drive

After you enter a filename for a transfer command, Word searches for that file in the default drive, which is preset by Word. If Word has been installed on a hard disk drive, the default drive is the hard disk drive. If the computer has two floppy drives, the default drive is drive B.

The default disk drive is changed with the Transfer Options command (see Fig. 15-1). To change the default directory, select the Transfer Options command and then enter the path name of the directory that contains (or will contain) data files. Unfortunately, the Transfer Options command does not change the default directory permanently. Thus, each time you start Word with a new document, you have to specify the default directory again. If no directory is specified, Word stores and retrieves files in the directory from which the program is started. For instance, on the computer on which this book was written, a batch file was created that switches to the Word document directory, then starts Word. Starting Word only involves entering the command WORD on the command line wherever you are in relation to the directory structure of your hard drive. A batch file that automatically places

```
IL                                                              =CHAP15.ASC=JI
TRANSFER OPTIONS setup: C:\X\BOOKS\WORD
                save between sessions: Yes(No)
Enter path or press F1 to select from list
Pg2 Li10 Col       {&·Afte...¶¶¶}     ?                         Microsoft Word
```

15-1 The Transfer Options setup designates the default directory where Word looks for document files and other files.

the operating system in the subdirectory with the data files saves some typing and time as you load and save files.

When you reach the Transfer Options command menu, you see the default drive and default path displayed in the setup: field. If you wish to change the default drive or change the path, enter the changes in the setup field. The drive specification must be in the proper format. The drive name must be followed by a colon (:) as in A:. Likewise, if you change the path, the path name must obey the proper format.

When you do not have the data disk in the default drive or when you are outside the document directory, it is a good idea to let Word know this information via the Transfer Options command. By changing the default drive or default directory to the drive or directory containing the data disk, you can edit files on the data disk without entering the disk drive specification each time a Transfer command is executed.

File directories

When a command field asks you to enter the name of a file, it is sometimes helpful to list the files stored on the disk. It is impossible to remember all the files stored on each disk; listing the files stored on a disk helps you to remember the names of files with which you are planning to work.

To list the document files stored on the default disk, simply press F1 while in the command field of a Transfer command. Word lists all the document files in the default drive. Remember that document files are ordinarily files with the .DOC extension (though you can save document files with any extension or no extension). One of these document files can be entered into the command field by highlighting the filename with the arrow keys and pressing Return.

Word can produce directories of files on other disks. To view a file directory from a disk drive other than the default drive, place the drive specification (A:, B:, C:, and so on) in the command field (do not hit Return) and press F1. This tells Word that you want to see the directory on another disk drive. The document files in the named disk drive are listed.

Using wildcards

Wildcards can be used to list specific files in a directory. Wildcards were discussed in Chapter 11, in conjunction with the Search and Replace commands. If you know your operating system well, you probably know the * and ? wildcards.

In Word, as in the operating system, the question mark (?) can be used as a wildcard to substitute for any single character. The asterisk (*), in turn, substitutes for any string of characters. By using wildcards, you can expand or restrict the files listed in the directory.

For example, the Transfer Load command is programmed to list only document files (files with the .DOC extensions). If you want to list all the files on the disk, type *.* into the filename: field and then hit F1 (do not hit Return before pressing F1). Word expands the wildcards to fit every possible filename, providing you with a list of all the files on the disk.

Wildcards can also be used with drive specifications. For example, suppose you needed to list your files in drive A. You could enter the drive specification A: and add wildcards *.* (see Fig. 15-2). Typing A:*.* in the filename: field and then pressing an arrow key lists all the files in drive A.

```
                        Wildcard to see list of all filenames

TRANSFER LOAD filename: *.*█                read only: Yes(No)

Enter filename or press F1 to select from list
Pg1 Col        {}                                      Microsoft Word
```

15-2 The * and ? wildcards can be used to list files. Wildcards can also be used to list selected documents.

Loading the document

Documents in Word are loaded with the Transfer Load command. By now you should be familiar with loading documents. Execute the Transfer Load command, and enter the name of the file you wish to load.

Before a document is loaded in Word, Word checks whether another document is being edited by Word. If a document is being edited, Word clears that document and then loads the document named in the Transfer Load command. Before Word clears the old document, it checks whether changes in the old document have been saved on a disk. Word safeguards against accidental work loss by checking for unsaved editing changes in the old document. If work is about to be lost, you are warned and asked permission to continue with the process (see Fig. 15-3).

```
        start-up learning time considerably. Remember, several
        of our word processing staff will be first-time
        computer users.

   2.   Hardware █
                                                   ═EXAMPLE.DOC═
TRANSFER LOAD filename: b:wdchap9.doc       read only: Yes(No)

Enter Y to save, N to lose edits, or Esc to cancel █ ── Overwrite protection
Pg1 Col5       {}                                      Microsoft Word
```

15-3 If you try to load a document while working on a document that has not been saved, Word gives you a chance to save the current document.

In response to Word's warning, you can press Y to load the document and lose the edits, or press the Esc key to abort the Transfer Load command. After pressing Esc, you can save the old document, and then retry the Transfer Load command.

In the past, you have started Word and then used the Transfer Load command to bring up a document for editing. However, you can name the document for editing when starting Word. Skipping the Transfer Load saves time. Next time you want to run Word and edit a document, type WORD YOURFILE and hit Return, where YOURFILE represents the filename of the document.

Protecting your document

The read only: command field (see Fig. 15-4) of the Transfer Load command has been ignored until now. The read only: command field has two settings: Yes or No. The read only setting is usually No, indicating that the file can be loaded, edited, and saved under any filename. If the document is saved under its original name, the edited document replaces the original, unedited document. When the read-only setting is Yes, a file can be loaded and edited, but when it is saved, it must be given a new name to preserve both the new and edited file and the old and unedited file. Thus, the Yes setting is especially useful when you are working with boilerplate documents.

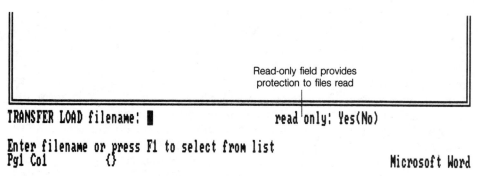

15-4 The Transfer Load menu read-only setting allows a file to be edited, but a new filename must be used to save it.

The status line after loading a document

When a document is loaded, Word's status line shows the total number of characters and pages in the document. The number of pages and the number of characters give you an idea of the length of the document.

Oversized documents

The documents you edit should not be more than 20 pages long. There are several reasons to restrict large documents. First, there might be insufficient memory in the computer to edit large documents.

Second, a large document takes much longer to load and save than a short document. If you only want to make changes on one or two pages in the document, the time used to load and save the extra pages is wasted.

Third, long documents such as manuscripts, reports, and theses, should be broken down into smaller sections, like chapters. Breaking a long document down into chapters helps to organize your thoughts and ideas. Thus, restricting the length of your documents might improve your writing style. Figure 15-5 shows how to determine the document size.

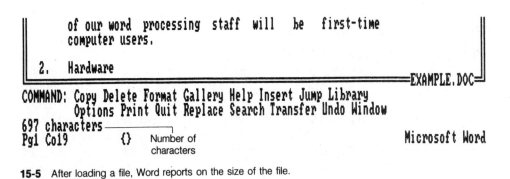

15-5 After loading a file, Word reports on the size of the file.

Clearing the document

When you wish to clear a window without having to quit Word, trigger the Transfer Clear command. The two options in the Transfer Clear menu are Transfer Clear Window and Transfer Clear All. The Transfer Clear Window command, as the name implies, clears only the currently active window. If you want to clear some other window besides the currently active one, the number of the window you desire to clear must be entered when executing this command.

The Transfer Clear All command not only clears all documents and style sheets in Word, it also closes any window splits that have been made. Employing the Transfer Clear All command leaves Word in a pristine state, as if you had just entered Word. This pristine state permits use of the Transfer Options command.

When a document is cleared out of memory by either Transfer Clear command, Word conscientiously checks the document, the active glossary file, and the attached style sheet. If Word finds any unsaved editing changes, you are prompted to save the file.

Saving documents

The Transfer Save command saves the latest version of a document. The process of saving documents should be very familiar by this point. When executing the Transfer Save command, you must enter the filename under which the document is to be saved. The document at this point is saved onto the disk without affecting the document being edited by Word.

If the document being saved is a version of a file stored on the data disk, several actions take place. First, the file containing the earlier version of the document is changed to a backup file (a file with the same filename, but with the extension .BAK). If a backup file from a previous session exists, it is erased. The document is then saved under original filename (with the .DOC extension, if no other extension is specified).

For example, suppose you have a document called LETTER.DOC. After editing it, you decide to save the document. Word renames the original LETTER.DOC file LETTER.BAK and stores the new version of the letter as LETTER.DOC. This system of maintaining backup copies from previous sessions is extremely useful, especially if you make mistakes while editing and need to recover an earlier version of the document.

If Word attempts to save a file under a filename shared by a file already on the disk, the second file is discarded. The document being saved is then stored in its place. This process is called *overwriting* a file.

Word doublechecks that you intend to overwrite the file by asking you to enter Y to overwrite file. Press Y only if you do not mind losing the other file, otherwise hit Esc and find another name for your file.

Word processing for programmers

A special feature of the Transfer Save command which is a boon for programmers is the format: field. The options in this field are Word, text-only, text-only-with-line-breaks, and RTF (rich text format) as shown in Fig. 15-6. So far, you worked with formatted files. Word, however, is perfectly happy dealing with unformatted files as well. Unformatted fields are loaded and saved with the Transfer Load and Save commands.

```
⊫──────────────────────────────────────────CHAP15.ASC⇛
TRANSFER SAVE filename: C:\X\BOOKS\WORD\CHAP15.ASC
                        format:(Word)Text-only Text-only-with-line-breaks RTF
Enter filename
Pg7 Li20 Co51      {Microsoft·}       ?                    Microsoft Word
```

15-6 When saving a file, you can save it as a Word document file (formatted), an ASCII file (unformatted) with or without line breaks, or an RTF file.

Unformatted files (text-only and text-only-with-line-breaks) are files consisting only of characters (letters, numbers, and symbols), Tab, Return, and Newline characters. Unformatted files contain only standard ASCII text. You can use unformatted files as input to other software packages that work with ASCII text. Unformatted files created by Word can serve as programs. Thus, you can write programs in BASIC, Pascal, COBOL, Fortran, and other languages with Word. You can also develop command files for dBASE with Word.

RTF files are files saved in an intermediate state of formatting that makes Microsoft text files more easily understood by other word processing programs.

Deleting files

Unless you have an inexhaustible supply of floppy disks, at some time or another you must delete your outdated and useless files. Files can be removed with the Transfer Delete command. It is more expedient to learn the Word Transfer Delete command to dispose of unwanted files, but is better to learn the operating system DEL erase command. The DEL (also called ERASE) command can delete one file or a group without requiring you to run Word.

When you are employing the Transfer Delete command, be very careful about what you delete. If the Transfer Delete command is used without proper caution, you could lose hours of work or essential parts of the Word program. Word does not allow files loaded or saved in the current session to be erased with the Transfer Delete command. This feature is intended to avoid accidental erasure of current work. To delete a file with Word:

1. Type Esc, T, and D to use the Transfer Delete command.
2. If you want a list of document files on the disk, press F1.
3. Type the name of the file you wish to delete (or highlight it in the list) and press Return.

Renaming files

The Transfer Rename command can change the filenames of documents. The Transfer Rename command is less powerful than the operating system RENAME command, which can be used to change the names of any file in the system and can change the names of several files at once. The Transfer Rename command only renames the document file currently being edited by Word.

To rename a document, load it into memory and execute the Transfer Rename command. A new filename should be entered in the filename: field. A list of the names of the files on the disk can be retrieved by pressing F1. The list is used so that the new filename selected does not already belong to file on the disk (files may not be given names of files already present on the disk).

Merging documents

While editing documents, you can add the contents of one document to another. This process might be useful while composing form letters or creating a document separated into different files. Word has provided for this possibility with the Transfer Merge command.

To use the Transfer Merge command, first load the document to which you wish to merge a file. Move the cursor to the location in the document where you wish to place the contents of the second file. Execute the Transfer Merge command. A prompt appears asking for the name of the file to be merged into the active document. You can either type in the filename or choose the filename from a list.

Once the correct filename has been selected, press Return. This causes a copy of the file selected to be inserted into the active document directly in front of the cursor. Remember that only a copy of the file selected has been merged into the current document. The Transfer Merge command and any later editing changes will not affect the file that was merged.

Print commands

In addition to the Transfer commands, Word also offers a number of advanced Print commands and options (see Fig. 15-7). Basic Print commands for selecting printers and printing documents were examined in Chapter 6. This section concentrates on advanced features such as direct and indirect printing, queued printing, pagination of documents, and the preview facility.

```
┕                                                            ═CHAP15.ASC┙
PRINT: Printer Direct File Glossary Merge Options Queue Repaginate preView

Prints document in the active window
Pg9 Li20 Co22      {x}              ?                          Microsoft Word
```

15-7 The Print menu controls the printing of documents.

The Print Printer command

The command that actually prints the active document is the Print Printer command. When this command is executed, Word first formats the document currently loaded in Word according to the print options. The document is then printed.

If you wish to stop a document while it is being printed ("kill a print job"), press the Esc key. Word prompts you to enter Y to continue or Esc to cancel. Pressing Y will resume printing where Word stopped. Pressing Esc will halt the printing, advance the paper to the next page, and return to the main menu.

When printing documents, a document might use fonts and print styles the printer cannot reproduce. If the printer is incapable of producing some fonts or print styles, Word uses the printer's special features to approximate the correct format.

Print Direct

The Print Direct command is used when you wish to be able to print characters directly from the keyboard. After the command is executed, every character typed in from the keyboard is immediately printed by the printer. This command is useful for quickly typing short documents and for typing envelopes on a printer. It turns your computer into a kind of typewriter.

The Print File command

The Print File command prints the current file to disk as a printer file. This does not affect the original document nor does it print the document. The file produced

170　*Advanced Transfer and Print commands*

by the Print File command can be printed later with the operating system COPY or PRINT commands.

To use the Print File command to convert a copy of a document into a printable file, first load the document file into Word. Select the Print Options command and change the printer driver to match the printer you plan to print your document on. The printer driver is listed in the printer: field on the Print Options menu.

Execute the Print File command. You are prompted to enter a filename for the printer file. Be sure to avoid entering a filename shared by another file. You might wish to add to the filename a special extension such as .PRN to distinguish it as a printer file. Press Return, and a printable file is created.

The Print File command is useful when you wish to print a document on a printer other than the printer connected to your computer. You might own a Star Micronics SG-10 dot matrix printer, a fine dot matrix printer, but you want to print your document in a camera-ready format on your friend's Star laser printer. To transport your document to your friend's printer, change the printer driver to one of the Star emulations, such as a Diablo daisy wheel or an Hewlett-Packard LaserJet drive, with the Print Options command. Then select the Print File command to create a printer file. Next, take your data disk to your friend's computer and use the operating system PRINT command to print the file.

Print options

The Print Options menu (see Fig. 15-8) command has been reviewed in Chapter 6. At that time, the fields printer:, paper feed:, and setup: were set so that you could print documents. You might now set more advanced print options. These advanced options fields are graphics resolution:, copies:, draft:, hidden text:; summary sheet:, range:, page numbers:, widow/orphan control:, queued:, and duplex:.

```
PRINT OPTIONS printer: HPLASER           setup: LPT1:
       model: LaserJet Series II         graphics resolution: 300 dpi
       copies: 1                         draft: Yes(No)
       hidden text: Yes(No)              summary sheet: Yes(No)
       range:(All)Selection Pages        page numbers:
       widow/orphan control:(Yes)No      queued: Yes(No)
       paper feed: Continuous            duplex: Yes(No)
Enter printer name or press F1 to select from list
Pg10 Li47 Co14    {S}            ?                       Microsoft Word
```

15-8　The Print Options menu sets the hardware to which Word is prepared to send the printout, and controls such items as print queues, printing portions of a document, and printing hidden text.

The graphics resolution determines the number of dots per inch your printer will place on the paper. The next option, copies, determines the number of copies of your manuscript will produce. However, a photocopier can produce multiple copies of a document much faster and cheaper than a printer. The draft option, if selected, informs Word that the current printout is only a rough draft. The printout will not contain any changes in font style or size. Any character assigned special character formats are printed, but without the character formats. The printout will contain the correct line and page breaks. The draft option allows you to create a preliminary copy of a document in minimal time.

The hidden text option allows you to specify whether hidden text should be printed or not. Summary sheet specifies whether the summary sheet that appears ordinarily when you save a document, providing valuable information like creation date and last editor, should be printed out along with the document.

The range field of the Print Options command determines what pages of the document are printed. If you select the All option, the entire document is printed. If the Selection option is chosen, only the part of the document that has been highlighted (selected) by the cursor is printed. If the Pages option is chosen, only the page numbers set in the page numbers: field are printed.

The page numbers field is where you list the page numbers of the pages that you wish to print. Consecutive numbers can be separated by colons (:) or hyphens (-). Nonconsecutive numbers are separated by commas (,). All three symbols can be used together. For example, 2-5 prints pages 2 through 5; 7,9 would print pages 7 and 9, and 2-5,7,9 would print pages 2 through 5, 7 and 9.

Widow/orphan control, when set to Yes, causes Word to format the manuscript intelligently to prevent single lines of paragraphs from appearing at the tops or bottoms of pages. The queued option enables you to put printing jobs on a queue. If the queued option is set to Yes, Word creates a print queue.

A print queue enables you to edit a document while printing a second document. You might place a number of print jobs in the queue. Each print job is printed consecutively until the queue is emptied. Thus, you could place a number of documents in the queue and then let your printer run unattended while you work on other more important things. Queue operations are affected by the Print Queue command.

The print queues are generally desirable. However, they must be employed with caution as print queues require space on the data disk. If you print a large document when you have little space on the disk, you might run into problems because of insufficient disk space.

The final option is duplex. If your printer is capable of two-sided printing, this command triggers your printer to print on two sides.

The Print Queue command

The commands in the Print Queue menu (see Fig. 15-9) are used when the print queue option is in effect. The four subcommands are Continue, Pause, Restart, and Stop. When the print queue is not in operation, you can stop the printer from printing a document by pressing the Esc. When a print queue is in operation, the Print Queue Stop command must be used to stop the printer.

```
┌─────────────────────────────────────────────────┐
│                                                 │
│                                                 │
│                                                 │
│                                                 │
│                                                 │
└─────────────────────────────────────────────────┘
```

PRINT QUEUE: **Continue** Pause Restart Stop

Resumes printing after Pause command
Pg1 Col   {}   Microsoft Word

15-9 The Print Queue menu is useful when printing many documents or when you want to print a document and continue editing a document.

Word cancels printing of a queued document when you execute the Print Queue Stop command. To start printing the document once again, employ the Print Queue Restart command. After this sequence of commands Word starts printing the document from the document's beginning.

If you do not wish to abandon the printing process but would like to suspend the printing process, select the Print Queue Pause command. The Print Queue Pause command temporarily halts the printing process. To commence printing after pausing, select the Print Queue Continue command. The Print Queue Continue command orders Word to finish printing the document. Print Queue Restart is used to restart printing the currently queued document from the beginning.

The Print Repaginate command

The Print Repaginate command does not print out documents, but performs some of the other functions as the Print Printer command. After the Print Printer command is selected and before a document is printed, Word goes through the document and updates the page breaks. Updating the page breaks is called *pagination*.

The Print Repaginate command paginates the document. Executing the command updates page breaks in the document. The Print Repaginate command is used when you wish to examine the page breaks in a document before the document is printed. The Print Paginate command also prepares the document for the Jump Page command.

A document that does not have page breaks cannot use the Jump Page command. Repagination adds page breaks to a document; making the Jump Page command usable.

If your document has several titles interspersed with the text and you do not want the titles to fall at the bottom of the pages, you should repaginate the document before it is printed. After the document has been repaginated, you can jump through the document checking the position of each title on each page. If a title lies too near the bottom of a page, you can move the title by inserting extra blank lines with Return. The better solution is the keep together command on the

Format Paragraph menu. Selecting the heading and the following paragraph and using the keep follow command ensures that the heading is moved with the paragraph, if the paragraph is shunted to the next page by pagination.

If you want Word to repaginate automatically, select Yes for the paginate option on the Options menu.

Print preview

An option available for users of graphic displays is preview. Select Page preView with Esc, F, V. You will see a graphic display of two facing pages (see Fig. 15-10). You can flip through your manuscript with the PgUp and PgDn keys.

15-10 The Print Preview option allows you to see what your document looks like on paper, and provides another layer of menus that allows direct setup and printing from the Print Preview screen.

The Print preView option provides yet another menu. Exit returns you to the edit screen. Jump allows you to enter a page number or bookmark to jump to. Options allows you to specify whether you prefer to preview a single page, two pages, or only facing pages (an even-numbered page on the left and an odd-numbered page on the right). Print provides you with the ability to print from the Print preView menu, to the printer, or a file. The Print preView Print Options menu is the same as the familiar Print Options menu seen earlier in this chapter.

The ability to see your work before it is committed to paper is a great advantage. Because you can quickly and easily examine the format of every page, your printing errors will probably be markedly reduced.

Summary

In this chapter, you have gained the following skills:

- Reading a directory of the files stored in the default disk drive and other disk drives.
- Loading, saving, deleting, and renaming document files with the Transfer commands.
- Direct printing from the keyboard with the Print Direct command.
- Indirect printing with the Print File command.
- Manipulating Printer queues.
- Updating page breaks in a document with the Print Repaginate command.
- Previewing documents with the Print preView command.

CHAPTER 16

Using style sheets

A style sheet is used to format selections of text or to format an entire document. A style is any combination of character, paragraph, or division formats. A style can be assigned to any selection of text. For example, a style could be created for document titles that centers a line of text and assigns the PicaD font with a font size of 16 to characters in the title.

Two skills are needed to use style sheets. First, you must know the Gallery menu commands to be able to view, edit, and create style sheets. Second, you must be able to attach style sheets to a document and then assign a style to a section of text. This chapter uses one of the sample style sheets supplied with Word to demonstrate how style sheets are attached and how styles are assigned. The chapter also shows how a style sheet can be loaded and viewed (see Fig. 16-1). Chapter 17 shows how style sheets can be created and edited.

Indirect formatting with style sheets

Indirect formatting with style sheets has three main benefits. The first advantage is speed. Because you can create your own styles and formats, you can save time by using customized formats. Instead of assigning long, complicated formats to a document with Word's extensive menu system, you can assign your customized formats. These formats can be assigned to text in the document with just three keystrokes.

The second benefit is consistency. A document formatted with a style sheet

```
FORMAT STYLESHEET ATTACH: C:\WORD4\NORMAL.STY

Enter filename or press F1 to select from list
Pg1 Col          {}                                         Microsoft Word
```

16-1 The Format Stylesheet Attach command attaches style sheets to a document so that styles can be used to format the document.

takes all of its formats from the style sheet. If you write many documents, you can use the same style sheet to give each document the same format.

The third advantage is flexibility. When you decide to change the format of a document, it is not easy to reassign all the formats with Word's Format commands. If, however, you use style sheets to format the document, you can quickly reassign all the default formats. In fact, you can quickly compare two style sheets with a document to find the style sheet that looks best with the document.

One way to take advantage of the flexibility of style sheets is to employ a draft style while editing your document and then switch to the final style after the document has been edited. You could change the format of your document without affecting the text.

The major disadvantage of style sheets and indirect formatting is that style sheets are not easy to learn. Word has comprehensive facilities for producing styles and style sheets, but learning to use these facilities takes patients and diligence.

A second disadvantage of style sheets is that it takes considerable time to create a complete style sheet. A vast number of styles and formats can be set in a comprehensive style sheet. Selecting these styles and formats requires time.

In general, indirect formatting with style sheets is most useful for long documents. Direct formatting with the Word's preassigned keycodes is adequate for short documents.

Attaching and detaching style sheets

Before a style sheet can affect the format of a document, the style sheet must be attached to the document. The Format Style Sheet command attaches and removes style sheets from the document in the window as shown in Fig. 16-1. After you select the Format Style Sheet command; you can obtain a list of all the style sheets stored on the data disk by pressing F1. Style sheets files have the .STY extension.

Once a style sheet has been attached to the document, attaching another style sheet replaces the original style sheet. To detach a style sheet without attaching a second style sheet, select the Format Style Sheet command. When Word prompts you for the name of a style sheet, hit the Del (Delete) key until the command field is blank. Then press Return. Word proceeds to remove the attached style sheet. The style sheet is not affected and the document returns to Word's normal formats.

Word recalls if a document has been saved with a style sheet attached to it. If a document is saved with a style sheet attached, Word automatically attaches the same style sheet to the document when the document is loaded with the Transfer Load command. If you change the style sheet attached to the document, it is considered an editing change.

The Gallery menu

To view a style sheet, select the Gallery command from the main menu. The Gallery menu resembles Fig. 16-2. The Gallery command is a major part of Word. All editing of style sheets is performed with the Gallery menu. The command lineup includes the Gallery Copy, Delete, Exit, Format, Help, Insert, Name, Print, transfer, and Undo commands. The commands in the Gallery menu, however, work only with style sheets.

```
⌐                                                                    =FULL.STY⌐
GALLERY: Copy Delete Exit Format Help
         Insert Name Print Transfer Undo
Copies selected style(s) to scrap
                    {}                     ?                     Microsoft Word
```

16-2 The Gallery menu is used to create and edit style sheets.

Gallery commands are executed by pressing Esc and then selecting a command. Select the Gallery Exit command to return to the document editing screen.

Loading and unloading style sheets

A number of style sheets are provided with Word. One style sheet is named ACADEMIC.STY. To load and view the ACADEMIC.STY style sheet, utilize the Gallery Transfer Load command by pressing Esc and G to enter the Gallery and T and L to execute the Transfer Load command. If desired, a directory listing of the style sheets can be obtained by pressing F1 while in the command field filename: of the Gallery transfer Load command (see Fig. 16-3).

For practice, try loading the style sheet called FULL.STY or some other style sheet. Enter the Gallery menu, then press T and L to enact the Transfer Load command. Finally, type FULL.STY and hit Return to load the FULL.STY style sheet.

Once the FULL.STY style sheet has been loaded, it resembles Fig. 16-4. FULL.STY depicts a typical style sheet. The style sheet contains a number of individual styles, each of which is numbered on the extreme left. A style sheet can contain up to 125 styles.

Using style sheets

```
C:\X\BOOKS\WORD\PROGRAM\*.STY
ACADEMIC.STY      RESUME.STY        SIDEBY.STY        [A:]
APPEALS.STY       SAMPLE.STY        STATE.STY         [B:]
FULL.STY          SEMI.STY          [..]              [C:]
OUTLINE.STY
```

TRANSFER LOAD style sheet name: FULL.STY   read only: Yes(No)

Enter filename or press F1 to select from list (2582528 bytes free)
                    {}   ?   Microsoft Word

16-3 The Gallery Transfer Load command retrieves a style sheet from the disk. The style sheet can then be edited.

```
][L[·········1·········2·········3·········4·········5·········]·········7····]
│ 1    S/ Division Standard                   FULL BLOCK LETTER, 6" WIDTH   │
│      Page break. Page length 11"; width 8.5". Page # format Arabic. Top   │
│   ▌  margin 1.67"; bottom 1"; left 1.25"; right 1.25". Top running head   │
│      at 1". Bottom running head at 0.83". Footnotes on same page.         │
│ 2    LH Paragraph 10                        ADJUSTABLE LETTERHEAD SPACE   │
│      CourierPC (modern b) 12. Flush left, space after 2 li.               │
│ 3    RA Paragraph 14                   shift-↵  RETURN NAME, ADDR         │
│      CourierPC (modern b) 12. Flush left, space before 1 li (keep in one  │
│      column, keep with following paragraph).                              │
│ 4    DA Paragraph 7                                    DATE               │
│      CourierPC (modern b) 12. Flush left, space after 1 li (keep in one   │
│      column, keep with following paragraph).                              │
│ 5    IA Paragraph 11                        INSIDE ADDRESS/Mr. Jim Smith  │
│      CourierPC (modern b) 12. Flush left, Left indent 0.5" (first line    │
│      indent -0.5"), right indent 2.8" (keep in one column, keep with      │
│      following paragraph).                                                │
│ 6    SA Paragraph 13                        SALUTATION / Dear...          │
│      CourierPC (modern b) 12. Flush left, space before 1 li (keep in one  │
│      column, keep with following paragraph).                              │
│                                                              ═FULL.STY═   │
```

GALLERY: **Copy** Delete Exit Format Help
         Insert Name Print Transfer Undo
Copies selected style(s) to scrap
                    {}   ?   Microsoft Word

16-4 A style sheet displayed in Word (FULL.STY).

Style composition

The screen in Fig. 16-5 shows an example of a style. Each style is composed of two sections: the name and the description.

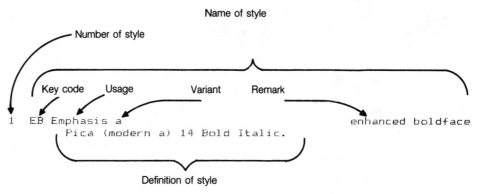

16-5 The components of a style name.

The name identifies and classifies a style. The description of a style provides a detailed account of the exact nature of a style. The individual formats of the style are listed in the description section.

A style name has four parts called the key code, usage, variant, and remark. The *key code* is a one or two-character code and is used to assign the style to text in the document. The *usage* identifies the general use of the style. The *variant* distinguishes between different styles with the same usage. The *remark* part is used to remind the user of the style's function.

Formatting documents with style sheets

To assign formats from a stylesheet, you must first attach the style sheet to the document. Then, you can assign the style sheet formats with the special style sheet key codes, or with the Format Stylesheet menu.

Once a style sheet is attached to a document, the formatting process for the document changes. It is still possible to use the direct format methods to format the document. Moreover, text can be formatted indirectly with the style names on the style sheet. If you decide to use direct formats to format parts of the document, note that direct formats are not affected by changes in the attached style sheet.

There are two methods to assign formats to the document. The formats can be entered directly with the Alt and format keys, or the formats can be entered with the Format command. The format keys allow you to format your document quickly, but the Format Stylesheet command gives you greater control over the formatting process.

Attaching or detaching style sheets

The Format Stylesheet Attach command removes the previous style sheet and attaches the specified style sheet to the document in the active window. Style sheets are attached by selecting the Format Stylesheet Attach command. Press F1 if you need a list of the style sheets stored on the disk. Finally, enter the name of the style sheet you want to use. Style sheet names have the .STY extension.

Once a style sheet has been attached to the document to the document, attaching another style sheet detaches the original style sheet. To detach a style sheet without attaching a second style sheet, select the Format Stylesheet Attach command. When Word prompts you for the name of a style sheet, hit the Del key until the command field is blank. Then press Return. Word removes the attached style sheet. The actual style sheet is not affected, and the document returns to Word's normal formats.

Word knows whether a document has been saved with a style sheet attached. If so, Word automatically attaches the same style sheet to a document when the document is loaded with the transfer Load command. If you change the style sheet attached to the document, it is considered an editing change.

Selecting text

The manner in which text is selected for formatting remains the same, whether or not a style sheet is attached to the document. Formats only affect the region highlighted by the cursor. If the region highlighted is too small for the format, the format applies to the smallest area of text containing the selected region that allows the format to be applied.

For example, suppose the style or format applies to paragraphs. If two paragraphs are highlighted by the cursor when the format is selected, both paragraphs possess this new format. If the selection is less than a paragraph in size, the format applies to all paragraphs that contain any portion of the selection.

Assigning styles with the Format Stylesheet commands

The Format Stylesheet commands are easier to use than format keys for assigning styles because you can list the formats available and do not have to remember a format code.

If you assign a format with the format keys, that format remains unaltered if the style sheet attached to the document is changed. Assigning these permanent formats causes the document to lose some of its flexibility.

To apply a format from the style sheet with the Format command, select the text to be formatted and choose the Format Stylesheet command from the main menu. The command menu resembles Fig. 16-6. Select the subcommand, character, paragraph, or division, to match the element of the document you wish to format.

```
FORMAT STYLESHEET: Attach Character Paragraph Division Record
Attaches style sheet
Pg1 Co1          {}                                    Microsoft Word
```

16-6 The Format Stylesheet menu used to attach a style sheet to a document, record new styles, or assign styles.

After making the selection, you are asked to enter a style. The style can be typed in directly or selected from a list. Press F1 and Word shows the list of styles on the style sheet that fit the element of Word you have selected. Figure 16-7 shows the paragraph formats on the FULL.STY style sheet. You can highlight the style you want with the arrow keys and press Return to carry out the command.

```
Character Standard                    UC Character 1 (UNDERLINED)
Character Summary Info ((C) 1984-6)




FORMAT STYLESHEET CHARACTER: Character 1

Enter character style variant or press F1 to select from list
Pg6 Li52 Co39      {.}              ?              ZM        Microsoft Word
```
16-7 The Format Stylesheet Character options on the FULL. STY style sheet.

As an exercise, suppose you want to underline several words in a document using the FULL.STY style sheet, but cannot remember the key code for underlining. To assign the format, highlight the words to be underlined, then select the Format Stylesheet Character command. Press F1 to list the formats available (see Fig. 16-7) and select the appropriate command, which happens to be UC (Underlined). Note that you could also have used the Format Character command to assign the PicaD (modern B) 12-point underlined font, although it would have taken several more keystrokes.

Assigning styles with format keys

To format the document with the format keys, use the Alt key to enter the required key codes. You enter the code for a style from the style sheet or the code for one of Word's predefined format keys. To format with a style from the style sheet, hold down the Alt key and enter the one- or two-character key code assigned to the style. Word formats the text according to the description of the style in the style sheet.

When a style sheet is attached to the active document, you might not be able to use the direct format keys or help key (Alt-H) as you did previously. If a style on the stylesheet uses the same letter for the first letter of its name as the Alt-key formatting combination, Word interprets your entry as a style sheet command and prompts you for the second letter of the style sheet keycode. Normal formatting keys and the help key can be selected after pressing Alt-X. By pressing Alt-X, you inform Word that you are not entering a key code for a style but rather a direct format key code.

For example, once a style sheet has been attached to the document, you can gain access to the help feature by pressing Alt-X-H. Likewise, instead of pressing Alt-B to assign the boldface character format, you can use Alt-X-B to assign format when a style sheet is attached to the active document. If you do not press Alt-X before pressing your format keys, the format keys can be mistaken for style key codes.

Default styles

When you are formatting a new document with a style sheet attached, Word automatically assigns a number of styles to elements of your document. These default styles are assigned by Word to eliminate the need to format large parts of your documents by hand. You can change these default formats at any time by formatting the document manually.

For example, when you attack a style sheet to a document, all paragraphs that have not been formatted by direct format commands are formatted by the style whose usage is Normal paragraph. Similarly, all unformatted divisions, footnotes, and running heads are automatically assigned default styles.

Remember, if you want to see the styles of the paragraphs in your document, select show style bar on the Options menu. The two-character style codes will appear in the margin to the left of the paragraphs in your document. Remember that there is a difference between loading a style sheet and attaching it. As you exit the Gallery menu with the Gallery Exit command, you are given the option of attaching the style sheet. If you miss this opportunity to attach the style sheet, use the Format Stylesheet Attach command to attach the style sheet. Attaching it puts all its formatting features into force. Loading it simply makes it visible in the Gallery menu for editing. In the next chapter, you will see how to create your own custom style sheet. By changing the defaults, you can made Word behave in a very individual manner.

Summary

From reading this chapter, you should be able to:

- Attach and detach style sheets from documents.
- Enter and exit the Gallery menu.
- Format a document with style sheet attached using format keys by pressing Alt-X followed by the desired code.
- Select text for formatting with styles.

CHAPTER 17

Creating style sheets

This chapter covers the process of creating style sheets. You will see all the commands in the Gallery menu to insert, delete, name, and format your own style names. You can then save, merge, and print the resulting style sheet. When you have learned all the techniques in this chapter and Chapter 16, you will become a master of style sheet use.

Entering the Gallery

While in the Gallery menu, you can view, create, and edit style sheets. Before constructing a new style sheet, you must first clear the existing style sheet with the Gallery Transfer Clear command. As in the Edit menu, the Gallery Transfer Clear command checks whether there are any unsaved editing changes on the style sheet being cleared. If there are any unsaved changes, Word warns you and gives you a second chance to save your work. For the chapter's example, execute the Gallery Transfer Clear command (Esc, G, T, C).

The Gallery Insert command is used to enter text in a style sheet. Select the Gallery Insert command (Esc, G, I). The screen should now resemble Fig. 17-1.

184 *Creating style sheets*

```
|                                                                              |
|                      Insertion from scrap by default                         |
|                                                                              |

INSERT key code: ▓               usage:(Character)Paragraph Division
       variant: 1                remark:
Enter one or two letter key code for style
                 {}                     ?                      Microsoft Word
```

17-1 The Gallery Insert command places a new blank style in a style sheet. The style can then be formatted so that it contains the desired character, paragraph, or division formats.

The Gallery Insert command allows you to enter the four settings of a style name: key code, usage, variant, and remark. For an example, you will be guided through the process of creating a style name for the footnote reference mark.

Creating a key code

The very first step in constructing a new style is to select a key code. A one- or two-character code is used to assign the new style to text in the document. The code is similar in function to Word's direct formatting commands (for instance, typing Alt–U underlines highlighted text). It is important to select mnemonic codes for styles, especially if a large number of style names will be used together.

Because you are creating a style for a footnote reference mark, a mnemonic key code would be FR. Enter the code FR into the key code: field of the Insert command. The screen should now resemble Fig. 17-2. Press the tab key to move to the next command field.

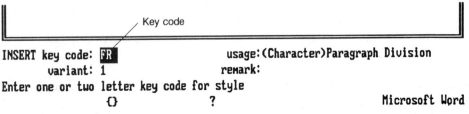

```
|                                                                              |
|                              Key code                                        |
|                                                                              |

INSERT key code: FR              usage:(Character)Paragraph Division
       variant: 1                remark:
Enter one or two letter key code for style
                 {}                     ?                      Microsoft Word
```

17-2 The key code field contains the style code used to directly assign style formats with the Alt key.

Word allows up to 125 styles on a style sheet. If you use one-character key codes, you are only be able to use 25 different styles (you cannot use key codes that begin with X). This is because one-character key codes block all key codes beginning with that character.

For example, if the key code M is being used, choosing the key code MA causes problems. When you attempt to press Alt–M, A, to assign a style, Word will stop as soon as you enter Alt–M. Word has no way of knowing that you intend to add another key, as the Alt–M portion is a key code by itself. Choosing a one-character key code thus blocks all two-character key codes beginning with that character.

You must not select keycodes that begin with X. Alt-X allows direct formats to be applied to documents with style sheets attached. If you choose a key code beginning with X, you will be unable to use Word's predefined direct formatting keys.

Selecting a usage

A response is now needed for the second part of the style name, the usage field. The usage field specifies whether characters, paragraphs, or divisions are affected by the style. For example, the paragraph usage is suitable for styles that affect paragraphs, titles, table of contents headings, index entries, outline headings, and other similar entities. The character usage is for styles that affect character formats, footnotes, page numbers, line numbers, summary information, and other character-oriented text.

Because this style formats footnotes, choose the character usage. Use Space and Tab to select the character usage.

Choosing a variant

The third part of a style name is the variant: field. The letter or number variant given a usage distinguishes between different style names that have the same usage. For example, Normal Division A and Normal Division B are both division formats, but their different variants tell Word that they are different styles. Normal Division A might have Arabic numerals for page numbers while Normal Division B might have Roman numerals for page numbers.

To see the usable variants, move the cursor to the variant: field and press F1 (see Fig. 17-3). You can select the variant from the list displayed with F1. Once the desired variant is highlighted, press Tab to select the variant. The variant: field can be left blank if you do not care to choose a specific variant. If the field is left blank, Word chooses a default variant. The default variant is either variant a, or variant 1 if variant a does not exist.

Page number	Line Number	Footnote ref	Summary Info
Line draw	Annotation ref	1	2
3	4	5	6
7	8	9	10
11	12	13	14
15	16	17	18
19	20	21	22
23			

```
INSERT key code: FR                      usage:(Character)Paragraph Division
        variant: Footnote reference      remark:
Enter variant or press F1 to select from list
        {Character 1 }    ?                              Microsoft Word
```

17-3 The character variants that can be used by a style. The variants determine what type of characters, paragraphs, or divisions are affected by the style.

In the footnote example, you are creating a style for footnote reference markers. Because you want this to be the default style for footnote reference marks, the variant should be footnote reference. Move to the variant field and type a and hit Tab. Then highlight Footnote ref on the list of variants and press Tab.

In Word, you can define up to 29 character styles, 74 paragraph styles, and 22 division styles. Only one usage and variant combination can exist in a style sheet at one time. The usage and variant of a style identifies it. The total number of usages and variants is 125. Thus, 125 is the maximum number of styles allowed on a style sheet.

Using variants to update styles in a document

The variant is important when altering styles in a document. For example, the footnote variant affects all footnotes in a document. Thus, all footnotes in the document attached to the current style sheet adopt the format defined in the footnote style. You are making the footnote style a superscript character, so all footnotes in the document and all footnotes added to the document in the future will adopt this style. If the footnote style in the style sheet is changed to boldface underline, then all footnotes in the document will adopt the boldface underline character format.

Similarly, the running head paragraph variant affects all running heads in a document, the heading paragraph variant affects outline headings, and the standard paragraph variant affects all paragraphs that have not been formatted. If you use paragraph variant 3, then all paragraphs assigned this style can be reformatted by changing the corresponding style on the style sheet.

Adding a remark

The last step in naming a new style is to add a comment to the style. Any descriptions may be entered in the remark: field of the Insert command. This step is optional, but can clarify a style's function by supplementing the description of the style given by the usage field. The remark is an opportunity to reveal the nature of the style.

For the style you are creating, it would be redundant to include a remark that the style affects footnotes. The usage Footnote reference more than adequately describes the use of the style. Because you intend to make the footnote reference mark a superscript, make it clear in the remark field. Press Tab until the cursor is in the remark: field; then type superscript. Finally, press Return to insert the style. The screen should now look like Fig. 17-4.

Formatting styles

Once a style is named, Word enters the name of your style into the style sheet. Along with the name is a description of the format of the style as shown in Fig. 17-5. This description, Courier (modern a) 12, is listed beneath the name of the style (your description might be different). Where did this format originate?

Word is designed to select default attributes for a style as soon as it is named.

Formatting styles 187

```
][••••••••1•••••••••2•••••••••3•••••••••4•••••••••5•••••••••]•••••••••7•••••]
1   FR Character Footnote reference          superscript
        Courier (modern a) 12.
◆
```

```
GALLERY: Copy Delete Exit Format Help
         Insert Name Print Transfer Undo
Select style or press Esc to use menu
              {Character 1 }   ?                    Microsoft Word
```

17-4 The Gallery screen after the sample style has been created.

```
Courier (modern a)              CourierPC (modern b)
LinePrinterPC (modern g)        LinePrinter (modern h)
```

```
FORMAT CHARACTER bold: Yes(No)    italic: Yes(No)         underline: Yes(No)
          strikethrough: Yes(No)  uppercase: Yes(No)      small caps: Yes(No)
          double underline: Yes(No)  position:(Normal)Superscript Subscript
          font name: Courier      font size: 12           font color: Black
          hidden: Yes(No)
Enter font name or press F1 to select from list
              {Character 1 }   ?                    Microsoft Word
```

17-5 The Gallery Format command is used to assign character, paragraph, and division formats to styles.

The format is chosen according to the usage of the style. Once a format is selected by Word, it is listed below the name of the style.

If you are satisfied with the default format Word offers, you might consider the job done. However, if you wish to implement formatting attributes of your own, use the Gallery Format command. The Gallery Format command does not format text as does the Format command in the Edit menu. Instead, the Gallery Format command only edits styles. You want the footnote reference mark to be a raised character (superscript), so you need to change the format of the style you have created. First, use the arrow keys to highlight the style you have selected, then choose the Gallery Format command.

In the Gallery Format menu, the selection of commands given depends on whether the style applies to a character, paragraph, or division. If it was a character, as in the footnote example, you are taken directly to the Gallery Format Character command. If you had selected a paragraph style, you would have been given the following options: Character, Paragraph, Tabs, Border, and position. If you were formatting a division, you would have been given the following selections: Margins, Page-numbers, Layout, and line-Numbers. Thus, it would be impossible for you to select a format that does not affect your style.

Because the use for your style is Footnote reference, Word automatically selects the Gallery Format Character menu. Once you have entered the Gallery Format Character options menu, you will see that the screen is exactly like the Edit Format Character menu.

Select the Superscript option in the position: field in the same manner you would in the Format Character command on the main menu: use the Tab key to move the highlight to the position field and then use the Space to select Superscript. Press Return and the format of the style on the screen switches to show the new formats.

The difference between the Gallery Format and the Format commands is subtle. Text is not formatted in the Gallery menu as it is in the main menu. Instead, formats are assigned to the styles being formatted. Only when the styles area assigned to text in the document do the formats take affect.

Recording styles from a document

The Format Stylesheet Record command allows you to create a new style by recording the formats used in a character, paragraph, or division in a document. The recorded style is automatically placed in the style sheet without using the Gallery menu. To record a new style, follow these steps:

1. Highlight the text from which you want to record a style.
2. Press Esc, F, S, and R for the Format Stylesheet Record command (or press Alt–F10).
3. Enter an appropriate key code.
4. Set the usage, variant, and remark fields.
5. Press Return to add the newly formed style to the current style sheet.

As shown in step 2, pressing Alt–F10 is equivalent to selecting the Format Stylesheet Record command and can be used as a shortcut.

Revising a style with the Record command

The Format Stylesheet Record command can be used not only to enter new styles, but also to revise existing styles. Styles are revised in the same manner as they are created. To revise a style, highlight the text containing the appropriate style, press Esc, F, S, F (or Alt-F10), enter the key code of the style to be revised, set the usage, variant, and remark fields, and finally press Return.

Editing styles

Styles on a style sheet can be edited using the Gallery commands, just as text in a document can be edited. Styles can be deleted, inserted, and moved around, just like text. Copies of styles can be made and then altered to form different styles. In addition, styles can be renamed and reformatted as desired.

Deleting styles

A style can be deleted with the Gallery Delete command or the Del key. To delete a style, simply highlight the style and then press the Del key. More than one style can be deleted at once if the cursor is extended. Deleted styles are placed in the scrap.

Moving styles

Once a style has been deleted with the Gallery Delete command or the Del key and placed in the scrap, it can be inserted into the style sheet with the Gallery Insert command or the Ins key. Either of the two actions places the style in the style sheet at the cursor position. By using a combination of the Del and Ins keys, styles can be moved from location to location on the style sheet.

Copying styles

Copies of styles can be placed in the scrap with the Gallery Copy command. The Gallery Copy command is not used in quite the same way as the Copy command on the main menu. In a style sheet, there can be no exact duplication of styles, as each usage and variant combination represents one and only one style.

The Gallery Copy command is still a useful command. Styles can be copied into the scrap and then inserted at another location in the style sheet. The name and format of the style can be changed to create a new style. This takes less effort than designing a complex style from scratch. The Gallery Copy command makes it easy to create variants of styles, which might only have minor differences between them.

Changing a style sheet

Once a style has been selected, the key code, variant, and remark can be changed with the Gallery Name command. To change the key code, variant, or remark of a style, highlight the style with the cursor, then select the Gallery Name command. You see the same menu brought up by the Gallery Insert command. The default options, however, are those of the original style. To change any parts of the name, simply re-enter the parts. After the Name command is carried out, the style has the new name.

If the formatting attributes of a style need to be changed, simply highlight the style and reapply the Gallery Format command as shown in Fig. 17-6. The original options is the default options in the options fields. By entering new options, you can change the formats assigned to the style.

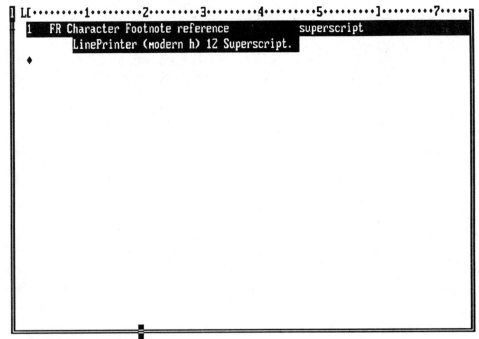

17-6 The screen after the style has been formatted. Note that a deleted or copied style is placed in the scrap.

Undoing editing changes

A final editing feature of the Gallery menu is the Undo command. Like the Undo command in the main menu, the Gallery Undo command reverses the last editing change made. The Undo command can even be used on itself, negating the effects of a previous Undo command.

Saving and retrieving style sheets

Style sheet files can be manipulated in the Gallery menu in much the same way document files can be manipulated in the main menu. With the Gallery Transfer commands, style sheet files can be loaded, saved, or even merged into one another. With the Gallery Print command, style sheets can be printed in the same manner as documents.

Saving a style sheet

Once the style sheet has been created, it can be saved with the Gallery Transfer Save command. Select the Gallery Transfer command; the screen should now resemble Fig. 17-7. The Gallery Transfer commands function in much the same manner as the corresponding commands in the Transfer menu under the main menu.

17-7 The Gallery Transfer menu manipulates style sheet files. The menu can store style sheets on disk and retrieve style sheets from a disk file.

The style sheet can now be saved in Word's files by using the Gallery Transfer Save command. The Gallery Transfer Save command operates in the same manner as the main menu Transfer Save command. Enter the Gallery Transfer Save menu, then enter the filename under which you want the style sheet stored. Style sheets must possess the extension .STY.

Other Transfer commands

Many command fields in the Gallery Transfer commands require a filename to be entered. Within these fields, the files on the disk can be listed by pressing F1. The

Gallery Transfer commands only list style sheet files (those with the extension .STY). The Transfer commands under the main menu only display document files.

Most Transfer commands in the Gallery menu perform functions equivalent to those commands in the Transfer menu under the main menu. The Gallery Transfer Load command, for example, loads style sheets instead of documents. The style sheets are, in turn, loaded into the Gallery, instead of the Edit window, for viewing and/or editing.

The Gallery transfer Rename command assigns a new filename to the style sheet currently loaded in the Gallery. The Gallery Transfer Clear command clears the style sheet loaded in the gallery and has the same safety feature as the Edit Transfer Clear command. You must confirm your order is you have any unsaved editing changes in the style sheet. The Gallery Transfer Merge command reads the styles of another style sheet file into the current style sheet.

Two Gallery Transfer commands are exactly the same as the corresponding commands in the main menu. These are the Gallery Transfer Delete and Gallery Transfer Options commands. The Gallery Transfer Delete command is used to remove files from the Word disk. The Gallery Transfer Options command is used to set the default drive for Word. Detailed descriptions of all of these Transfer commands can be found in Chapter 14.

Other Gallery commands

The Gallery Help command is the exact same command found in the main menu. It can be invoked either through executing the Gallery Help command or by pressing Alt-H.

The Gallery Print command prints out the style sheet loaded in the gallery (the active style sheet). A paper copy of the style sheet and the key codes for each style can be very useful when you are editing a document. The style sheet is printed according to the options selected in the Edit Print Options command. If you need to change the printer options, it is necessary to return to the main menu with the Gallery Edit command.

Summary

Chapter 17 covered the following points:

- The four components of a style name: key code, usage, variant, and remark.
- Creating a style name.
- Formatting a style with the Gallery Format commands.
- Editing a style sheet with the Gallery Copy, Name, Delete, and Insert commands and the arrow keys.
- Moving and Copying styles in a style sheet with the Gallery Delete and Gallery Copy commands and the Ins and Del keys.
- File operations with style sheets and the Gallery Transfer commands.
- How to print a style sheet with the Gallery Print command.

CHAPTER 18

Merging documents

Perhaps one of the greatest inventions of American business is the form letter. Form letters can vary in quality from the letters that look as if they were badly photocopied and half the words are faded and illegible, through the letters that look neat, begin with a line like "Dear Sir" and end with a printed signature, to the letters that begin with "Dear Mr. Jones" or "Dear Mr. Smith" depending on who will be receiving the letter. The best form letters are personalized, look classy, and do not resemble a mass mailing sponsored by your local flea market. Although these polite form letters might not convince you to empty your pockets for a new frozen yogurt machine, they do look presentable.

Word contains a mail merge program that enables you to insert names, addresses, and assorted phrases into a form letter automatically. The merge program combines a letter or similar document with data fed from a separate file. The data file must consist of ASCII characters. Word can be used to create the data file or the data can be retrieved from programs like dBASE or Lotus 1-2-3. dBASE works with ASCII files, and 1-2-3 has a routine that converts spreadsheets into ASCII files. Merging documents can be divided into four separate steps:

194 *Merging documents*

1. Create a document, just as you would without the merge facilities.
2. Insert merge commands and merge variables. This designates sections of the text that will be grafted to the text from a separate file or via the keyboard.
3. Create a data file containing the data that will be inserted. The data file can be created by Word, dBASE, or another program that works with ASCII files.
4. Load the text document with the Transfer Load command. Use the Print Merge command to commence printing. Word will proceed to print all versions of the document.

Designating merge commands

Figure 18-1 depicts a typical document ready for merging. The words delineated by «and» denote merge commands and merge variables. These commands instruct Word where to get the data to be inserted, and where to insert the data. This chapter introduces you to the elementary merge commands first. The advanced merge commands appear in the subsequent chapter.

```
«data customer.dat»   Merge data command
June 20, 1984

Dear «lastname»:———Merge variables

Your address change has been acknowledged and updated.
Please inform us if the address listed below is incorrect.

    «street»
    «city», «state» «zip»

US Magazines is offering a special subscription rate to our
new magazine US Computers. US Computers provides behind the
scenes reporting at all the computer manufacturers, from IBM
to Apple from Microsoft to Lotus. Order now and get twelve
copies for just $15.95.

Sincerely yours
                                                        MTEST.DOC
COMMAND: Copy Delete Format Gallery Help Insert Jump Library
         Options Print Quit Replace Search Transfer Undo Window
Edit document or press Esc to use menu
Pg1 Co16        {}                                   Microsoft Word
```

18-1 A typical letter that incorporates several merge variables and a merge command.

The symbols « and » can be created by holding down the Alt key and typing 174 or 175 (on the numeric keypad). Depressing Alt and typing 174 creates «. Depressing Alt and typing 175 creates ». The special brackets can also be created by holding down the Ctrl key and pressing either [or]. The square brackets ([and]) are generally found directly to the left of the Return key.

If you wish to practice merging a file, enter the text appearing in Fig. 18-1 into a document. Once you have finished copying Fig. 18-1, type Esc, T, S, address and hit Return. This saves the document under a file named ADDRESS.

Merge variables

Figure 18-1 contains several merge variables. The merge variables indicate where text is to be placed in the document. Each variable has a different name. For example, the merge variable «lastname» retrieves the last name of a person from the database, and the merge variable «street» retrieves the street address of this person. The merge variable names correspond to names appearing in the *header* of the database.

Merge variables can be placed anywhere in a document. The same merge variable might appear many times in a document. The order of the merge variable does not affect merging. Note that the merge variables' names have no significance. The names can be any combination of letters and numbers. The variable names used in the example were chosen because they tell you the type of information being entered in the document.

Note that if the merge variable stands for a number, it can be used in an arithmetic function in Word. The number printed is the merge data number plus, minus, times, or divided by another number. For example:

   Your last check bounced, please remit $«amntdue+15» immediately.

Arithmetic functions can also be useful for calculating an employee's salary or the total price of a product. Even two different merge variables can be added (multiplied, divided, or subtracted), provided they are both numbers. For example, you could enter the following into a form letter:

   At «wage» an hour, for «time» hours, you will receive «wage*time».

Word is also able to make comparisons. This is addressed in Chapter 19.

Creating a data file with Word

The data file contains data that is inserted in the document when the Print Merge command is selected. The data file can be created with Word or another program that generates ASCII files. Any data file can be edited, like a document, by Word. Thus, if the data is out of date, it can be updated with Word.

Figure 18-2 depicts a typical data file. The top line is called the *header*. It designates the various groups of data, called *fields*, in the data file. The lines beneath the header are called *records*. The records contain data to be inserted in the document when the merge command is selected.

196 *Merging documents*

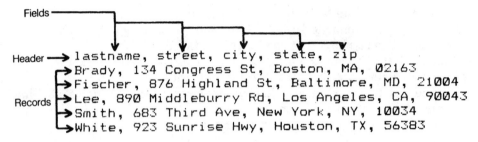

18-2 An example of a data file created by Word.

Below the header are lines of data to be inserted in the document when the document is merged. The data is arranged according to a pattern dictated by the header. In this scenario, the customer's last name always comes first. Following last name is street, city, state, and zip. Each record must obey the order dictated by the header, otherwise, the data is not merged into the document in the appropriate order.

Commas are used to separate each field in a record. The Return key is used to separate each record in the data file. A record can extend for hundreds of lines as long as the end-of-paragraph marker generated by the Return key only comes at the end of the record and does not appear anywhere within the record.

Several restrictions must be observed when creating a data file:

- Entries in a record must be separated by commas.
- Every record must end with a paragraph marker (Return character).
- Entries that contain quotation marks or commas, like $3,671.35 or "The ChipWich Kid", must be surrounded by quotation marks.
- Each record may contain up to 256 fields.
- The field names within the header must be 64 characters or less in length.
- Field names must be made up entirely of letters and numbers, and must begin with a letter.

As long as you abide by these ground rules, creating a data file should be easy. Simply use Word to create the file as you would an ordinary document. A common error to avoid is placing too few or too many entries in a record. Each record must have the exact number of entries called for by the header.

Once the data file has been created, it must be saved on the disk. The name of the data file must match the name listed in the «DATA filename» on the first line of the document waiting to be merged. The data file should be saved on the same disk (and directory) as the document. This enables Word to find the two files when it is printing the form letters.

For this chapter's example, you should enter the data depicted in Fig. 18-2. After the data has been entered, type Esc, T, S, customer.dat, and hit Return. This saves the data on a disk.

Printing a merged document

After the document and data file have been properly prepared, the document can be merged. To print a merged document, follow these steps:

1. Use the Transfer Load command to load the document.
2. Select the Print Options command (Esc, P, O) and set the print options.
3. Select the Print Merge command. Word will begin printing the merged document.

For practice, print out the document portrayed in Fig. 18-1. You must have a printer connected to your computer to execute the steps in this exercise. Press Esc, T, L, and type address and hit Return. This loads the letter called ADDRESS.DOC. The letter appears on the screen. Next, type Esc, F, M, and hit Return to begin the printing of the document. A letter for each record is produced. The word Merging... appears on the message line indicating that the file is being merged.

If you wish to cancel the merging at any time, press Esc to halt the printing. The message line prompts you to enter Y to continue, or Esc to cancel. At this point, you can abandon the merge operation by pressing Esc a second time, or you can resume the merge operation by pressing Y.

Printing to a disk file

Another option for printing a series of form letters is to use the Print Merge Document command to create a series of form letters in a disk file. Follow these steps:

1. Use the Transfer Load command to load the document.
2. Select the Print Merge Document command (Esc, P, M, D).
3. Enter a filename for the new merged document when prompted.
4. Press Enter to effect the merge.

The advantage of this command is that you can carefully inspect the resulting form letters for the sort of embarrassing typos and malapropisms that occur when simple, tiny errors are placed in the data file. For instance, a letter was received at a religious center called Christ Church that began with the greeting, Dear Mr. Church. A magazine subscription clearing house sweepstakes mailing was sent to a man living in Studio City, California. Either through a typo, or a data entry person's inattention, the letter was addressed to Stupid City and it began simply: Dear Stupid.

Commas and quotation marks

You can include commas and quotation marks within an entry by surrounding the entire entry with quotation marks. For example:

Williams, Mark

Should be designated by surrounding the entry with quotation marks:

"Williams, Mark"

Likewise:

Acme Computers, Inc.

Must be delineated with quotation marks:

"Acme Computers, Inc."

In addition, caution must be exercised when entering data that incorporates quotation marks. Thus the line:

"The Greek Sheik"

Becomes:

"""The Greek Sheik"""

Similarly:

Daniel "The Stomach" Carter

must be enclosed in double quotation marks:

"Daniel ""The Stomach"" Carter"

Using header files

If you are creating a data file with a data management program, you should place the header in a file separate from the data file. You should also place the header in a separate file if the same header is used by many different data files. This *header file* can be created with Word. A minor change is required in the current document (shown in Fig. 18-1) to include a header file. The «DATA» command in the document must be changed to the following format:

«DATA headerfile, data file»

Note the comma separating the two filenames.

The header file contains the field names and their positions in the data file. For example, the original data file had the following header:

lastname, street, city, state, zip

This line can be placed in a separate header file, and the header in the original data file depleted. Although a separate header file is not practical in this scenario, it is when your data files are generated by a database program.

To review, add a header file to the current merged document. If the document address is not loaded, load the document (press Esc, T, L, and type address and hit Return). Replace the top line with «DATA CUSTOMER.HED, CUSTOMER.DAT». The document should now resemble Fig. 18-3.

Any name can be used to describe the header and data file. The .DAT ending

```
┌─[········1·········2·········3·········4·········5·········]·········7·····┐
│ «data customer.hed▮ customer.dat»
│ June 20, 1984
│
│ Dear «lastname»:
│
│ Your address change has been acknowledged and updated.
│ Please inform us if the address listed below is incorrect.
│
│     «street»
│     «city», «state» «zip»
│
│ US Magazines is offering a special subscription rate to our
│ new magazine US Computers. US Computers provides behind the
│ scenes reporting at all the computer manufacturers, from IBM
│ to Apple from Microsoft to Lotus. Order now and get twelve
│ copies for just $15.95.
│
│ Sincerely yours♦
│
└─────────────────────────────────────────────────────MTEST.DOC─┘
COMMAND: Copy Delete Format Gallery Help Insert Jump Library
         Options Print Quit Replace Search Transfer Undo Window
Edit document or press Esc to use menu
Pg1 Co19        {}                                    Microsoft Word
```

18-3 A document with a data command that calls upon a header file and a data file.

on the data file and the .HED ending on the header file were chosen to clarify the role of these two files.

After the original document has been changed, you should create the header file shown in Fig. 18-4. Save the document ADDRESS and clear the screen (type Esc, T, S, hit Return and then Esc and type T, C, Y). Place the following line at the first line of the header file: lastname, street, city, state, zip and hit Return. Save the header file (type Esc, T, S, and customer.hed and hit Return).

18-4 A header file created by Word.   `lastname, street, city, state, zip`

Finally, the original data file must be updated. Load the data file (type, Esc, T, L, hit Return and Y). Delete the first line. Save the data file (type Esc, T, S, and hit Return).

If you wish to print the new merged files, follow the directions under the section "Printing a merged document" in this chapter.

Merging data files from other programs

Data files created in dBASE and 1-2-3 can be used with Word in merging form letters. The only caveat is that the program must create ASCII data files in which the fields are separated by commas, semicolons, or tabs, and the records are separated by carriage returns. Because these files do not contain a header, and because inserting a header might ruin the file for use with the original database, you will have to use the procedure outlined earlier in this chapter for using a header file in order to merge a database data file.

Summary

By now you should know how to:

- Designate merge variables with « and ».
- Create a document with merge variables and the data command.
- Create a merged disk file for editing and review before the letters are printed.
- Use header files.
- Print a merged document with the Print Merge command.

19
CHAPTER

Merge commands

Word's merging facilities include a short list of commands that can be placed in the document. The Set, Ask, and If commands are useful when creating form letters. The Include and Next commands aid in creating tables and lengthy documents.

The Set and Ask commands

The *Set* and *Ask* merge commands permit the user to enter text from the keyboard while the document is being printed. Because the data is entered while the document is being merged, you can avoid the use of data files.

Using the Set merge command

The Set merge command prompts the user to enter information once, before any documents are printed. The data entered is used repeatedly in each document. The date is often designated by the Set merge command. Setting the date is especially convenient when you plan to send a form letter on a number of different dates. A Set merge command seeking the amount received from a customer would resemble this:

《set amountrec=?》

Figure 19-1 depicts a typical document incorporating the Set merge command. Experiment with the Set command by creating this document; then print the

Merge commands

```
«data customer.hed, customer.dat»
«set date=?» «date»


«lastname»
«street»
«city», «state»  «zip»

Dear «lastname»:

Thank you for your order.  The parts ordered, unfortunately,
are not in stock.  Our stock will be replenished in five
days.  We plan to ship your order within eight days.


Sincerely yours,

«set name=?» «name»
Acme Truck Parts♦
                                                         NOSTOCK.LET
COMMAND: Copy Delete Format Gallery Help Insert Jump Library
         Options Print Quit Replace Search Transfer Undo Window
Edit document or press Esc to use menu
Pg1 Li1 Col      {}                              Microsoft Word
```

19-1 A Set merge command that asks the user to input a name.

document with the Print Merge Printer command. (The data file and header file used in this example were created in Chapter 18.)

Just before the document is merged and printed (and after the Print Merge Printer command has been selected), you are prompted to enter the text you want included in the letter. This is your cue to enter the date. If today's date were 12 October 1991, you would type 12 October 1991 and hit Return. After you press the Return key, Word resumes the merge operations and continues printing.

When the document is merged, Word prompts you for the text with a generic message that doesn't say very much about the information you should enter. Someone not intimately familiar with the document would probably be confused by the message. You can very easily program Word to type Please enter today's date. To add this special message, change the first line in the document to the line:

«set date=? Please enter today's date»

The next to last line in the letter may also be changed to generate a message when the second Set merge command is encountered. The new and improved line is listed below. You can program Word to say anything as long as it fits within the message line.

«set name=? Enter your name»

The question mark in the Set merge command can be replaced by an entry such as «set item=intro-course». This is helpful when there are a number of repetitive phrases in a document (see Fig. 19-2). Any reasonable number of Set and Ask commands can appear in a document.

```
«set co=Third National Semiconductor Company, Inc»

Dear Sir:

It is a pleasure doing business with «co». «co» is prompt
at paying bills, has beautiful stationary, and a classy
corporate headquarters.

I especially want to thank «co» for the helping Acme Truck
Parts obtain sufficient supplies of the VLSI 9011 chip for
our environmental control computers.


Sincerely yours,

Mark Wilson
Acme Truck Parts
                                                          =3NATSEMI.LET=
COMMAND: Copy Delete Format Gallery Help Insert Jump Library
         Options Print Quit Replace Search Transfer Undo Window
418 characters
Pg1 Li17 Co17   {}                                        Microsoft Word
```

19-2 A Set merge command that has a predefined value.

The Ask merge command

The Ask merge command prompts the user to enter data each time a document is merged. If you print 10 copies of a document, the Ask merge command prompts you to enter data 10 times. After the data is entered, that version of the document is printed.

The Ask merge command can be useful in a number of ways. You might be sending a letter to a number of people and wish to personalize the letter by adding a different paragraph to each letter. You might want to send a form letter to a handful of people and do not wish to create a data file. Or you might have a data file, but do not wish to add a field to it for the merge routine.

The formats for the Ask merge command and Set merge command are identical. A typical Ask merge command appears below:

«ask quantity=?»

For practice, enter the document listed in Fig. 19-3. The document incorpo-

```
Sept 19, 1984
«ask lastname=?» «ask street=?» «ask city=?» «ask state=?»
«ask zip=?»

«lastname»
«street»
«city», «state»  «zip»

Dear «lastname»:

Thank you for your order of «ask items=?» «items». The order
is being shipped by sea and should arrive within six weeks.


Sincerely yours,


Seafarers Trading Co.

COMMAND: Copy Delete Format Gallery Help Insert Jump Library
         Options Print Quit Replace Search Transfer Undo Window
Edit document or press Esc to use menu
Pg1 Li18 Co21    {}                                    Microsoft Word
```

19-3 Several Ask merge commands that ask for the last name, address, and items ordered by the recipient of the letter.

rates several Ask commands. Once the document has been created and a suitable data file is available, use the Print Merge command to generate hard copies.

While the document is being printed with the Print Merge command, Word prompts you for data for the Ask command. You are prompted (again with a very generic prompt) to enter the information to be merged. Once the prompt appears, you must enter some text. If you do not want to enter text, simply press the Return key. The process is repeated for each document printed by the Print Merge command. If you print 20 copies of a document, each Ask command prompts you to enter data each of the 20 times.

The prompt used with the Ask command is not very helpful, but to create a more informative prompt, enter the Ask command as follows:

«ask quantity=? Enter quantity ordered by customer»

Figure 19-4 contains prompts for each Ask merge command used in Fig. 19-3. The basic difference between the Set and Ask merge commands is that Set establishes a value, such as a date, that is used across all the printed documents. You are only prompted for it once. The Ask merge command requests an item of information that is probably different for each document printed, thus you are prompted for an entry each time the document is merged. When you are using it without a data file, it appears to initiate a continuous loop. It requests information and print

```
Sept 19, 1984
«ask lastname=? customer's last name» «ask street=? street
address» «ask city=? city» «ask state=? state» «ask zip=?
zip»

«lastname»
«street»
«city», «state»  «zip»

Dear «lastname»:

Thank you for your order of «ask items=? items ordered»
«items». The order is being shipped by sea and should
arrive within six weeks.


Sincerely yours,
```

19-4 The same document as in Fig. 19-3, except the Ask commands have prompts displayed when Word executes the commands. The prompt tells users what data is required for the field.

documents until the end of time (or the end of your patience). To terminate the merge, respond to the Ask merge command prompt by pressing the Esc key twice.

The If command

The *If* merge command allows you to send conditional messages. For example, if you wanted to send messages to subscribers who had renewed their subscriptions different from the messages sent to subscribers who had not, one solution would be to separate the renewals from the nonrenewals and print two sets of letters.

A data management program like dBASE can easily divide a database into two distinct data files and then print each data file separately. If you have a data file designed by Word, it is impossible to separate electronically the data file into two groups. The If command, however, can distinguish between the two groups and prints two different letters with the same data file. A typical If merge command resembles:

«If state="NY"»New York residents must pay sales tax. Your invoice has been updated to reflect this fact.«else»Out of state residents pay no sales tax.«endif»

The If merge command contains three parts: «If state="NY"», «else», and «endif». Within the three parts are two phrases; in this scenario the two phrases are New York residents must pay sales . . . and Out of state residents pay . . . . One of the two phrases is printed during merging, depending on whether the state field indicates the recipient lives in the state of New York.

The first part,《If state="NY"》, determines which of the two phrases is printed. The word "state" represents a merge variable. The merge variable can be set by an Ask or Set command, or the merge variable can be set from a data file. The statement state="NY" is evaluated by Word. If the state is NY, the statement is true. If the state is not NY, the statement is false. When the statement is true, the first phrase is printed. When the statement is false, the second phrase is printed. Thus, the first part controls the entire If merge command.

The If merge command can test a number of different criteria. Some additional examples of the If merge command follow:

- 《If category="Library"》US Magazines offers special subscription rates for non-profit libraries. Send us a letter on your stationary for a quote.《else》The annual subscription fee is $14.00.《endif》
- 《If graduate="Y"》Your Alma Mater《else》Podunk University《endif》
- 《If received=" "》As a new subscriber《else》Renewing subscribers《endif》
- 《If type="relative"》 members《else》friends《endif》

The If merge command can be simplified by eliminating the 《else》 part. For example:

《If state="MA"》Residents of Massachusetts must pay state sales taxes on all items except textbooks. 《endif》

In such a merge the first part, state="MA", is evaluated. If it is true, the phrase Residents of Massachusetts . . . is printed. If the first part is false, nothing is printed. Figure 19-5 incorporates several If merge commands.

Testing numbers with If

The If command can also test integers. Be careful when working with integers because integers can be stored in a text format or in a numeric format. Thus, "50" is very different from 50. If the integer is in a numeric format, the integer can be tested in six different ways:

```
>    greater than
<    less than
=    equal to
<>   not equal to
<=   less than or equal to
>=   greater than or equal to
```

If the integer is in text format, only equality can be tested.

The If merge command can be used with numbers in a variety of ways as illustrated below:

- 《If quantity>50》A special ten percent discount is granted to bulk orders《endif》

```
┌─────────────────────────────────────────────────────┐
│ Sept 19, 1984                                       │
│                                                     │
│ Dear «lastname»:                                    │
│                                                     │
│ Thank you for your order of «items-ordered». The order is │
│ being shipped by «if mail="L"»surface and should arrive  │
│ within six weeks. «else»air and should arrive within six │
│ days. «endif» «if paid="Y"» Thank you for your advance   │
│ payment. «else» An invoice is enclosed. «endif»      │
│                                                     │
│                                                     │
│ Sincerely yours,                                    │
│                                                     │
│                                                     │
│ Seafarers Trading Co□                               │
│                                                     │
│                                       ═SHIPORD.LET═ │
└─────────────────────────────────────────────────────┘
COMMAND: Copy Delete Format Gallery Help Insert Jump Library
         Options Print Quit Replace Search Transfer Undo Window
365 characters
Pg1 Li16 Co21     {}                            Microsoft Word
```

19-5 The If merge commands enable data to be inserted conditionally in a merge document.

- «If income<19000»Your family should consider applying for «else»Your family is not eligible for «endif»
- «If stock<10»Please send «reorder-amount» of part number «partno». «endif»
- «If paidthru=60»It is time to renew your subscription «else»Thank you for subscribing to «endif»

Multiple If commands

Word can also handle If merge commands embedded within If merge commands. Embedding If merge commands increases the power of the If merge command, but also makes the command more complex. The number of If merge commands that can be embedded is limited.

   Two If merge commands are embedded in a third If merge command in the following command:

   «If amount-owed>100»«If received="June"»Your car loan payments have been two months late. «endif»«If received="May"»Your car loan payments have been three months late. «endif»«else» Please pay friendly loan service «amount-owed» dollars by the end of the month. «endif»

To dispense with the chevrons («») for the moment, here is an explanation of the command: Should (amount minus owed) be greater than 100, the statement is true and Word proceeds to the first phrase. In this example, the first phrase consists of two other If merge commands.

If received does equal June, then both conditions are true and Word prints Your car payments are two months late. This If command statement has no Else statement., so if received is anything but June, nothing is printed.

However, Word immediately proceeds to the second embedded If statement. Out of all the non-June possibilities rejected by the first embedded If statement, if received happens to equal May, you have two true conditions again, so the statement Your car loan payments have been three months late is printed. There is no Else clause here, either, so if received is anything but May, nothing is printed.

If (amount minus owed) is less than 100, however, it doesn't matter if the two embedded conditions are true. The outer condition being initially false, it is not possible to have two true statements in the scenario. Word skips immediately to the Else clause associated with the outer If command and the message "Please pay friendly loan service . . . " is printed, along with the value in amount-owed.

As you can see, the position of each If merge command determines the order in which it is processed. If merge commands can be arranged in a hierarchical fashion. In fact, other merge commands can be embedded within an If merge command.

The Skip command

The *Skip* command is used in conjunction with the If merge command. The Skip command causes Word to ignore the current record and jump to the next record. Thus the current record is not printed and the next record is printed unless it, too, is skipped. The Skip command appears in an If command as follows:

   «if amountowed=0»«skip»«endif»

When the statement amountowed=0 is true, the Skip command is executed, causing the present record to be bypassed. The Skip command is useful when you wish to print selected records from a database.

Note that you can also select records from the database using the database software package commands. For example, dBASE users can use the COPY and the FOR command to select records from a database and copy them to a secondary database. Word can then be used to print merged documents from the secondary database.

The Next command

The *Next* merge command can be used to merge several records into a single document. Until now, you were only able to merge one record in a document. Organizing several records can be helpful in comparing records or creating tables.

With the Next merge command, you could get a quick report of 10 subscribers. Although this is not necessarily a boon to form letters, it is a merge command of great value when printing mailing lists or mailing labels.

Figure 19-6 depicts a document that uses several Next merge commands to form a table. Figure 19-7 contains the printout of such a document.

```
«data income.dat»

        ESTIMATED INCOME FOR 1985

The Computer Works expects to gain 90% of its income from
five software programs.  The programs are:

Program Name         Est Gross Sales      Type of Program

«progname»           «estsales»           «progdesc»
«next»
«progname»           «estsales»           «progdesc»
«next»
«progname»           «estsales»           «progdesc»
«next»
«progname»           «estsales»           «progdesc»
«next»
«progname»           «estsales»           «progdesc»]
                                                           ESTINCOM.DOC
COMMAND: Copy Delete Format Gallery Help Insert Jump Library
         Options Print Quit Replace Search Transfer Undo Window
Edit document or press Esc to use menu
Pg1 Li18 Co51    {}                                        Microsoft Word
```

19-6 The Next merge command enables data from several database records to be placed in a document.

```
                ESTIMATED INCOME FOR 1985

The Computer Works expects to gain 90% of its income from
five software programs.  The programs are:


Program Name         Est Gross Sales      Type of Program

FastCalc             54,300               Electronic Worksheet
FastDOS              12,600               DOS utilities
FastTalk             21,800               Communications
FastDraw             17,100               Business Graphics
FastHorses           13,500               Horse Racing Game.
```

19-7 The merged printout of the document shown in Fig. 19-6.

The Include command

The *Include* merge command is not very useful in producing form letters. However, it can help organize manuscripts, theses, and other lengthy documents. The Include command can combine several different documents into a single document.

The ability to combine different documents into one permits editing of a large document in several parts. Separating a large document into parts is advantageous because it is easier to edit short documents. Large documents take a long time to load and save.

Furthermore, it takes a long time to print selected pages in a long document, because Word must read and format each preceding page before the selection is printed. Thus, if you want to print pages 45 to 49, Word must read and format pages 1 through 4 before printing the desired five pages.

Figure 19-8 demonstrates one possible use of the Include merge command.

```
«include chap1.frm»
«include chap2.frm»
«include chap3.frm»
«include chap4.frm»
«include chap5.frm»
«include chap6.frm»
«include chap7.frm»
«include chap8.frm»

COMMAND: Copy Delete Format Gallery Help Insert Jump Library
         Options Print Quit Replace Search Transfer Undo Window
Edit document or press Esc to use menu
Pg1 Li9 Col      {}                                    Microsoft Word
```

19-8 The Include merge commands can link different documents into a single document.

Summary

By the end of the chapter, you should know how to:

- Get data from the keyboard with the Set and Ask commands in a document.
- Use prompts with the Set and Ask commands.
- Place If merge commands in a document.
- Add data from several different records to one document with the Next merge command.
- Combine different documents with the Include merge command.

CHAPTER 20

Word to WordStar and back again

Before there was Word, there was Wordstar. WordStar was so good that for years it was the number one selling word processing package for personal computers. It was virtually the only alternative in the ancient days of CP/M, when Z-80 Kaypros ruled the world of personal computers.

Making the conversion

Although both Word and WordStar are capable word processors, they are not totally compatible. They can't share files and their operation, even on the same computer, is very different. Nevertheless, documents written in Word can be edited by WordStar, and Wordstar documents can be edited by Word. How is this possible, if their files aren't compatible? Microsoft has developed a conversion program that converts WordStar documents into Word documents and back again. Unfortunately, you have to purchase this program from Microsoft separately.

WordPerfect, another popular word processor (in fact, king of the hill, now that WordStar has slipped in popularity), is shipped with a conversion program that converts text files to and from WordPerfect format, as well as among a number of other program formats, usually through a two-step process, such as DCA to WordPerfect, then WordPerfect to WordStar.

Most word processors (Word, WordStar, and WordPerfect are among them) can save and load pure ASCII documents. Unfortunately, these files lose all their formatting. You would be transferring the naked text from one to the other, and in the process you would be losing footnotes, graphics, page formatting, and a myriad other details that would make the conversion such a headache, it would hardly be worth the trouble except for the sake of sharing a text file.

Other options

User groups and shareware distributors are a likely source of software for converting files from one format to another. A few years ago a company called Systems Compatibility Corporation released software known as Word Exchange that converted files among virtually all popular word processing formats. Your dealer might be able to locate it for you.

Sprint, a word processor from Borland International, is shipped with a very powerful conversion utility. One reviewer noted that Sprint would be well worth its price if all it had to offer was this conversion utility.

Nearly all word processors other than Word are shipped with some sort of conversion program and it is hard to imagine why Microsoft did not follow this industry trend by providing one. Previous versions of Word (through 3.0) included a converter.

CHAPTER 21

The spelling checker

Spelling checkers are great for poor spellers, but they cannot correct grammar, tense, or syntax. In general, a spelling checker can only find misspelled words, but Word's Spell utility is an elegant spelling checker that finds not only misspellings but instances of incorrect punctuation. The program is useful but cannot replace proper proofreading.

A spelling checker finds the "misspelled" words tox, thr, and Texarkana. Tox and thr are not words and should be corrected. However, Texarkana is a name that Spell would flag for correction. The spelling checker finds all words that are not in its list of correct words. Many words and most proper nouns are not in the list.

Furthermore, if you use the word "machine" when the word "distant" was appropriate, Spell cannot determine that "machine" is out of context. The word "machine" is spelled correctly and is therefore correct in the eyes of the spelling checker.

Thus, a spelling checker cannot replace careful editing. A spelling checker is good at quickly finding misspellings (or typos) and nothing else.

214   *The spelling checker*

How Spell works

Spell maintains a dictionary of words against which it compares words in the document. When you perform a spelling check, Spell compares each word against the words in the dictionary. If a word in the document matches a word in the dictionary, Spell assumes that word is correct. If a word in the document does not match a word in the dictionary, Spell assumes that word is misspelled. If the unmatched word is correct, that word can be added to the dictionary so that future occurrences of the word are ignored.

When Spell is finished with the check, it lets you review all the words in the document not found in the dictionary. Spell gives you a chance to correct the errors and review possible correct spellings for the misspelled words. There are two main tasks which you perform in Spell: checking documents and adding words to the Spell dictionary.

Starting Spell

Whether you are using a single floppy disk drive, two floppy disk drives, or a hard disk determines how you should start the spelling checker. Performing a spelling check on a 10-page document using two floppy disk drives takes several minutes.

Press Esc, L, and S and you go to the speller. If you are using a floppy drive system, you are prompted to switch disks.

The main menu

Spell's running screen resembles Fig. 21-1. The Spell main menu contains six commands: Correct, Add, Exit, Ignore, Options, and Undo. Commands are se-

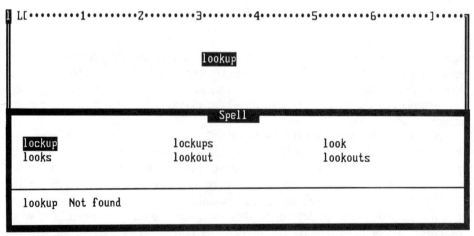

21-1   The Library Spell main menu.

lected in the same manner in both Word and Spell. The initial character of the command is typed to select that command or you can click on the command with the mouse pointer. Each command is discussed in the next section.

Correct

When Word finds a misspelled word, it tries to locate other possible correct spellings. If the Spell utility finds the word "splel," for instance, it suggests the options shown in Fig. 21-2. From the list provided, use the cursor keys or the mouse pointer to select the word that matches what you intended to spell and then click on Correct or type C to substitute the highlighted word for the misspelling in the text. You can also click on Correct and then type in the correct spelling. When you press Return, the correction is substituted.

```
spell      spiel      spill
spells     spiels     spleen
spelt      spills     cpl
splent     spelled    speller
spieled    spieler    spleens
scope      spelts     spilled
spiller    spinel
```

21-2 Suggested correct spellings for "splel."

Add

As in the case of Texarkana, the Spell utility often finds words that ought to be in the dictionary. To place them in the dictionary, click on Add or type A.

Exit

When you are through with the Spell utility, click on the Exit option or type E to return to the editing screen.

Ignore

If you edit documents on a wide variety of topics, your dictionary might become huge and unwieldy. To avoid filing it with technical words of narrow usefulness like "640K" and "ramdisk," you can tell Word to simply ignore all instances of the word. Click on Ignore, or type I.

Undo

Undo undoes a correction. If you insert the suggested word and have second thoughts, click on Undo or type U.

Summary

Upon completing this chapter you should know:

- That Microsoft Spell can correct spelling and identify punctuation errors, but it cannot locate or correct grammatical errors.
- How to run Microsoft Spell and use its various commands.

CHAPTER 22

Dictionary management

You can use Spell without knowing how to edit previous corrections, add words to the dictionaries or the change the settings governing the checking process. However, if you plan to use Spell regularly, you should learn about Spell's dictionaries and the Correct, Add, Exit, Ignore, Options, and Undo commands.

Changing corrections

The Correct, Add, Exit, Ignore, Options, and Undo commands are used to review marked words during the proofing phase. Undo returns you to the last word marked for correction. If you corrected the word, the original spelling appears, and you have the option of correcting it again.

Suppress the word "received" is marked for correction, and you accidentally press I, triggering the Ignore command. You could go back to "received" by using the Undo command (by tapping U when the Library Spell menu appeared again. You can only move back one word with the Undo command. If you find you have made terrible, wide-spread errors, simply clear the document out of memory and reload the original version (assuming you haven't made other enormous editing changes).

Adding words to the dictionaries

While you are correcting the words in a document, you might add words not in Spell's vocabulary to one of three dictionaries: the Standard, Document, and User dictionaries. When the word is added to a dictionary, the Library Spell Utility recognizes the word in the future and does not cull that word from the document. You do not actually add new words to the Library Spell dictionary, although it might appear that way. The words are actually added to a file called UPDAT-AM.CMP, which is treated as if it were part of the standard dictionary. To add a word culled from a document to a Spell dictionary:

1. Select the Add command before selecting either the Ignore or Correct commands.
2. Select the dictionary to which you want to add the word.

You might add groups of words to a Spell dictionary by using Word to create a document consisting of words to be added to dictionaries. Then use Spell to check the document. Use the Add command on each word in the document you wish to include in a dictionary.

The three dictionaries

When the Library Spell command checks a document, it first consults the standard dictionary. If the word is not in the standard dictionary, Spell checks the UPDAT-AM.CMP update dictionary discussed in the previous section. If Spell does not find the word in the standard dictionary or the update dictionary and a document dictionary exists, Spell looks in the document dictionary. Finally, if it has been unsuccessful so far in finding the questionable word, Spell checks the user dictionary. If the word does not appear in any of the four dictionaries, the word is flagged and displayed for changes. The next sections briefly summarize the role of the three accessible dictionaries.

Standard The standard dictionary is the main dictionary Spell uses to check all possibly misspelled words culled from the document. Added to this dictionary is the supplemental dictionary. Although technically they are separate, these two dictionaries can be thought of as one. Words you use frequently that are not included in the standard dictionary should be added to it. For example, if you were a technical writer engaged in writing about some topic on the cutting edge of technology, you might regularly encounter words not found in the standard dictionary. These words should be added to the standard dictionary.

Document The document dictionary is a dictionary attached to the document you are checking. The dictionary is used whenever that document or a document by the same name is checked. If a word is unique to a document, the word can be added to the document dictionary or not added to any dictionary. When you choose to ignore a word, Spell automatically places the word in a temporary dictionary, not the document dictionary. For example, suppose you were writing a letter to Mr. Rajid Kapor. Mr. Kapor's name appears several times in the letter. Because "Kapor" is not in the Spell dictionaries, Spell culls the word and asks whether it is correct. When you select the Ignore command, Spell adds "Kapor" to the temporary dictionary and skips it whenever it is encountered in the text. Because you do not plan to write to Mr. Kapor in the future, you do not want to add "Kapor" to the document, user, or standard dictionary. When you add a word to a document dictionary, Spell places the word in a dictionary attached to the document. If you thought you would make some additions to Mr. Kapor's letter and then check the letter a second time with Spell, you would want to add the words to the document dictionary.

If you are familiar with your operating system, you can use an existing document dictionary to check a new document. The document dictionary has the same filename as the original document and a .CMP extension. For example, if your letter is KAPOR1.DOC, the document dictionary would be KAPOR1.CMP. If the filename document dictionary matches the filename of a document being checked by Spell, that document dictionary is used during the checking process. The RENAME or COPY command can be used to change the filename of the document dictionary.

User The user dictionary is a dictionary created by the user that contains words unique to some documents. A user dictionary is used to check special documents. Suppose you write about the Maxwell-Boltzmann speed distribution or the number of Glial cells in the left hemisphere of the brain, or perhaps you write about early Incan architecture or write legal documents. These documents contain many words specific to their field and not encountered by the layman. Spell flags words like "Incan" that might be commonplace in your work but not so in the work of a nuclear physicist or a stock broker. You can create special user dictionaries for different fields.

General principles

The more words in Spell's dictionaries, the longer it takes to look up a word. Thus, it would be inefficient to create a single dictionary with all the esoteric terms used in all the arcane specialities of the world. For example, if you had a dream spelling dictionary containing every conceivable word, it would miss many misspellings and typos. It is more practical to divide the terms from the standard words by placing the terms in user dictionaries.

To use a user dictionary, you must select the Options menu. You are prompted for the name of the dictionary to use. Any words added to the user dictionary with the Library Spell Add command are placed in the designated user dictionary. If no user dictionary is designated, the words added are placed in a user dictionary called SPECIALS.CMP.

The options

The three options that control the checking process and their default settings are:

Lookup:	Quick(Complete)
Ignore all caps:	Yes(No)
Alternatives:	(Auto)Manual
Check punctuation:	(Yes)No

Lookup tells Spell whether or not to assume that the first two letters of all words in the document are correct. The default setting is complete, which means Spell does not assume the first two letters are correct. Changing this option to Quick reduces the number of possible spellings Spell must review to check a word's spelling. As the number of possible spellings decreases, so does the time required to perform a spelling check.

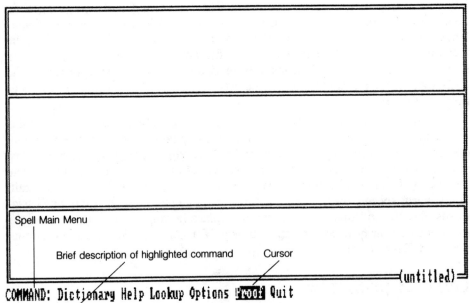

22-1 The Correct Spell command looks for alternative correct spellings of the misspelled word.

The option Ignore all caps tells Spell whether or not to check words that consist entirely of capital letters. For example, abbreviations like IBM, MBTA, USDA, and LCD are checked when this option is set to No. If you do not want such words to be marked, use the Yes setting. However, you must take responsibility to check these acronyms. You might avoid marking such words in the future by adding them to the Spell dictionary.

The option Alternatives allows you to see the various spelling alternatives Word suggests when it finds an incorrect setting if it is left Yes. If this is turned to

No, and an incorrect spelling is encountered, you are given the option of changing to the most likely spelling (not displayed) or using the menu to ignore the word or add it to the dictionary.

The final option is to use the speller to locate incorrect punctuation. This is yet another improvement in the spelling utility that double-checks your work. Perhaps some future release will include a grammar and usage checker, but even checking punctuation is a great advance over most word processor spelling utilities.

Editing your dictionaries

All the dictionaries except the standard dictionary can be edited as if they were simple document files (including the UPDAT-AM.CMP file). Load the dictionary with the Transfer Load command. Edit it to remove any unwanted words (no matter how vigilant you are, some misspellings will probably creep in, unless you never use the Library Spell Add command).

Summary

When you have finished Chapter 22, you should know:

- How to use the Undo command to change the most recent correction back to the original spelling.
- How to use Spell's three dictionaries.
- How to use the Options command to control the checking process.
- How to edit your dictionaries.

23
CHAPTER

Other library commands

The Library Run command allows you to run operating system commands from within Word. The Library Hyphenate command automatically hyphenates multi-syllabic words in a document. Hyphenating allows you to have more even right margins in left-adjusted documents and more evenly spaced letters in fully justified texts.

Automatic hyphenation

Most writers (and readers) prefer text to be *ragged right*. But this option can look inelegant, as in the following lines:

> General Washington crossed the
>
> Delaware River during a
>
> Christmas Eve assault on the enemy.

In this instance, the right is a little too ragged. It looks sloppy. But consider the following:

General Washington crossed the

Delaware River during a Christ-

mas Eve assault on the enemy.

The Library Hyphenate command hyphenates words in a document. Figure 23-1 shows the Hyphenate menu.

```
LIBRARY HYPHENATE confirm: Yes No        hyphenate caps: Yes No
```

23-1 Library Hyphenate command menu.

Words can be hyphenated automatically or manually. When words are automatically hyphenated, Word determines where the hyphenation will occur. The routine usually (but not always) finds the appropriate point for the hyphenation.

If you don't trust Word to hyphenate appropriately, you might tell Word to let you review hyphenation. During this procedure, Word finds each word that should be hyphenated, suggest a point in the word where the hyphen should be placed, and allows you to move the hyphen or simply opt not to hyphenate that particular word.

The file HYPH.DAT is used to perform hyphenations. HYPH.DAT must be on the same disk and in the same directory as the Word program files.

Hyphenating automatically

Follow these directions to hyphenate a document.

1. Move to the point in the document where you want hyphenation to start. If you want to hyphenate the entire document, take the cursor to the beginning of the document before calling up the command. You can hyphenate any contiguous section of the document by highlighting that section and then selecting the Library Hyphenate command. If you have already hyphenated part of a long document, it is better not to waste time rehyphenating that part of the document.
2. Type Esc, L, and H to select the Library Hyphenate command.
3. Press N to invoke automatic hyphenation. Press Y if you wish to hyphenate manually. See the next section for additional information.
4. If you do not wish to hyphenate words that are capitalized, press Tab, N This option is useful if you do not want to hyphenate names, proper nouns, and the first word of a sentence.
5. Press Return to begin hyphenating.
6. Press Esc if you wish to halt hyphenation before the end of the document.

Hyphenating manually

When you are hyphenating words manually, Word picks out all words that require hyphenation. When a word that should be hyphenated is found, you are prompted to respond Y to insert the hyphen, N to skip the word, or use the arrow keys to highlight the position where the hyphen ought to be inserted. Although you can pick the spot for the hyphen, Word overrules any hyphenation that violates the right margin. Press Y when the hyphenation meets your requirements.

Press Esc to cancel the hyphenation command.

Operating system commands from Word

The Library Run command enables you to give operating system commands while in Word. If you are using Word and you want to save a file, but you have no formatted disks available, you can use the Library Run command to issue the FORMAT command. You can COPY disks or files, use EDLIN, or any other operating system command or utility from within Word.

Certain operating system command take up a lot of memory. If your computer has insufficient RAM, the command will not run. If you are operating from a floppy disk, COMMAND.COM must be on the disk before you can use the Library Run command.

When you use Library Run, at the end of the operation of the operating system command, you are prompted to press any key to return to Word. To run programs other directories and off the operating system's path, include the complete path and filename.

Summary

In this chapter, you saw:

- How to use the hyphenation command manually and automatically.
- How to run operating system commands from within Word.

CHAPTER 24

The thesaurus

To a writer, a thesaurus can be an invaluable resource. To the rest of us, a thesaurus is a practical way to prevent repetition in our writing. A thesaurus is a simple text of synonyms. The one shipped with Word contains 220,000 synonyms. If, for example a document contained the word "document" too often, you could look for synonyms for "document" with the Library thEsaurus command. A search for synonyms reveals deed, paper, title, text, words, certificate, credential, instrument, license, pass, and permit. The thesaurus is best used with a hard disk so that words can be referenced without swapping disks.

Looking up words in the thesaurus

Entering and using the thesaurus is easy. To begin, move the cursor to the word for which you want to find a synonym. Then choose the Library thEsaurus command (press Esc, L, E). If you are using a hard disk and the thesaurus is in the same directory as the Word program (this is how the setup program installs it), Word automatically loads and runs the thesaurus utility. If the file can't be found, Word instructs you to insert the thesaurus disk. Place this disk in drive A, and Word proceeds to find the synonyms if any can be found. If you are operating from a floppy system, Word prompts you to replace the document disk with the thesaurus disk. When you follow this instruction, do not forget to replace the thesaurus disk with the document disk when the word search is finished.

When the thesaurus utility is called up, you see a screen similar to the one in Fig. 24-1. If the list of synonyms is too large to display, the word MORE: PgDn

```
┌─────────────────────────────────────────────────────────────────┐
│ TWICE IN PARADISE IS ONE TOO MANY                               │
│                                                                 │
│     In the opening act of Twice in Paradise, Karl Gruber        │
│ overshadows the other actors. Normally, an actor would be       │
│ proud of accomplishing this act. In Mr. Gruber's case, this     │
│ is not so. To say Mr. Gruber's actions are stiff would be       │
│ an injustice to the public. Mr. Gruber would do better if       │
│ he were a piece of wood and not acting at all. Why he has       │
│ chosen theatre as his profession remains a mystery probably     │
│ even to those around him. He belongs next to the fireplace,     │
│ the mantle, or even in place of the mantle itself.              │
├═══════════════════════════ Word Finder Thesaurus ═══════════════┤
│ act:                                              MORE: PgDn    │
│ noun • accomplishment, achievement, acquirement, action, battle,│
│         deed, doing, event, exploit, feat, stunt, thing, trick; │
│      • farce, make believe, parody, performance, show, sketch,  │
│        skit;                                                    │
│      • law, legislation, measure, ruling, statute.              │
│ verb • function, go, perform, run, work;                        │
│      • ape, copy, emulate, follow, imitate, lip synch, mime,    │
│        mimic, mock, model, mouth, pantomime, parody, pattern,   │
│        take off;                                                │
│      • assume, bluff, counterfeit, fabricate, fake, feign,      │
│        imitate, invent, make believe, play, pretend, put on,    │
│        sham;                                                    │
│ ↑↓←→:point       ENTER:replace       ESC:exit    CTRL-F6:look up│
└─────────────────────────────────────────────────────────────────┘
```

24-1 Selecting the Library Thesaurus command finds synonyms for the highlighted word. When synonyms are found in Word's thesaurus, they are displayed on the screen in this manner.

appears. You can scroll through a long list with the PgUp and PgDn commands. When using the mouse, move the pointer to the left of the screen and guide the screen up or down using the scroll bar.

To choose a synonym from the list provided by Word, move the cursor with the arrow keys to the synonym you want and press Return, Word removes the original word and replace it with the highlighted synonym. If there are no words that look appropriate, you can exit the thesaurus by pressing Esc and no replacement is made. If you are using a mouse, you can click on the replacement word to make the selection.

If no synonyms can be found, Word informs you and provides a short list of words it considers similar in spelling, which you might then use to access the thesaurus. Sometimes words are not indexed, while words very similar in spelling and meaning are.

Note that a list of all possible commands in the thesaurus is always displayed in the thesaurus window. The commands necessary to finding a synonym are:

1. Move to the word you want to replace. Either select the word or place the cursor on it.
2. Press Esc, L, and E to select the Library thEsaurus command.
3. Select a synonym from the list of words provided.
4. Press Return.

A hands-on example

Let's suppose that you are writing a review of a play. You find that your piece contains the word "act," "action," and "actor" too often, and you must find an alternative. (To follow this example, type in the document shown in the top half of Fig. 24-1). To find a synonym, move the cursor to the word "act" in the document and press Esc, L, E Move the highlight within the thesaurus window with the cursor keys. "Act" is a word with many synonyms, so you need to use the PgDn key to find a few more options. Move the highlight to the word "feat," and the screen will resemble Fig. 24-1: half the screen contains the text, half the thesaurus, and the proper word is highlighted. Finally, to replace "act" with "feat" and return to the document, press Return. The word "act" disappears and "feat" takes it place, using the same capitalization and format, and the thesaurus window closes.

Advanced options

If the exact word is a form of another word, the thesaurus provides synonyms of the root word only. For example, if you wanted synonyms for "computing," the thesaurus only displays synonyms of "compute."

If no synonym can be found for a word, an alphabetized list of words that matches the word you are looking up in spelling appears. To look up the highlighted word, press Ctrl-F6. For example, suppose you just obtained a list of synonyms for "compute" (see Fig. 24-2). Now you want to view the synonyms for the word "figure," which is the closest word in the thesaurus list to what you want to say.

24-2 The synonyms found by the thesaurus for the word "computing." The thesaurus automatically searches for synonyms for the root word.

230 *The thesaurus*

Figure 24-3 portrays a new list of synonyms. If you wish to return to the previous list of synonyms, press Ctrl-PgUp. This capability of the thesaurus can help you when you have a concept in mind, but cannot come up with the exact word that describes the concept. You can chase down the exact word through associational chains, zeroing in on it quickly by navigating thesaurus screens, selecting words that most closely match the meaning you want.

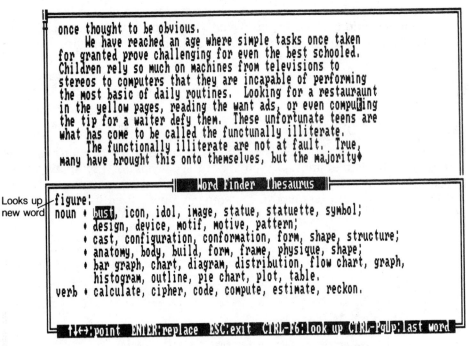

24-3 You can find the synonym of a synonym of a word with the Ctrl-F6 command.

Summary

After reading this chapter, you should be able to:

- Find a synonym for a word in a document with the thesaurus.
- Use the commands in the thesaurus menu to look up words in the thesaurus itself.

25
CHAPTER

Drawing lines

Most of us have seen line drawings used in various texts, but few of us realize how effective they can be for any document. Obviously, line drawings are essential for charts. A line drawing can also enhance any report, tabbed column, or even a table of contents. You might even want to create diagrams for papers with Word's line-drawing commands.

The three forms of line drawings are lines drawn with direction keys, borders around paragraphs, and vertical lines with the Tab key. Each one serves a different purpose, so you should choose carefully.

Line drawings are available through the Ctrl-F5 (Line draw) command. Some printers, particularly inexpensive ones, cannot print lines. In this case, dashes, colons, and plus signs are used.

Line drawing with the arrow keys

The simplest form of line drawing is accomplished with the arrow keys. The arrow keys allow you to draw horizontal and vertical lines around any text you choose (see Fig. 25-1).

To begin drawing lines, press Ctrl-F5. LD appears on the status line at the bottom of the screen. The following keys are used for line drawing:

    Ctrl-F5   Toggles on/off line drawing mode.
    Left, Right Draws horizontal lines.
    Up, Down   Draws vertical lines.

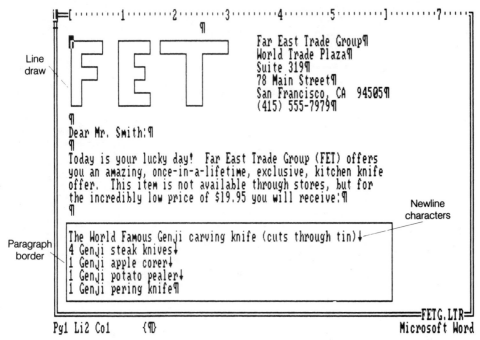

25-1 An example of line drawing in a document. The Ctrl-F5 command activates and deactivates line drawing.

Home	Draws a line from the cursor to the left indent.
End	Draws a line from the cursor to the right indent.
Esc	Cancels line drawing mode.

After a line drawing has been entered, it can be edited like any other text. If you are typing text on the same lines as the line drawing, it is easiest to enter the text while in the overtype mode, so that the line drawings are not disturbed by inserting text. F5 toggles overtype mode. While in LD, use the direction keys to move. Pressing Return has no effect.

Erasing Lines

Editing a line drawing is the same as editing text. To erase lines, first exit line drawing by using Ctrl-F5 or Esc. Then, move to the line you wish to delete and press Delete. You can also use F6, Shift-F6 (column selecting), or the mouse to highlight a section of a line drawing for deletion. To delete a small section of a line without disturbing the entire line drawing, switch to overtype mode (F5), move the cursor to the place where the deletion should begin, and press the Space bar over any line characters you want to erase.

Moving and copying lines

Frequently, you might want to move line drawings from one point in the document to another. Line drawings are copied and inserted just like ordinary text: highlight the line drawing and press Esc, C, and hit Return to copy the line drawing to the scrap. Move the cursor to the new location where the line drawing is required and press Ins or Esc, I, and hit Return to place the line drawing into the text.

Changing the line draw character

A straight line may be the most direct path between two points, but it can be boring. If you choose to draw with another character, such as a colon, a period, or some other character, you can change the line draw character by pressing Esc and O to access the Options menu. Then change the setting of the linedraw character: to your choice of characters. You can simply type in the character you want to use, or, with the option highlighted, press F1 and see an array of line draw schemes.

Paragraph borders

A paragraph border encloses an entire paragraph. This can be helpful both in headings and in highlighting important information. A paragraph border can be an entire box, or any part of a box as seen in Fig. 25-2. Word computes the size of the box and formats accordingly. The box remains with the paragraph until you remove it. The entire paragraph, box included, can be moved, copied, or deleted.

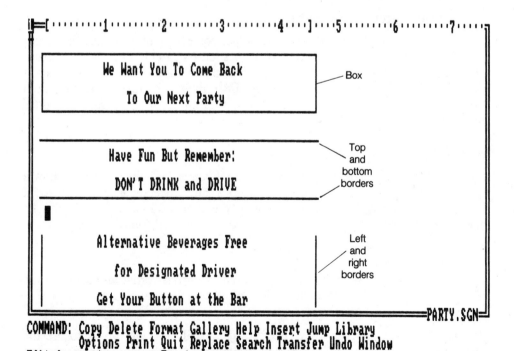

25-2 Examples of paragraph borders created by the Format Border menu.

Creating and deleting paragraph borders

The Format Border command controls the creation and removal of paragraph borders. To create a paragraph border, follow these steps:

1. Highlight the paragraph you want enclosed.
2. Press Esc, F, and B to select the Format Border command.
3. Choose either Box or Lines under the Type option.
4. If you chose lines under the type option, choose on which sides to print borders by selecting Yes or No, under Left, Right, Above, and Below.
5. Choose Normal, Bold, or Double, for the line style option. (Double and bold print only if available on your printer.)
6. Press Return to create the paragraph border.

To remove a paragraph border:

1. Highlight the enclosed paragraph.
2. Press Esc, F, B, to select the Format Border command.
3. Choose None under the Type option to remove the entire border, or if the Lines setting was chosen under the Type option, choose No under Left, Right, Above, and Below to remove the corresponding border lines.
4. Press Return to execute the command.

Editing bordered paragraphs

A bordered paragraph can be edited (deleted, copied, or moved) like any other paragraph. Simply move the cursor to the desired paragraph. Highlight the paragraph to be edited. Press Del to remove the paragraph and place it in the scrap. If you are only copying the paragraph, press Ins immediately to put the paragraph back in place. Then put the cursor in the new location for the paragraph and press Ins again.

Enclosing groups of paragraphs

Groups of paragraphs are also easy to enclose. Figures 25-2 and 25-3 show how a series of paragraphs can be enclosed. Figure 25-2 shows several paragraphs enclosed in a single box, while Fig. 25-3 shows paragraphs enclosed in a series of boxes. To enclose a series of paragraphs in a series of boxes or lines, follow these steps:

1. Highlight the paragraphs you want enclosed.
2. Press Esc, F, B
3. Choose Box under the Type option of the Format Border menu. Or choose Lines and select the combination of all four lines as before.
4. Press Return to enter the sides of the paragraph.

The easiest way to enclose a group of paragraphs in a single box is to use the newline character, Shift-Return instead of Return, to separate the paragraphs and then select the Format Borders command to place either a box or selected lines around the group of paragraphs. This technique was used in Fig. 25-1.

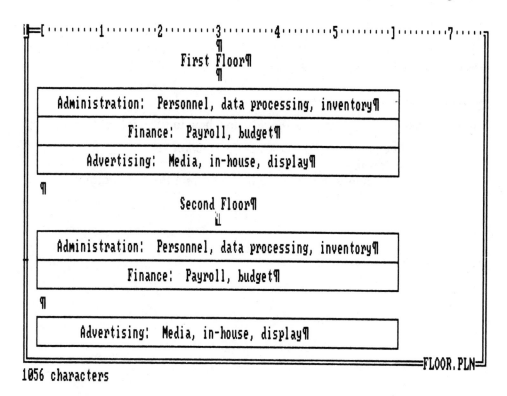

25-3 Additional examples of paragraph borders created by the Format Border menu. Word places a single line between boxed paragraphs.

A single box can be placed around a sequence of paragraphs by using the Lines setting to place individual lines around each paragraph. Thus, the first paragraph would have a top, right, and left border. The last paragraph would have a bottom, right, and left border, and all the paragraphs in between would have left and right borders only.

Note that if two adjacent paragraphs have different paragraph formats, they can automatically be placed in separate borders. The specific conditions that cause paragraphs to be placed in separate border lines are as follows:

1. The paragraphs have different indent settings.
2. The paragraphs have different border styles.
3. The space before and space after settings in the Format Paragraph menu has inserted a space between the paragraphs.

Shading, color, and background shading

Note that in addition to the border selections in the Format Border menu, you have selections for color, shading, and background shading. These additional enhancements allow the box to be set aside from the text with a shading or color. The color option is not available on many printers, obviously, but printers capable of placing varying densities of shading on the page behind print can make up for the lack of color with a very attractive screen to draw attention to text.

Summary

After completing the chapter, you should know how to accomplish the following:

- Create line drawings with the Ctrl-F5 function key.
- Edit line drawings.
- Enclose paragraphs in borders with the Format Borders command.

CHAPTER 26

Sorting

Sorting arranges text and numbers into easy-to-read lists organized according to some principle. Names can be alphabetized, for instance, and numbers can be sorted into ascending or descending order. Sorting is an efficient way to organize, file, and list names or numbers in tables, paragraphs, and data. Sorting is especially useful when you are alphabetizing names or ordering data in a table. A word of caution about sorting is in order, however. Some large texts can tie up your machine's memory, so it is best to save large documents before sorting them.

The Library Autosort command enables you to sort columns of text or numbers. To sort a list, follow these steps:

1. Highlight the complete list.
2. Press Esc, L, and A for the Library Autosort command.
3. Select the appropriate settings for the options by, sequence, case, and column only.
4. press Return to sort.

Figures 26-1 and 26-2 show the same list of names and addresses. Figure 26-1 is an unsorted list, while Figure 26-2 is a sorted list. The method Word uses to determine the sorted order of a list is very intuitive. Word sorts a list by ranking rows according to the first character in each row. If the first character matches in two rows, then the second character is checked to determine the order of the rows.

Sorting

```
╔[·······1·······2·······3·······4·······5·······6·······7··]··
║ Potential Supporters ¶
║
║
║ Last      First     Address            City           State   Zip¶
║ White     Janet     613 Cherry Ln      Boston         MA      02280¶
║ Lincoln   Alfred    34 Oak St          Trenton        NJ      07665¶
║ Goldberg  Karen     110 Missouri Ave   St Louis       MO      63250¶
║ White     Guy       17 Fir St          Fairfax        VA      22032¶
║ Smith     Kate      612 Government Sq  Boston         MA      02280¶
║ Martin    Craig     12 Franklin        Cambridge      MA      02139¶
║ Davis     Eileen    P. O. Box 4        Decatur        GA      01334¶
║ White     James     14 Jocelyn Place   Deer Park      NY      06656¶
║ Blair     Vanessa   11 Beach Rd        Miami          FL      04342¶
║ Powell    Vickie    9 Cowden Pk        Nashville      TN      03718¶
║ Chang     Winston   873 Hillside Ave   San Francisco  CA      94410¶
║ White     Jocelyn   Pilgrim Bldg       Plymouth       MA      02716¶
║ Smith     Guy       110 76th St        New York       NY      10021¶
║ White     Joe       99 Park Way        Boston         MA      02170¶
║ Smith     Karen     1683 Sunnyside Dr  Redwood City   CA      94389¶
╚═══════════════════════════════════════════════════════SUPPORT.DOC═

LIBRARY AUTOSORT by: Alphanumeric  Numeric   sequence:(Ascending)Descending
                    case: Yes(No)         column only: Yes(No)
Select option
Pg1 Li19 Co71   {Blair→...¶¶¶§}                        Microsoft Word
```

26-1 The Library Autosort command can sort paragraphs or lines in a database. The items to be sorted must be highlighted before the Library Autosort command is selected.

```
╔[·······1·······2·······3·······4·······5·······6·······7··]··
║ Potential Supporters ¶
║
║
║ Last      First     Address            City           State   Zip¶
║ Blair     Vanessa   11 Beach Rd        Miami          FL      04342¶
║ Chang     Winston   873 Hillside Ave   San Francisco  CA      94410¶
║ Davis     Eileen    P. O. Box 4        Decatur        GA      01334¶
║ Goldberg  Karen     110 Missouri Ave   St Louis       MO      63250¶
║ Lincoln   Alfred    34 Oak St          Trenton        NJ      07665¶
║ Martin    Craig     12 Franklin        Cambridge      MA      02139¶
║ Powell    Vickie    9 Cowden Pk        Nashville      TN      03718¶
║ Smith     Guy       110 76th St        New York       NY      10021¶
║ Smith     Karen     1683 Sunnyside Dr  Redwood City   CA      94389¶
║ Smith     Kate      612 Government Sq  Boston         MA      02280¶
║ White     Guy       17 Fir St          Fairfax        VA      22032¶
║ White     James     14 Jocelyn Place   Deer Park      NY      06656¶
║ White     Janet     613 Cherry Ln      Boston         MA      02280¶
║ White     Jocelyn   Pilgrim Bldg       Plymouth       MA      02716¶
║ White     Joe       99 Park Way        Boston         MA      02170¶
║
╚═══════════════════════════════════════════════════════SUPPORT.DOC═
Pg1 Li20 Co1   {Blair→...¶¶¶§}                         Microsoft Word
```

26-2 The lines sorted by the Autosort command. Compare with Fig. 26-1. Note how the first name was used to sort the Whites and Smiths.

The Library Autosort options

The options under Library Autosort determine how sorting rearranges text, numbers, uppercase and lowercase letters, and columns in a selection. Figure 26-3 illustrates the different results obtained by changing the Autosort settings. The sequence option determines whether Word sorts by ascending or descending order. Ascending order sorts lists from A to Z and from 0 to 9. Descending order sorts lists from Z to A and from 9 to 0. The default setting is Ascending.

```
≡[········1·········2·········3·········4·········5·········6·········7····]¬
 AlphaNumeric     AlphaNumeric     AlphaNumeric     Numeric¶
 Ascending        Ascending        Descending       Ascending¶
 Case No          Case Yes         Case No          Case No¶
 --------------------------------------------------------------¶
 .009              .009             Bldg 101         .009
 .34               .34              Beach Rd         .34
 101 Avenue        101 Avenue       beach ball       101 Avenue
 105               105              avenue           ave
 107               107              Avenue           Ave
 12090             12090            ave.             Beach Rd
 1356              1356             ave              ave.
 6,890             6,890            Ave              avenue
 623-7891          623-7891         Area Code 212    beach ball
 Area Code 212     Area Code 212    623-7891         Avenue
 ave               Ave              6,890            Bldg 101
 Ave               Avenue           1356             105
 ave.              Beach Rd         12090            107
 avenue            Bldg 101         107              Area Code 212
 Avenue            ave              105              623-7891
 beach ball        ave.             101 Avenue       1356
 Beach Rd          avenue           .34              6,890
 Bldg 101          beach ball       .009             12090
                                                     ═SORTDEMO.DOC═┘
Pg1 Li22 Co40    {1}                             CS      Microsoft Word
```

26-3 Separate columns can be sorted with the Autosort command by setting the column-only field to Yes.

The case option indicates whether Word should discriminate between upper- and lowercase letters. When the setting is No, Word treats uppercase and lowercase as equal. It would sort the list Arlington, arguable, and Arbuckle as Arbuckle, arguable, Arlington. If the case option is set to Yes, Word separates uppercase letters from lowercase letters. Because their ASCII value is lower, uppercase letters would come first. The list would be sorted as Arbuckle, Arlington, arguable. The default setting is No.

The by: option determines whether Word treats the list as numbers or as text. If the Alphanumeric setting is used, the order of the list is determined by the first character in each row. If the Numeric setting is used, Word finds the first number in each row and orders the rows by the value of that number. The Alphanumeric setting is the standard setting.

When sorting addresses, telephone numbers, zip codes, and other entries that include both numbers and text (like "4A"), always use the Alphanumeric setting. When sorting entries that just text, you must use the alphanumeric setting. When entries are just numbers and should be sorted in numeric order, use the Numeric setting. When sorting numbers, always be sure that there are no spaces or tabs before or after the numbers. If there are spaces or tabs included in a sort, Word considers some of the entries to be text entries and sorting will not place those numbers in numeric order.

The column only option designates whether Word sorts the entire table (the No setting), or simply a column in the table (the Yes setting). Figures 26-1 and 26-2 show an entire table that was sorted by setting column only to No. Figure 26-3 shows a table whose columns were sorted by setting column only to Yes. Remember that a column can be highlighted by pressing Shift-F6 to activate column selection and then using the cursor keys to highlight the entire column. Note that records longer than one line cannot be sorted with the Yes setting. If a record does not fit on a line, try changing the margins to accommodate the record. The column only setting is normally No.

Sorting paragraphs

Paragraphs can be sorted by placing a number before each paragraph in the sequence. The number should correspond to the desired order of the paragraphs (see Figs. 26-4 and 26-5). Then highlight the paragraphs to be sorted. Select the Library Autosort command and choose Numeric under the by option. The paragraphs will be sorted numerically.

Undoing a sort

The Undo command undoes only the most recent command. Therefore, if you decide that the sort was a mistake, you must select Undo immediately, before issuing any other editing command. Press Esc then U to invoke the Undo command.

Summary

In this chapter, you have seen how to sort:

- In ascending or descending order.
- Just within a column, or the entire row.
- Ignoring or taking into account case and mixtures of numbers and letters.

```
┌─[······1······2······3······4······5···]······7···─┐
│ Swimming Pool Rules:¶                               │
│ ¶                                                    │
│ 1 Guests Must Sign in at the Front Desk¶            │
│ ¶                                                    │
│ 3 No Street Shoes on Deck¶                          │
│ ¶                                                    │
│ 6 No Radios¶                                        │
│ ¶                                                    │
│ 9 The Swimming Pool Is Open Daily from 12:00 P.M. to 8:00
│ P.M.¶                                               │
│ ¶                                                    │
│ 5 No Horseplay, Spitting or Offensive Language¶     │
│ ¶                                                    │
│ 4 No Running¶                                       │
│ ¶                                                    │
│ 7 No Diving at Shallow End¶                         │
│ ¶                                                    │
│ 2 Children Under 12 Must Be Accompanied by an Adult Unless↓
│   They Pass a Swim Test    ¶                        │
│ ¶                                                    │
│ 8 Adult Swim Is from 6:00 P.M. to 8:00 P.M.▮        │
└·····················································RULES.SWM─┘
```

2126 characters

Numbers by which the
paragraphs will be sorted

26-4 Paragraphs can be sorted by placing a number before each paragraph.

```
┌─[······1······2······3······4······5···]······7···─┐
│ Swimming Pool Rules:¶                               │
│ ¶                                                    │
│ 1 Guests Must Sign in at the Front Desk¶            │
│ ¶                                                    │
│ 2 Children Under 12 Must Be Accompanied by an Adult Unless↓
│   They Pass a Swim Test    ¶                        │
│ ¶                                                    │
│ 3 No Street Shoes on Deck¶                          │
│ ¶                                                    │
│ 4 No Running¶                                       │
│ ¶                                                    │
│ 5 No Horseplay, Spitting or Offensive Language¶     │
│ ¶                                                    │
│ 6 No Radios¶                                        │
│ ¶                                                    │
│ 7 No Diving at Shallow End¶                         │
│ ¶                                                    │
│ 8  Adult Swim Is from 6:00 P.M. to 8:00 P.M.¶       │
│ ¶                                                    │
│ 9 The Swimming Pool Is Open Daily from 12:00 P.M. to 8:00
│ P.M.¶                                               │
│ ♦                                                    │
└─────────────────────────────────────────RULES.SWM─┘
Pg1 Li95 Co1    {.}                       Microsoft Word
```

26-5 The document after the number has been sorted. Compare with Fig. 26-4.

CHAPTER 27

Mathmetical calculations

Word allows you to perform basic mathematical calculations on numbers in a document. Word's built-in calculator adds, subtracts, multiplies, divides, and computes percentages. Word uses the following symbols:

+ (or no symbol)	Addition
− (or parentheses)	Subtraction
*	Multiplication
/	Division
%	Percent

The symbols are used with numbers to form equations. If an equation does not contain a symbol, Word assumes you intend to add numbers in the equation. Some examples of equations are as follows:

3+5
12*7
2-6⅜*10%
104 23 16

244 Mathematical calculations

99 ⅔
6·5 2 1

To calculate an equation, first highlight the complete equation, then press F2. Word computes the equation and places the answer in the scrap. You can then move the cursor to where you want the answer, press Ins. Figure 27-1 illustrates the steps required to calculate an equation in a document. Note that you can highlight text surrounding an equation and press F2 to calculate whether or not the text contains nothing but numbers. For instance, highlighting the entire previous sentence and pressing F2 yielded the answer 2, the sum off all the numbers in the sentence. Be careful of this, though. Obviously, it would be easy to include numbers you don't intend to be part of the calculation.

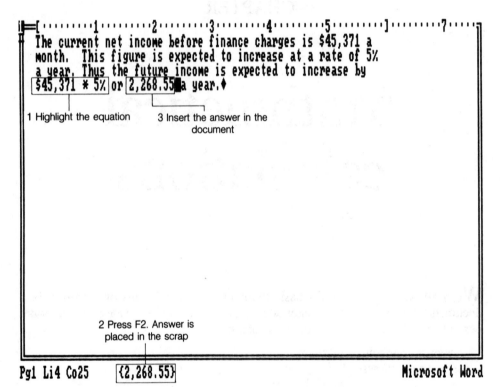

27-1   The F2 (Calculate) command calculates equations in a Word document and places the result in the scrap.

Word can compute a result that contains up to 14 digits. A longer answer generates an error message. Word will calculate equations with intermediate values over 14 digits in length; however, the result placed in the scrap is limited to 14 digits.

Columns

Columns of numbers can also be placed in equations and calculations can be performed on them (see Fig. 27-2). To calculate a column equation, follow these steps:

1. Press Shift-F6 to activate Column Selection and highlight the entire column of numbers and symbols with the direction keys.
2. press F2 to calculate the equation and place the answer in the scrap.
3. Move the cursor to where the answer should be inserted.
4. Press Ins to insert the answer into the document.

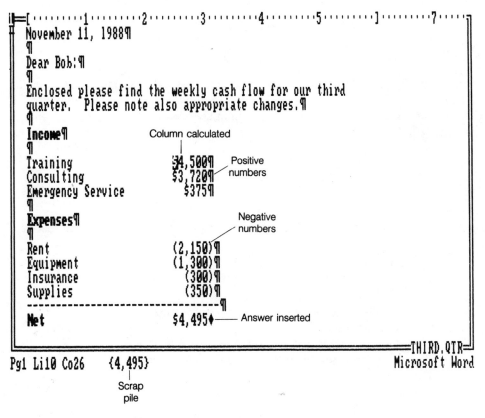

27-2 Columns can be added using the F2 (Calculate) command.

How Word performs calculations

Word uses a very intuitive approach to calculating equations. You should know about some special cases in case they are applicable to your work. Remember that if no symbol is used, Word adds the numbers in the equation.

Word performs calculations in this order: percentages, multiplication or division, addition or subtraction. You can use parentheses to change this order. You might find this confusing because earlier in the chapter, it was said that parentheses can be used to indicate negative numbers. Parentheses only mark a single number as negative. If more than one number is within parentheses, the numbers are treated as an expression and calculated first, ahead of percentages and multiplication/division. If more than one set of parentheses is placed around a single number, it is still considered negative.

Word calculates in floating-point arithmetic. Calculations on equations containing only integers produce results with two decimal places. The answer is expressed in the least possible decimal places without sacrificing accuracy, as shown:

$6/2 = 3$
$5/2 = 2.5$
$5/3 = 1.67$

If an equation contains numbers that are not integers, Word yields an answer equal in decimal places to the number in the equation with the most decimal places. If the answer requires more decimal places than are used in the equation, the answer is rounded:

$12.02/6.01 = 2.00$
$12.0200/6.01 = 2.0000$
$12.02/6 = 2.00$
$12.0200/6 = 2.0033$

Commas in numbers are retained in the answer. Dollar signs are not retained.

Summary

In this chapter, you learned:

- To calculate from numbers embedded in the text.
- To insert the results from the scrap.
- To calculate a column of figures.
- To use parentheses to indicate negative numbers or to prioritize calculations.
- To use decimal places and round numbers.

CHAPTER 28

Using outlines

Outlining brings back memories of high school English and mandatory reports. Regardless of how your teacher affected you, outlines are very effective for organizing your thoughts about a paper or speech. Word enables you to create outlines before you begin a document, as well as after you have begun one.

An outline begins with headings. Headings represent broad subjects and usually appear flush left (see Fig. 28-1). Often, headings actually appear in the document itself, such as the heading "Outlining" and "Editing headings" in this chapter. Subheadings further define and appear below their headings, but may or may not appear in the document. Headings and subheadings appear on different levels. Levels are indicated by the amount of indention given a heading, by the outline numbering scheme, and by the level indicated on the status line when in outline mode.

Body text appears below a heading or subheading and is text that (one hopes) pertains to the heading. Body text can be of any length, but is usually a brief paragraph or collection of paragraphs. Body text can be an expansion of the heading, an explanation of details, or any other form of text. If you begin with a document and switch to the outline mode, the entire document begins as body text. Body text can be converted to headings, and headings can be converted to body text. Figure 28-2 shows all the keys needed to work with outlines.

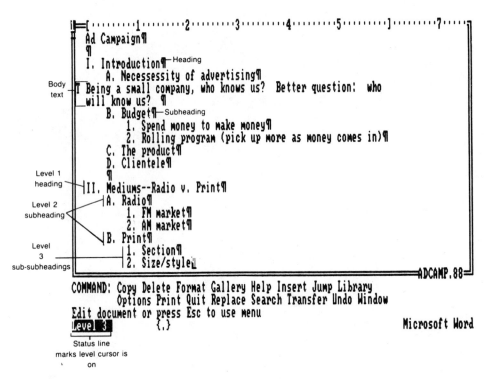

28-1 Outlines can be manipulated while in the outline organize (Shift-F5) or outline view (Shift-F7) modes.

Key	Function
Shift-F2	Switch to outline mode
Shift-F5	Outline mode to organize mode
Alt-0	Lower heading level
Alt-9	Raise heading level
Alt-P	Create body text
− (on key pad)	Collapse headings
Shift-−	Collapse body text
+	Expand headings
Shift−+	Expand body text
*	Expand all headings below
Ctrl−+−#	Expand headings to specified level

28-2 A list of keys used to edit outlines.

Outlining

To enter the outline mode, press Shift−F2. Outline mode is on when the level of the current heading appears in the lower left corner of the screen. To exit outline mode, press Alt−F2 again.

To create a heading, press Shift-F2 to enter outline mode and type the heading. Press Return. To create subheadings or body text, you need to change levels. Alt-0 and Alt-9 change the level of a heading. Alt-0 lowers the level of a heading and increases the indention. Alt-9 raises the level and reduces the indention. The indention level is the most obvious visual cue telling you the level of the heading.

Adding headings and body text to outlines is very intuitive. To create new headings, move the cursor to the spot for the heading, type the new heading, and press Return (this same action applies to subheadings as well). Word lines that heading up with the heading immediately above it. If necessary, use Alt-9 and Alt-0 to change the level of the heading. IF you insert the heading in body text, Word also considers it body text. If Word interprets your new heading as body text, press Alt-9 to convert it to a heading.

To add body text, move the cursor to the end of the heading under which the body text should appear and press Return. Then press Alt-P. This addition differentiates body text from the heading. A T appears in the left margin to remind you that this is body text. Now type your text.

Word only allows a certain sequence of levels. Pressing Alt-9 repeatedly makes the heading the highest level possible. Pressing Alt-0 repeatedly will make the heading the lowest level possible. Word usually makes the heading the appropriate level automatically. For example, suppose part of your outline looks like Fig. 28-3. Word does not permit you to change "Townhouses" from a level 4 heading to a level heading because "Dorms," which immediately precedes it, is level 3. Similarly, Word does not allow you to change "On Campus" from level 2 to level 1 because the heading immediately after it is level 3, "Dorms." Thus, if you wanted to change the level of "On Campus," you must edit other portions of the outline.

```
              I. Housing
                  A. On Campus
                      1. Dorms
                          a) Townhouses
                          b) Co-operatives
                  B. Off Campus
```

28-3 An example of permissible outline levels.

Numbering headings and paragraphs

Because most outlines contain numbers, Word automatically numbers an outline (see Fig. 28-1). Pressing Esc, L, N, and hitting Return gets Library Number Update which automatically numbers the outline. If the outline is new, the command adds numbers to all the headings. If the outline has been edited, the command updates the numbering. Outline numbers can be removed by pressing Esc, L, N, R, and hitting Return for the Library Number Remove command.

Word uses upper- and lowercase Roman numerals (I, II, III or i, ii, iii), upper- and lowercase letters, Arabic numerals (1, 2, 3), and legal numbers (1.1, 1.2, 1.3). Figure 28-4 shows the default formats for each level in an outline. Note that levels 7

250 *Using outlines*

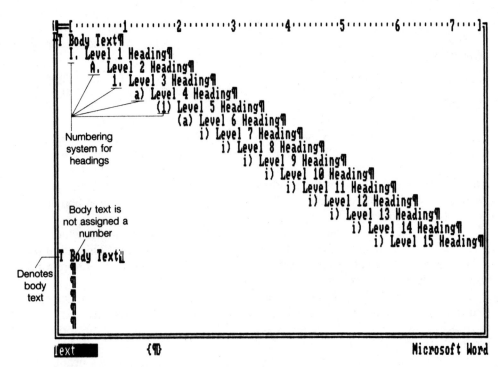

28-4 Word allows more heading levels than you will ever need. The first seven levels use different formats.

and greater all use lowercase Roman numerals. The numbering format Word uses can be changed by typing the numeral or letter format you want at the first heading in that level. Then, press Esc, L, N, and hit Return.

For example, suppose you want to change the numbering of level 4 from lowercase letters to lowercase Roman numerals. Move to the first level 4 heading in the outline and type i. at the front of the heading. To renumber the outline then press Esc, L, N, and hit Return.

For those who want practice, try creating the example in Fig. 28-1. To begin, press Shift-F2 to enter outline mode. Now type Ad Campaign and press Return twice. You've typed your first heading, which appears at level 1. Type Introduction to enter your second heading. Press Return once more and press Alt-0 to lower the cursor one level. Type the subheading Necessity of advertising. The screen should now match Fig. 28-4. According to the bottom of your screen, you are now at level 2.

Continuing with the example, press Return and Alt-P to create space for body text. Type in the body text shown in Fig. 28-1. Press Return and Alt-9 to exit the body text and return to level 2 for your next subheading. Continue until you complete the outline in Fig. 28-1 (or use your own). To complete the outline, press Esc, L, N, and hit Return to number the headings. Use this example to practice editing, renumbering, and/or collapsing and expanding.

Editing headings

Outlines can be edited using the same keys that were used to edit documents, or outlines can be edited in the more powerful and slightly more complex *organize* mode. Organize mode allows you to jump between headings on the same level. By skipping over body text and subheadings, organize mode enables you to find, delete, insert, copy, and even sort headings more quickly than any other method.

```
╔═[·········1·········2·········3·········4·········5·········]·········7····╗
║ Ad Campaign¶                                                               ║
║ ¶                                                                          ║
║ Introduction¶                                                              ║
║     Necessity of Advertising¶                                              ║
║ ◆                                                                          ║
║                                                                            ║
║                                                                            ║
║                                                                            ║
║                                                                            ║
║                                                                            ║
║                                                                            ║
║                                                                            ║
╚════════════════════════════════════════════════════════════════════════════╝
 Level 2            {}                                         Microsoft Word
```

28-5 The practice document for the chapter.

To enter organize mode, press Shift–F5. As soon as you enter organize mode, Word automatically highlights a heading. Organize appears at the bottom left of your screen when the organize mode is on. To exit from the organize mode and return to outline, press Shift–F5 again.

When organize mode is on, the direction keys help you move from heading to heading. Figure 28-6 shows how the direction keys perform when the organize mode is on. Once you highlight a section using these keys, you can perform the usual editing commands: delete, insert, copy, formatting characters, sorting, and other tasks.

Key	Function
Up, Down	Previous and next heading, stays on same level
Left, Right	Previous and next heading, regardless of level
Home	Previous heading at next higher level
End	Last subheading at next lower level
F6	Activates extend selection mode and highlights all subheadings and body text below heading
F6 and Down	All headings at same level

28-6 The keys used to move the cursor and select text when the outline organize mode is on.

Collapsing and expanding

Collapsing and expanding help you to look at the basic structure of your outline. They allow you to reduce (collapse) sections to just one heading, minus subheadings and body text. Similarly, the entire outline can be reduced (collapsed) to any desired level of headings (see Fig. 28-7). A collapsed portion is restored when it is expanded.

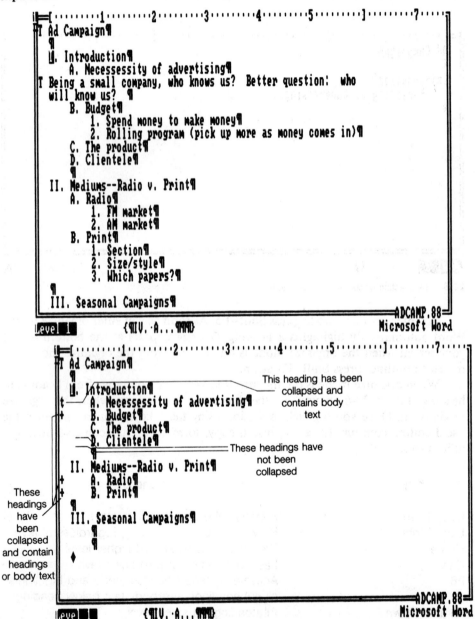

28-7 Outlines can be collapsed or expanded to help you review an outline and its contents.

The Minus and Shift-Minus keys collapse headings. The Plus, Shift-Plus, and Multiply keys expand headings. The Minus key appears on the numeric keypad and must not be confused with the Dash key. The Plus key also appears on the numeric keypad and should not be confused with the Plus-Equals key on the normal keyboard. The Multiply key is the asterisk key on the numeric keypad. If you press the wrong key, a minus, plus, or multiplication sign is typed into the text.

To collapse all subheadings and body text below a heading, move the cursor to that heading and press the Minus key. To collapse only the body text directly below a heading, move the cursor to that heading and press Shift-Minus. A plus sign or lowercase t appears before a heading that has been collapsed. The plus sign reminds you that the heading contains undisplayed subheadings or body text. The lowercase t indicates that the heading contains collapsed body text.

Expanding a collapsed heading displays subheadings and body texts that appear below the heading. To expand a collapsed heading, press Plus. Pressing Plus only retrieves subheadings in the next level below the heading. If you need to expand a series of all levels under a heading, press Multiply. To expand only a piece of body text directly below a heading, press Shift-Plus.

The Ctrl-Plus key combination enables you to expand or collapse all headings in a document to any level between 1 and 7. To perform this global expansion or contraction, press Ctrl-Plus. Word prompts you to enter a number between 1 and 7. Now type the number of the level you want displayed. Word displays all headings within that level or a higher level (a higher level has a lower level number). Ctrl-Plus collapses headings and body text, but only expands headings.

A selection of an outline can be collapsed or expanded by highlighting that section of the outline and then pressing Minus, Shift-Minus, Plus, Shift-Plus, or Multiply. Keys like F6 and Shift-F10 can be useful in highlighting sections. This method is especially useful for expanding the body text in a section. For example, if you wanted to expand the body text in the entire document, you would press Shift-F10, Shift-Plus.

Converting an existing document to an outline

Another approach to outlining is to convert an existing document into outline form. Depending on how large your file is, this conversion might end up being a lot of work, but it might prove useful. Outline mode can help break text down into workable parts, while organize mode can help you edit quickly.

Press Shift-F2 to enter outline mode. Until you assign levels, the entire file is marked as body text. If you make the first paragraph a heading, subsequent paragraphs will remain body text. Continue to assign levels in outline mode, then switch to organize mode for easy editing.

Moving through your text while in organize mode is extremely fast. Once you have assigned levels, you can collapse everything to a specified level. For example, press Ctrl-Plus-1 to show only those headings at level 1. Your text then looks like a simple outline. Now you can jump from heading to heading and expand each heading individually to edit. Press Shift-F10 to highlight all headings, then press the Multiply key to expand all collapsed headings. Press Shift-Plus to expand all collapsed body text and return your file to its original (and possibly cluttered) state.

Using the outline style sheet

The outline style sheet included in the Word software package contains a number of special formats for outline headings. The Word outline style sheet assigns character formats as follows: level 1 and level 2 headings are boldface, level 3 headings are underlined, and level 4 headings are italicized. Chapters 16 and 17 explain in detail how to work with style sheets.

You can assign the default outline styles by carrying out the following steps:

1. Press Esc, F, S, and A for the Format Stylesheet Attach command.
2. If you do not have a hard disk, place the disk containing the outline style sheet in the B disk drive. The Word utility disk normally contains the outline style sheet.
3. Type outline and hit Return.

You can either modify the factory version of the OUTLINE.STY style sheet or you can write your own from scratch. Chapters 16 and 17 explain how to create style sheets.

Printing

Word prints an outline as it appears on your screen. Headings and body text are displayed on the screen are printed. Word does not print collapsed headings and body text, nor does it print symbols in the selection bar.

The F11 and F12 Keys

The larger keyboards are now equipped with F11 and F12 keys, which are very useful in editing an outline. F11 collapses a heading and Shift-F11 collapses body text. F12 expands a heading while Shift-F12 expands body text and Ctrl-F12 expands the whole outline.

Summary

After reading this chapter, you should be familiar with:

- Using Shift-F2 to enter outline mode.
- Entering and deleting headings and body text.
- Changing levels with Alt-9 and Alt-0.
- Using Alt-P and Alt-9 to convert headings into body text and body text into headings.
- Editing headings.

CHAPTER 29

The document retrieval system

The document retrieval system facilitates storing and retrieving Word document files. The document retrieval system displays a list of files within a given directory for your review (see Fig. 29-1). You can load any of the files displayed on the list.

The power of document retrieval is that you can instruct Word to display certain files, making it easier for you to locate a special file. For example, suppose you need a document and know that either Ralph or Lillian wrote it, but you cannot remember the name of the file. You could tell Word to display all the documents written by Ralph or Lillian and then search those documents manually until you found the appropriate one. Similarly, suppose you wanted to review all the files written before June 1990 that have the keyword "accounts" on the summary sheet. You could check each file by loading it and reading it to see if it were the correct file, or you could use the document retrieval system to bring up all the pre-June 1990 files that have "accounts" in the keyword field on the summary sheet.

In order to be able to harness the force of document retrieval, your must fill in the summary sheets when saving files. Chapters 6 and 15 show how to save files. In this chapter, you are taught how to enter information into a summary sheet when saving

```
Path: C:\X\BOOKS\WORD
C:\X\BOOKS\WORD\CODE1.DOC      C:\X\BOOKS\WORD\MTEST.DOC
C:\X\BOOKS\WORD\DUMMY.DOC      C:\X\BOOKS\WORD\PROMO.DOC
C:\X\BOOKS\WORD\EMPH.DOC       C:\X\BOOKS\WORD\RULER.DOC
C:\X\BOOKS\WORD\EMPH1.DOC      C:\X\BOOKS\WORD\RUNNHD.DOC
C:\X\BOOKS\WORD\EMPH2.DOC      C:\X\BOOKS\WORD\SCRAPSYM.DOC
C:\X\BOOKS\WORD\EMPH3.DOC      C:\X\BOOKS\WORD\SCROLL.DOC
C:\X\BOOKS\WORD\ESTINCOM.DOC   C:\X\BOOKS\WORD\SPELTEST.DOC
C:\X\BOOKS\WORD\FIG7-1.DOC     C:\X\BOOKS\WORD\TABS1.DOC
C:\X\BOOKS\WORD\FONT1.DOC      C:\X\BOOKS\WORD\TABS2.DOC
C:\X\BOOKS\WORD\FONT2.DOC      C:\X\BOOKS\WORD\TABS3.DOC
C:\X\BOOKS\WORD\LES.DOC        C:\X\BOOKS\WORD\TRIALFUN.DOC
C:\X\BOOKS\WORD\LESSON2.DOC    C:\X\BOOKS\WORD\USAGES.DOC
C:\X\BOOKS\WORD\LESSON3.DOC    C:\X\BOOKS\WORD\VARIANTS.DOC
C:\X\BOOKS\WORD\LESSON4.DOC


DOCUMENT-RETRIEVAL: Query Exit Load Print Update View Copy Delete

Press Spacebar to mark-unmark file, Ctrl+Spacebar to mark all, or Esc for menu
                                ?                           Microsoft Word
```

29-1 The Docment Retrieval menu and files in the current directory.

files. If you have not used summary sheets yet and want to use summary sheets with your existing documents, you can use the Update command on the document retrieval menu to enter new information and edit old information on summary sheets of existing documents.

Entering the document retrieval menu

The Library Document-retrieval command activates the document retrieval system. To start this utility, press Esc, L, and D. Figure 29-1 shows the document retrieval menu. While in this menu, you can load a document, print summary sheet statistics, or search for a document using summary sheet information.

When in the document retrieval system, press Esc to toggle between the menu and the list of documents. You can always select a command from the menu simply by pressing the key corresponding to the first letter of the command. If you want to select a file from the list and the cursor is on the menu, press Esc and the cursor returns to the list.

The Exit command returns you to editing the document. Use Exit to leave the document retrieval system.

Loading documents

Once in the document retrieval system, documents are easy to load. Simply select the document to load by using the arrow keys to move the selection to the file and then pressing Esc, then L for the Load command, moving the cursor with the arrow

Entering the document retrieval menu 257

key. Word displays the menu in Fig. 29-2. If you want to designate the file as a read-only file, change the read-only setting. Finally, press Return to load the file. Note that if you knew the name of the file you wanted to load, you could always have loaded the file with the Transfer Load command.

```
Path: C:\WORD4\
C:\WORD4\123LET.DOC              C:\WORD4\READHE.DOC
C:\WORD4\2ARNLD2.DOC             C:\WORD4\REPORT.DOC
C:\WORD4\2ARNOLD.DOC             C:\WORD4\RESUME.DOC
C:\WORD4\6FAMILY.DOC             C:\WORD4\RIGHTS.DOC
C:\WORD4\BULFINCH.DOC            C:\WORD4\RIVRSIDE.DOC
C:\WORD4\COMPTRAD.DOC            C:\WORD4\SPELTEST.DOC
C:\WORD4\CS145FIG.DOC            C:\WORD4\SPELVER4.DOC
C:\WORD4\DEC-RIV.DOC             C:\WORD4\SUPPORT.DOC
C:\WORD4\DEHAN.DOC               C:\WORD4\TARIFFS.DOC
C:\WORD4\EC980.DOC               C:\WORD4\TCW-CON.DOC
C:\WORD4\ESTINCOM.DOC            C:\WORD4\TEST.DOC
C:\WORD4\EXAMPLE.DOC             C:\WORD4\TEST1.DOC
C:\WORD4\KARATE.DOC              C:\WORD4\THO.DOC
C:\WORD4\LESSON.DOC              C:\WORD4\THO2.DOC
C:\WORD4\LESSON2.DOC             C:\WORD4\TRAFFIC.DOC
C:\WORD4\MATHISRL.DOC            C:\WORD4\TRASH.DOC
C:\WORD4\ORDERREC.DOC            C:\WORD4\TREES.DOC
C:\WORD4\PRACTICE.DOC            C:\WORD4\TYPOS.DOC
C:\WORD4\PROJSALE.DOC            C:\WORD4\WATERSDE.DOC

LOAD filename: C:\WORD4\123LET.DOC            read only: Yes(No)

Enter full filename or press F1 to select from list
DOCUMENT-RETRIEVAL                                       Microsoft Word
```

The highlighted document appears in the menu

29-2 Documents can be retrieved from the data disk by the document Retrieval command.

Printing summary sheets and selected documents

Word prints summary sheets, documents, or both, for files displayed in the document retrieval screen. Documents can also be printed using the Print commands in the Edit menu. The document retrieval system, however, is best at printing groups of files that are related by certain information in the summary sheets. For example, if you wanted to print all the documents written in the year 1990 by Carolyn, you would use the document retrieval system to make a list of all those documents and then select the Print command on the Document retrieval menu.

To print a document or summary sheet from the document retrieval screen, follow these steps:

1. Highlight the name of the file you want to print.
2. Select the Print command.
3. Select either Summary, Document, or Both to print the summary sheet only, the document only, or both the summary sheet and the document.

4. Choose Selection under the option Range.
5. Press Return.

If you want to print summary sheets and/or documents for a group of files, you must do the following:

1. Use the Query command to list the files you want to print.
2. Select the Print command.
3. Select either Summary, Document, or Both.
4. Choose All under the option Range.
5. Press Return.

Note that this sequence of commands prints information from all the documents displayed, so it is best to be careful with the Query command and select only those files that should be printed.

When printing, Word tries to fit each summary sheet heading on one line. If there isn't room, Word indents and continues on the next line. Word does not split summary sheet information between pages.

You can print summary sheets with the Print commands in the Edit menu. If you want to print a summary sheet when you print a file, press Esc, P, and O to enter the Print Options menu. Then select Yes under summary sheet. Word continues to print a summary sheet with each document until you change the summary sheet setting on the Print Options menu to No.

Entering and editing summary sheets

The Query command lists files according to information in their summary sheets. Thus, if you intend to use the document retrieval system, you must fill in the summary sheets when you save files and update the summary sheets when necessary. Figure 29-3 shows a summary sheet.

When Word saves a file, it checks if it is a new file. If the file is new, Word displays a new summary sheet, allowing you to enter information such as the author and a keyword. If you press Esc, Word leaves the summary sheet blank.

Summary sheets for existing files can be modified at any time with the Library Document-retrieval Update command. To use the Update command, enter the document retrieval system and bring up a list of files. Highlight the file you wish to update. Select the Update command. The summary sheet for the highlighted file appears at the bottom of the screen. Enter the summary sheet information, pressing Tab to move between fields. When the summary sheet has been appropriately modified, press Return.

Word automatically creates a summary sheet when saving a new file unless you turn off the option in the Options menu (see Chapter 13). The default condition is to create the summary sheet with each file. Word automatically enters the creation date when you open a file and a revision date each time you revise it.

Each field in the summary sheet should contain certain specific information. The author field contains the name of the writer of the document. The operator field contains a second name, such as the name of the editor, or reviser, of the document. The operator and author fields can each contain one or more names.

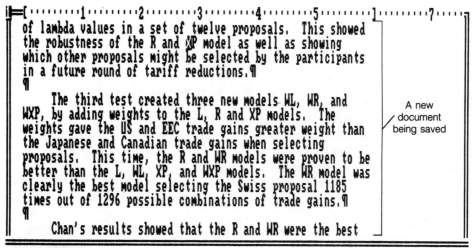

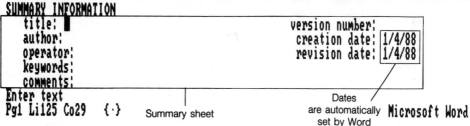

29-3 The information in the summary sheet is used by the Document Retrieval system to find certain document files.

The creation date and revision date are automatically entered by Word, but can be set manually. The title, version number, and comments fields contain the title, version number, and comments about the document.

The keyword field contains keywords pertaining to the document. Keywords for a paper on computer manufacturing might include chips, PC, circuit boards, IBM, and microprocessors. When searching documents using Query command's keyword field, simply enter one or more keywords. Query will select those documents that have keywords matching the ones specified in the Query summary sheet.

It is not necessary to enter information in each field. Enter information in only the fields that will be used to find the document or provide a summary of it.

Each field in the summary has a limit to the number of characters it can store. Word does not allow you to enter more characters than it can handle, but for those who want to know the limits, they are listed below:

title:	40
author:	40
operator:	40
keywords:	80

comments: 220
creation date: 8
revision date: 8
version number: 10

Selecting files with the Query command

The Query command controls which files appear in the list of files on the document retrieval screen. The Query command allows you to specify which files are listed by entering information into a special summary sheet connected to the Query command. For example, you can list documents written by Amy, Ron, or Laura. You could also list all the files written after 5/1/88 and before 11/1/88. If you wanted to be extremely precise, you could even search for all the files written by Amy or Ron between 5/1/88 and 11/1/88.

The process of searching for files is very similar to the process of searching for text with the Search and Replace commands. If you understand the Search and Replace commands (covered in Chapter 11), you should have an easy time understanding the Query selection process.

Searching for files with the Query command can be annoyingly time consuming. The search time depends on the number of files in the directory, the complexity of the search specified in the special summary sheet, and, of course, the speed of the equipment.

To search for files with the Query command, select the Query command from the Library Document-retrieval menu. The Query summary sheet appears at the bottom of the screen. Fill in the summary sheet using Tab to move from field to field. It is not necessary to fill the entire summary sheet: simply fill in the fields that will be used in the search and leave the remaining fields blank. When the summary sheet has been completed, press Return. After some careful searching, Word displays the list of files found by the Query command. A brief explanation of the important fields follows.

Query path

The Query path tells Word which directories and files to search for documents. Possible paths include C:\DIRECTORY\, which would list document files in a directory; C:\DIRECTORY*.*, which has the same action; and C:\DIRECTORY*.SFC, which lists all the files with the .SFC extension in the directory.

Author, operator, and keyword

Entries in the author, operator, and keywords fields can be quite lengthy. Unlike entries in the usual summary sheet, these fields can contain up to 80 characters each, including operators and multiple names. Figure 29-4 shows how AND and OR criteria can be used to select documents with multiple authors, operators, or keywords. For example, the phrase stocks&bonds in the keywords field accepts documents that contain both stocks and bonds as keywords. Likewise, the phrase GNP,budget in the document text field finds all the documents that contain the word

Character	Denotes
,	Or: Amy, Ron, Laura means: Amy or Ron or Laura
& or space	And: Amy & Ron means: Amy and Ron
~	Not: ~Ron means: not Ron (anyone but Ron)
?	Any single character: R?n means: Ron, Ran, Run . . .
*	Any number of characters: R*n means: Ron, Rain . . .
< (with dates)	Less Than: <5/1/88 means: before this date
> (with dates)	Greater Than: >5/1/88 means: after this date

29-4 Characters used to define rules for selecting documents with the document retrieval system.

GNP or the word budget anywhere in the document. This search can take some time to process.

Parentheses can further define a search. Items in parentheses are executed first. For example, the line Amy(Ron,Laura) instructs Word to search for Amy and (Ron or Laura) or files written by Amy and Ron or by Amy and Laura. Note that this criteria is very different from (Amy&Ron),Laura, which retrieves documents written by Amy and Ron or written by Laura.

Quotation marks are used to differentiate the characters from those found in filenames. For example, "Carter, Amy" means to search for the character string Carter, Amy. It does not mean search for documents written by Amy or Carter. Similarly, "Amy & Ron"&"Laura,Ashley" means search for documents written by Amy & Ron and Laura,Ashley.

Double quotation marks are necessary when quotations are used in a title. For example, """"Laura's"""" means "Laura's". A caret (^) is used to specify question marks or asterisks within a search. For example, Amy^? means you are looking for Amy?. Double carets are needed to search for a caret (^^).

Creation date and revision date

The creation date and revision date are used to search for document begun and revised on or relative to a specific date. These fields can contain up to 25 characters.

The characters < and > mean *before* and *after* in a document search. Thus, 12/10/90 means after 12 December 1990. Similarly, >11/15/87&<11/30/87 means to search for documents after 15 November and before 30 November 1987 (that is, documents created between 11/15/87 and 11/30/87).

Document text

The document text field specifies a special text string that must appear in a document. Word searches the entire document for this phrase, which can take a considerable amount of time. Up to 80 characters can be entered in this field. Word searches entire documents for the string in this field. This can be a time-consuming search. The characters in Fig. 29-4 can be included in the field in the summary sheet. Remember that text with quotation marks must be typed with double quotation marks. Thus Ron and Amy said Laura was "the best cook." must be written "Ron and Amy said Laura was ""the best cook."""

Case

The case field determines whether the case of the query string must be taken into account when searching for the matching string.

Changing the arrangement of the document list

The View command controls the amount of information displayed for each file in the list. The View command also controls whether the list is sorted by filename, author, creation date, or some other parameter. Normally, Word sorts the files by filename and displays only the filename. This type of display is called the *short* display.

The View command offers three types of views of files: short, long, and full. *Short* displays the filename only, as stated. This is the standard setting. *Long* displays the filename and two additional items from the summary sheet (such as the author and title or creation date and title). *Full* displays a list of filenames and the summary sheet of the file whose name is highlighted on the list. When the list is too long to be displayed on one screen, the arrow keys can be used to scroll the list.

The View command Sort by: option enables you to sort the directory list by directory (filename), author, operator, revision date, creation date, or size. To change the sorting criteria, choose the appropriate setting for the Sort by: option. Normally, View uses the Directory setting, causing files to be displayed in alphabetical order.

Summary

After reading this chapter, you should be familiar with the document retrieval system and be able to perform these tasks:

- Load a document from the document retrieval system.
- Update a summary sheet.
- Print a summary sheet.
- Use the Query command to display selected files in the document retrieval system.
- Change the information displayed in the document retrieval system.

30
CHAPTER

Indexes and tables of contents

No lengthy document is complete without a table of contents and/or an index. Word uses similar principles for both, so they are combined into this single chapter. Each section covers tables before indexes. The section on indexes refers you frequently to the section on tables, because the concepts are similar.

Before you can create either a table of contents or an index, you must alert Word to the material you want placed in them. Specific codes are used to denote this material. These codes are entered into your document in hidden character format, so they do not appear in the final draft and so that Word can distinguish the codes from normal text. Once the appropriate codes have been entered, a brief command tells Word to compile all the information. Word can create both tables and indexes from an outline or text.

Format adjustments for tables and indexes fall under the Library Table and Library Index commands, respectively. The Library Table command adjusts such things as page numbers and use of a style sheet. The Library Index command makes the same format adjustments with minor differences. Both commands can be used before, during, or after a table of contents or index is made.

Entries for tables of contents

To create a table of contents from text, you must use table codes. Table codes mark the text you want in your table of contents. This marked text is called an *entry*. You place a code before an entry and an endmark after an entry (see Fig. 30-1). The code for a table of contents is .c. (a "c" preceded and followed by a period).

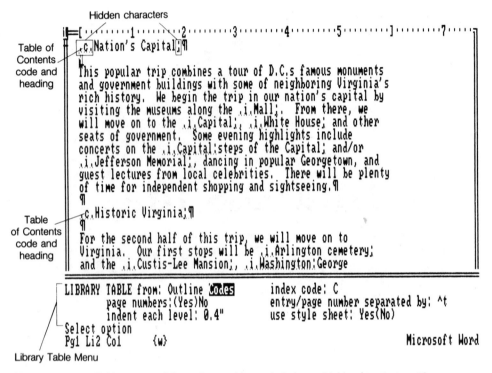

30-1 The Library Table menu and the codes used to create index and table of contents entries.

Using hidden text

Word requires the table codes to be entered in hidden character format so Word can distinguish then from normal text. Furthermore, you want to use hidden character format because hidden material can be made to appear on the screen, and turned off so it will not be printed.

Any portion of the entry can be made hidden text as long as the code is hidden text. The portion of the entry that is hidden text does not have to be printed. Thus, the table of contents entries do not have to correspond with titles in the document (although you usually want to use the titles as entries).

Obviously, you want to show hidden text while writing so you can see your headings. Be sure to turn off the hidden text later to avoid printing the codes. The steps to display hidden text while editing are as follows:

1. Press Esc then O for Options.
2. Select Yes under the show hidden text setting.

Now hidden characters are displayed. A dotted underline (or an underline, if you are working in text-mode) denotes hidden text. The steps to turn off printing of hidden text are as follows:

1. Press Esc, P, and O for Print Options.
2. Select No under the hidden text setting.

Entering a table code

The steps to enter a table code are:

1. Move the cursor with the arrow keys to the first letter of the word you want entered into the table.
2. Press Alt-E for hidden text (or Alt-X then E, if you are using a style sheet that uses Alt-E to install a style).
3. Type the code .c. before the entry.
4. Type one to four colons to indicate entry level, if the entry is a subentry.
5. Move to the space after the entry.
6. Type a semicolon, a Return, or a Ctrl-Return at the end of the entry.
7. If you used a semicolon and want to make the semicolon hidden text, do so.

If you want to create subentries, you must place a colon after the code .c. and before the entry. For example, if you wanted two entries to appear as follows:

News

    Television

You need to tell Word to indent the subentry Television one level. The table codes to do this are as follows:

    .c.News;

    .c.:Television;

For each level you want indented, type a colon. You can indent up to four levels. If you want an entry indented all four levels, type the following:

    .c.::::entry;

Including punctuation in entries

If you want to include additional punctuation in your entry, such as colons, semicolons, or even quotations marks, you need to enclose the entire entry in quotation marks. For example, the entry News: Domestic and International should appear as follows:

    .c."News: Domestic and International";

Quotation marks within an entry require double marks. For example, the entry News: "Domestic" and International should be written as follows:

.c."News: ""Domestic""" and International";

Also remember that colons are entered before the entire line of subentries. The previous entry is a second level subheading would appear like this:

.c.::"News: ""Domestic""" and International";

If you do not want a page number at the end of a specific entry, type a colon after the entry and before the semicolon. For example, consider the following entry:

.c.News:;

It causes News to appear as a heading with no page number as a reference. To review, here is a table of contents entry that combines the above instructions:

.c.:"News: ""Domestic""" and International":;

The colon in front means this entry is indented one level. The quotation marks are necessary to include punctuation; that is, the colon after the word News. The double set of quotation marks are necessary in order for Domestic to appear in quotation marks. Finally, the colon at the end means a number does not appear at the end of the entry in the table of contents.

A fast macro is available in the MACRO.GLY glossary file. Use the Transfer Glossary Load command to load the glossary. Then, simply highlight text to use in the table of contents and press Ctrl-T and then E. Word automatically enters the codes necessary to place the highlighted text in the table of contents.

Creating tables for illustrations and other tasks

You can create other kinds of tables, such as a table for illustrations or a table for chapter contents. The coding to create these tables is identical to the coding used to create the main table of contents except that the .c. code is replaced by some other letter. Word recognizes .c. as the code for the main table of contents, therefore you need to choose a different letter so Word can distinguish which entries go into which table. You cannot use the letters D, G, or L (these are reserved for linking documents, a graphics, and spreadsheets), or I (reserved for the index). You can use any other letters.

Suppose you wanted to create a table for illustrations. The table for illustrations contains the following entries:

GNP from 1950 to 1989 in the US

Savings Rates in Industrial Nations

The codes for these entries could be:

.f.GNP from 1950 to 1989 in the US;

.f.Savings Rates in Industrial Nations;

You need to use a separate code for each type of table in the document. Thus, if you had a table of contents, a table of figures, and a table of charts, you could use the codes .c., .f., and .t. When you compile a table, you must change the index code: setting of the Library Table command to match the code for the table entries (see the section on "Formatting Tables and Indexes" for details).

Creating a table of contents from an outline

You can create a table of contents from an outline very easily by first collapsing the outline to only those headings you want to appear in the table of contents (see Chapter 28). Then press Esc, L, and T to select the Library Table command and change the from option to the Outline setting. Set the remaining Table options. Finally, press Return to compile the table of contents.

Creating indexes

The essential difference between creating an index and a table of contents is the code. The index code .i. is typed before the entry. A semicolon is typed after the entry. You must enter the index codes in hidden character format so that Word recognizes the codes, and so that the codes can be displayed on the screen but not printed. The steps to make an index entry are as follows:

1. Move the cursor to the first letter of the word you wanted entered in the index.
2. Press Alt-E for hidden character format or Alt-X, E, if you are using a style sheet.
3. Type the code .i. before the entry.
4. Move to the space after the entry.
5. Type a semicolon, hit Return, or use Ctrl-Return at the end of the entry.
6. If you used a semicolon and want to make the semicolon hidden text, do so.

Thus a typical index entry would look like:

.i.Boston;

Entries, subentries, and punctuation

Type both entry and subentries on the same line. For example, to make Commercials an entry and Television a subentry, type the following:

.i.commercials:television;

Type internal punctuation directly in the entry. The following line:

.i.Commercials ¦ :"Endorsement";

is compiled as:

Commercials

  "Endorsement" 19

where 19 is the page number. As with a table, you can create index entries with or without page numbers. When you create subentries as in the example above, the subentry has a page number, but the entry does not. To create an entry and a subentry with a page number, type this:

.i.Commercials:

.i.Commercials ¦ :"Endorsement";

This is compiled as follows:

Commercials 17

   "Endorsement" 19

To create subentries without page numbers, type the entire entry on one line. For example, to create the following entry:

Commercials

   Television

      Early years 23

type:

.i.commercials:television:early years;

Sometimes you might want to include an entry in your index which does not appear exactly in your text. For example, your text might mention Personnel, but you might want to refer your reader to Administrative Services in your index. Although the original text does not make this reference, your entry should. Your entry should be:

.i.Personnel:See Administrative Services;

Similarly, if you wanted an entry that did not appear anywhere in the text, you could make up your own entry from scratch. Thus, if the text does not contain the word "consul," but refers to the concept, you could include an entry by typing the text .i.consul; in hidden text. You can place any portion of an entry in hidden character format, so if you do not want the entry to print, making it hidden and choosing not to print hidden text keeps it from being seen.

Compiling tables and indexes

Compiling means pulling something together. After you designate entries with character codes, you compile the table with the Library Table command by following these steps:

1. Press Esc, L, and T to select the Library Table command.
2. Set the from: option to Outline, if you are working from an outline, or Codes, if you are working from text.
3. Set the index code: to the letter corresponding to the code used in entries. The default letter for tables of contents is .c.

4. Set the remaining options.
5. Press Return to compile your table.

After the table has been compiled, Word places the results at the end of the document Word also places the codes .Begin Table C. and .End Table C. in hidden character format at the beginning and end of the table. Word uses these codes when recompiling the table of contents when the Library Table command is selected again. You can delete these codes or hide them by adjusting the Options show hidden text setting and the Print Options hidden text setting.

To compile a table that encompasses more than one file, you need to merge the additional files before you compile the table of contents. For example, if you are writing a book and each chapter is a separate file, you have to merge all the chapters before compiling the table of contents. To merge and compile, follow these steps:

1. Press Ctrl-PgDn to move to the end of the text.
2. Press Esc, T, and M for the Transfer Merge command.
3. Enter the name of the file to be merged.
4. Repeat steps 1 to 3 for each additional file.

Now all the files are merged into a single file. Compile the table as described previously.

To update an existing table, simply compile the table as described at the beginning of this section. Word asks if you want to replace the current table with a new table of contents. Type Y to replace the table, N to let the table stand, or Esc to cancel the operation.

Compiling an index

To compile an index:

1. Press Esc, L, and I for Library Index.
2. Make adjustments to the options.
3. Press Return to compile the index.

An index is arranged in alphabetical order. A table of contents arranges entries by page number. If you want an index arranged by page number, you can select the Library Table command, change the index code setting to .i. and press Return to process. This creates a table with all the index entries ordered by page number.

To create an index for more than one file, merge the other files with the Transfer Merge command as explained in the previous section. Then compile the entire file using the above steps. To update an existing index, compile the index with the Library Index command again, and replace the existing index with the new one.

Formatting tables and indexes

Formats can be adjusted either before or after you create a table or index. This section covers formatting for both tables and indexes because they are similar. The options on the Library Table and Index menus adjust the formatting for a table or an index.

To format a table or index, select the Library Table command or Library Index command. Adjust the format options on the Library Table or Library Index command. Adjust the format options on the Library Table or Library Index menu and press Return. If this is a new table or index, Word compiles it with all the set formats. If this is an update of an existing table or index, Word checks whether you want to replace the existing one with a new one. Choose Yes if you want Word to proceed and set up the new formats, otherwise, choose No.

The options under Library Table cover index codes, page numbers, separator characters, subentries, and style sheets (see Fig. 30-2). The index code tells Word about the table code. The normal table of contents code is .c., but as explained earlier, another letter, (other than .d., .g., .l., or .i.) can be used for different tables. Change this option to the appropriate code when compiling different kinds of tables.

The page numbers field determines whether page numbers are printed on pages at the right of entries. The default setting is Yes. Select No if you do not want the numbers in your table. Use the Format Division Page-numbers command to number the document pages containing the table of contents.

The entry/page # separated by: field sets what is between your entry and the page number. Word fills this space with a tab, but you can replace the tab with characters such as a series of periods (known as a *dot leader*), one or more spaces, or some other string of characters. Type in the new characters in place of the default ^t. If these characters do not appear on your screen, press Esc then O for options and select Partial or All under show non-printing characters.

The indent each level: field refers to subentries. A subentry is normally indented .4 inches to the right of the main entry. To change this indention, type a new measure in place of 0.4".

The use style sheet: field asks whether you are using a style sheet or not. Word assumes you are not. If you choose Yes under this field, Word ignores subentry indentions and uses the paragraph styles for tables or indexes in the style sheet.

Index

To adjust settings for an index, choose the Library Index command by pressing Esc, L, I (see Fig. 30-2). The entry/page # separated by:, indent each level:, and use style sheet: options are the same in both the Library Index and the Library Table menus, except that the Library Index normally indents subentries .2 inches.

The cap main entries: field automatically capitalizes the first letter of the index entry and leaves all other cases alone. If you select No, Word does not adjust capitalization.

Adding page numbers to an index

•The Format Division Page-numbers or Format Running head command can add page numbers to an index. An index is typically numbered with Arabic numerals, which continue the page number sequence used in the text itself.

Formatting tables and indexes 271

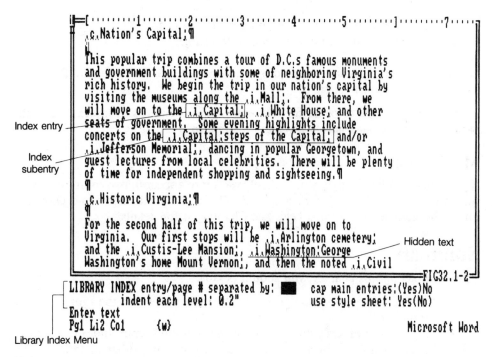

30-2 The Library Index menu can construct indexes for documents.

Adjusting the page number column and leader characters in tables

The default ^t setting under the entry/page # separated by field is set so that page numbers in a table appear in a column six inches from the left margin. You can change this distance and change the leader characters separating the entries and the page numbers with the Format Tab command. To make these changes, follow these steps:

1. Highlight the entire table of contents.
2. Press Esc, F, T, and R for Format Tab Reset-all.
3. Press Esc, F, T, and S for Format Tab Set.
4. Under Position:, type in the point where the page number column should appear.
5. Set the leader char: field.
6. Choose Right under the alignment: field.
7. Press Return.

Continuous and multiple page references

If you have an entry which refers to a series of pages, you can create a continuous page reference by simply entering two or more index entries. Similarly, you can create a reference to two or more pages by including two or more index entries. The steps to create a continuous entry are as follows:

1. Type your entry at the beginning of the subject.
2. Type the same entry at the end of the subject.
3. Compile your index.
4. The two pages are separated by a comma. Delete the comma in the index and insert a hyphen.

This denotes a range of pages for that entry. If you wanted to indicate separate pages, then you would simply leave the comma in the index.

Multiple columns in indexes

If your index is long enough, you probably want it to appear in two columns. To do this, press Esc, F, D, and L for the Format Division Layout menu and choose 2 under the number of columns field. See Chapter 14 for details.

Summary

After completing this chapter, you should be able:

- To generate tables of contents with the table codes and the Library Table command.
- To generate indexes with the index codes and the Library Index command.
- To assign hidden format to codes, semicolons, and other material in the document that should not be printed.
- To define entries and subentries for table and index entries.
- To create illustration tables, chapter tables of contents, and other document tables by using different table codes.
- To set the Library Table options.
- To set the Library Index options.

CHAPTER 31

Printing line numbers and revision marks

Legal document features include line numbers and revision marks. They can be useful in many other settings besides the law office. Figures 31-1 and 31-2 display uses of line numbers and revision marks.

Line numbers

The Format Division Line Numbers command allows you to print arabic line numbers in the margin of your text. The line numbers do not appear on your screen, but appear in a printout. To add line numbers for printing, follow these steps:

Printing line numbers and revision marks

```
╒═[·······1·······2·······3·······4·······5······]······7···╕
│ This form has been written to help you understand your
│ rights as a tenant living in a vacancy decontrolled housing
│ accommodation.  In some cases you may have somewhat
│ different rights than what are described here; if you have
│ any questions regarding your tenancy, please visit the Rent
│ Equity Board, City Hall, Room 505 or call us at 555-1324.
│
│ To determine if you live in a vacancy decontrolled unit call
│ the Renty Equity Board.  Units become vacancy decontrolled
│ after a rent-controlled tenant vacates voluntarily and the
│ landlord receives a Vacancy Decontrolled Certificate.  When
│ the unit is decontrolled the landlord may raise the rent,
│ subject to the tenants' grievance rights.  Once decontrolled
│ and totally vacated, the landlord may negotiate a new rent,
│ at any amount, with the incoming tenants.
│
│ A tenant living in a vacancy decontrolled unit has many
│ rights and protections; however, the tenant must file a
│ petition at the Rent Equity Board before the Board can ♦
╘═══════════════════════════════════════════════════RIGHTS.DOC═
FORMAT DIVISION LINE-NUMBERS: Yes No           from text: 0.4"
        restart at:(Page)Division Continuous    increments: 1
Select option
Pg1 Li10 Co56    {·}                           Microsoft Word
```

- Status line
- Line number cursor is on

```
 1    This form has been written to help you understand your
 2    rights as a tenant living in a vacancy decontrolled housing
 3    accommodation.  In some cases you may have somewhat
 4    different rights than what are described here; if you have
 5    any questions regarding your tenancy, please visit the Rent
 6    Equity Board, City Hall, Room 505 or call us at 555-1324.
 7
 8    To determine if you live in a vacancy decontrolled unit call
 9    the Renty Equity Board.  Units become vacancy decontrolled
10    after a rent-controlled tenant vacates voluntarily and the
11    landlord receives a Vacancy Decontrolled Certificate.  When
12    the unit is decontrolled the landlord may raise the rent,
13    subject to the tenants' grievance rights.  Once decontrolled
14    and totally vacated, the landlord may negotiate a new rent,
15    at any amount, with the incoming tenants.
16
17    A tenant living in a vacancy decontrolled unit has many
18    rights and protections; however, the tenant must file a
19    petition at the Rent Equity Board before the Board can
```

Line numbers in margin

31-1 The Format Division line-Numbers menu adds line numbers to a document. This feature is useful in legal documents.

1. Press Esc, F, D, and N for Format Division line-Numbers.
2. When the line-Numbers menu appears, select Yes.
3. After the settings on the menu are correct, press Return.

The three settings on the line-Numbers menu are from text:, restart at:, and increments:

Word automatically prints line numbers .4 inches from the left margin. You can adjust the position of the line numbers by entering a new number under the from text: field. The number must be smaller than the left margin for Word to print line numbers.

Word normally begins the line number count with 1 at the top of every new page. To change this procedure, use restart at: and either select Division to start the count with each new division, or select Continuous to number the lines consecutively throughout the document.

Line numbers are normally printed on each line. Word does not skip any lines when printing line numbers. Using the increments option on the Format Division line-Numbers menu can alter the frequency of line numbers: they can be placed at every fifth line, for instance, by entering 5 at this option.

Adding revision marks

Revision marks indicate deletions and insertions made to a document without altering the original text. Revision marks are extremely useful when you are working on a document with a group of people. The marks enable you to designate any alterations in the original document so the next person who reads the document can determine if the original text is better than the modified text.

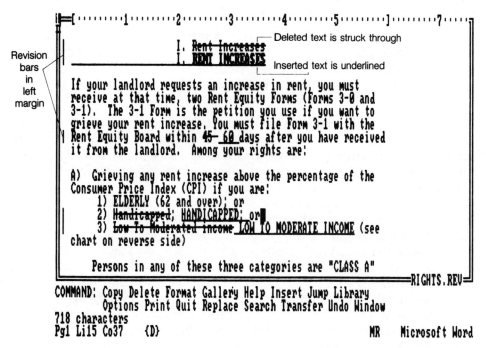

31-2 Revision marks can be placed in a document to indicate changes made. Revision marks are useful when several people are editing the same document.

```
                    I. Rent~Increases    ─Deleted text
_____I. RENT INCREASES ───Revised text            | Revision
                                                                   bars
If your landlord requests an increase in rent, you must            on
receive at that time, two Rent Equity Forms (Forms 3-0 and         right
3-1). The 3-1 Form is the petition you use if you want to          margin
grieve your rent increase. You must file Form 3-1 with the
Rent Equity Board within 45- 60 days after you have received     |
it from the landlord. Among your rights are:

A)   Grieving any rent increase above the percentage of the
Consumer Price Index (CPI) if you are:
     1) ELDERLY (62 and over); or
     2) Handicapped; HANDICAPPED; or                              |
     3) Low-To-Moderated-income LOW TO MODERATE INCOME (see
chart on reverse side).

     Persons in any of these three categories are "CLASS A"
Tenants.

31-2   Continued
```

When you use revision marks, Word designates text that was deleted in the editing process with the strikethrough character format. Text that is inserted is marked with underlining or some other user-defined character format. Additionally, Word places a vertical bar in the margins next to any line that contains inserted or deleted text. You can search for these revisions and print them to show changes from draft to draft. To include revision marks when editing a document, follow these steps:

1. Press Esc, F, M, and O for the Format revision-Marks Options menu.
2. Select Yes under add revision marks: to include revision marks in the document.
3. Set the inserted text: and revision bar position: options.
4. Press Return to see revision bars in the left margin.

The inserted text: and revision bar position: options control the place and style of revision marks. The revision bar position: option determines whether vertical lines are placed in the margins to show edited lines in the printout. Left, Right, and Alternate place vertical marks in the left column of the document window. When printing, the Left and Right options place revision marks in the left and right margins of the printout. The Alternate option causes Word to print the mark in the left margin of even-numbered pages and in the right margin of odd-numbered pages (thus placing them farthest from the binding of a bound document. The None setting is the default setting, which causes Word to forgo the use of the marks in the margins.

The inserted text option lets you choose the character format taken by inserted text to distinguish it from surrounding text. The default is underlining.

Word displays MR in the status line when you are using revision marks. You cannot use Overtype mode while in MR, You cannot backspace into old text, but the Del key works as usual.

Searching for revision marks and canceling revisions

The revision-Marks Search command finds and highlights the next occurrence of revised text in a revision-marked document. This is extremely useful when working with a lengthy document that contains widely separated revisions. To use the revision-Marks Search command, press Esc, F, M, and S. The Search command does not remove the revision-Marks menu, so a search can be repeated by pressing S again. Press Esc when you find the hunted revision, and you are ready to return to editing mode. The Shift-F4 (repeat last search) command can also be used to repeat a search for a revision mark.

To remove revision marks, first highlight the portion of the text from which to remove the revision marks. Then press Esc, F, M, and R for the Format revision-Marks Remove command. This command leaves the changes intact but removes the revision marks.

The Format revision-Marks Undo-revisions command removes the revisions made to a selection of text and restores the original text. When this command is selected, struck-through text is restored, new text is deleted, and revision marks are removed. To undo revisions, highlight the text whose revisions you wish to eradicate. Then press Esc, F, M, and U to trigger the Undo-revisions command.

Summary

By this point, you should know how to accomplish the following:

- Include line numbers in a printout.
- Place revision marks in a document.
- Remove, undo, and search for revision marks in a document.

CHAPTER 32

Macros

This chapter shows what macros look like, how to execute a macro, how to create a macro, and how to use the special macro commands. *Macros* are programs that you write to help perform repetitive and time-consuming tasks with Word. A macro program, like a typical document, contains a number of keystrokes. When a macro program is run, it gives Word a string of keystrokes to process just as if you typed those keystrokes at the keyboard. Thus, a macro can automatically give a prewritten list of commands to Word for processing as fast as possible.

Macro programs not only take the drudgery out of repetitive tasks, but they are also faster and more reliable than typing in the sequence of commands, because the macro program does not make mistakes.

For example, you could write a macro that deletes the next three words after the cursor. You could also write a macro that moves a line of text to the end of the document. More complex macros could be used to change the printer under the Printer Options menu, reassign the character fonts for the document, and then print the document (this is especially useful if you use two or more different printers). Similarly, you could write a macro to change the tab settings on the ruler line or change the settings on the Options menu. Because macros are best for helping with repetitive tasks, macros are most useful for those who use their word processor every day.

Macros are stored in glossary files. A familiarity with glossary files (Chapter 10) can help you learn macro programs. Note that style sheets are useful for setting formats for characters, paragraphs, and divisions. You can also use a macro to assign formats, but you should determine whether a macro or style sheet is better suited for your needs.

Running a macro

You will see how to run a macro by running one of the sample macros included with the Word 5.0 package. The macro 1-READING-FIRST describes some of the macros supplied with Word version 5.0. Use the Transfer Load Glossary to load MACRO.GLY, the glossary that contains all the prepared macros that came with your copy of Word. With no document loaded, or with an empty window active, click on Insert or press Esc and I and then F1 to see a list of available macros. Near the top of the list, you will see 1-README-FIRST. Use the mouse or cursor keys to highlight this macro and press Return. The macro prints on screen an explanation of the most popular macros. You would be wise to print out a copy of this document to use until the macros become second nature to you.

Before you run an unfamiliar macro, you should be sure to save your document file, because the macro might change your document in an unexpected way.

There are three ways to run a macro. Every macro can be run with the first two procedures. Only certain special macros can be run with the third procedure.

The first procedure is for use if you do not know the name of the macro and if you do not know its keypress, or if it does not have a keypress associated with it.

1. Move to the point in the document where you want the macro to begin.
2. Press Esc then I to select the Insert command.
3. Press F1 to view the list of available macros.
4. highlight the desired macro and press Return.

The second way to run a macro, if you already know the name of the macro, is by following these steps:

1. Move the cursor to the point in the document where you want the macro to begin.
2. Type in the name of the macro.
3. Press F3 (Expand glossary name).

The macro name is removed and the macro executed.

The third method is used if the macro has a keypress associated with it. Press Esc, I, F1, and look at the resulting list of macros. Many of them are followed by keypresses, such as <Ctrl-I>E. This means that you can run the macro simply by pressing Ctrl-I, E. Try it. Highlight a piece of text and enter the keypress. The computer automatically makes the highlighted text an index entry.

You can cancel a running macro at any time by pressing Esc.

For practice, run the macro called next_page.mac. As the name implies, this macro jumps to the next page. Press Esc, I, then F1 to list the items in the glossary MACRO.GLY. Use the arrow keys to highlight the command next_page.mac^<Ctrl J>N. Then press Return to execute the macro. If there is a next page in the document, the cursor jumps to that page. Try running the same macro with the F3 and Ctrl-J then N methods.

Creating macros by recording

Macros can be created by recording keystrokes or by writing the macros in Word and then placing them in a glossary. The recording method is the easiest and quickest method of creating macros. The writing method, however, must be used to create macros that use macro command words. Be sure to determine in which glossary file you intend to store a macro before creating a macro.

The recording method saves your keystrokes in a glossary buffer. Whatever you type is saved for the macro and processed as a command. If you are in the edit mode and type Esc then P, Word enters the Print menu and stores Esc and P in the glossary buffer. You should test the macro before attempting to record it, and you should test the macro on a test document so you do not accidentally delete some important information. You must be sure to anticipate every keystroke needed in the macro. For example, if you use the Transfer Load command, you must anticipate whether or not it is necessary to save the current document before the load command is executed.

Macros can be created with the recording method by following these steps:

1. Press Shift-F3 (Record macro) to begin recording the macro. RM appears on the status line while recording a macro.
2. Enter the commands and keystrokes as you would in a Word document. The commands and keystrokes are recorded.
3. Press Shift-F3 to halt recording. Word displays the message COPY to {}.
4. Type in the macro name.
5. If you want to include a macro control code, type a caret and then the code (for example, ^<Ctrl T>).
6. Press Return to store the macro in the current glossary.

The recording method is easy to use because it copies keystrokes from the keyboard. This method, however, also records any typographical errors, so it is difficult to use for long macros. The recording method also does not allow you to put macro command words in a macro. Usually a combination of the recording method and the writing method is best for writing long macros.

If you begin to record a macro and then make a mistake, you can cancel the recording process. After recording has begun, press Shift-F3 and then Esc to halt recording and not save the macro.

The macro name and macro control code

When you enter the macro name (step 4 above), you should pick a name that is not too long, but that describes the macro's function. A name that is short is quicker to type when running the macro. A name that is descriptive is easier to remember, enabling you to run it with the F3 function key.

The macro control code (step 5) provides a faster method for running a macro. When a control code is assigned to a macro, that macro can be run by simply typing in the control code. For example, if ^<Ctrl G> were type in, then the macro could be run by simply typing Ctrl-G. Word prevents you from assigning the same control code to more than one macro. The control code is optional, and step 5 can be skipped if you do not want to add a control code.

Practice recording a macro program

For practice, follow this example to create a macro to move a sentence to the end of the document. Enter a few sentences into an otherwise blank document and move to a sentence in the middle of the document when you record the macro. Press Shift-F3 to begin recording the macro. Now press Shift-F8, Del, Ctrl-PgDn, and Ins to move the sentence to the end of the document. Next, type Shift-F3 to halt recording of the macro. Finally, type movsent and hit Return to enter the macro name. The macro has been completed and placed in the glossary. Try running the macro now to test it.

Saving and retrieving macro programs

Macros are stored in glossary files. The Word software package includes several macro programs in the MACRO.GLY glossary file, but macros can be stored in any glossary.

When a macro is created, it is automatically placed in the glossary file in use. When you have finished creating macros, they are saved by pressing Esc, T, G, and S keys to select the Transfer Glossary Save command. The macros are thus saved with the glossary file. Therefore, you should load the glossary file in which you want to save the new macros before you create any macros. To load a fresh glossary file, use the Transfer Glossary Clear command to remove the current glossary file and then select the Transfer Glossary Merge command.

To retrieve a glossary containing macro programs, simply press Esc, T, G, and M keys to select the Transfer Glossary Merge command. Then, enter the name of the glossary file to be retrieved.

You can move a macro from one glossary to another by merging two glossary files together and saving the combined glossary file under an appropriate name.

Writing and editing macros

Fortunately, learning how to write macros is just as easy as learning how to record macros. Writing macros is more time-consuming than recording macros, however, because you must be doubly careful that the program you write does what you hope it will do. Writing macros, however, gives you the freedom to include comments, to edit macro programs, to condense some programs, and to add macro command names. These features are used extensively in long macro programs. To write a macro program, follow these steps:

1. Load a document into which the macro can be written.
2. Type in the macro program. Use the table in Appendix A to determine the names of the keys.
3. Highlight the completed macro program.

4. Press Esc, C, or Esc, D, to either copy or delete the macro from the document into the glossary.
5. Type in the name of the macro.
6. If you want to include a macro control code, type a caret and then the code (for example, ^<Ctrl T>).
7. Press Return to store the macro in the current glossary.

Entering key names

When writing a macro, you must type out the names of any special keys used in the macro. The key names are placed in brackets and are listed below. The macro that was used to move a sentence to the end of the document looks like this:

<shift f8><del><ctrl pgdn><ins

The code is the exact code you would have typed, had you used the writing method to construct the macro instead of the recording method.

For practice, enter a macro that assigns the boldface and underline format to the next four words. The macro is as follows:

<f8><f6><f8 3><alt b><alt u>

The first F8 highlights the current word. F6 activates the extended selection cursor. <F8 3> highlights the next three words (the equivalent of pressing F8 three times). A number can be placed after a key name to indicate repeated use of the key. Finally, <Alt B> assigns the bold format to the text and <Alt U> assigns the underline format.

Formatting single characters

Word does not allow you to format single characters with the direct formatting keys. The ability to format single characters is especially useful when working with footnotes. A macro can be written to enable you to format a single character quickly. The macro below assigns the superscript format to the character at the cursor but only works when the next character is the normal character format. To enter the macro, follow these steps:

1. Type in the macro: <f6><right><alt =><right><f6><left><alt space>.
2. Highlight the macro.
3. Press Esc then D to delete the macro.
4. Type super^<Ctrl S>.
5. Press Return to enter the macro.

By assigning a macro control code, you can invoke this macro program by simply pressing Ctrl-S.

Editing a macro

Macros can be edited by inserting a copy of the macro into a document, editing the macro, and then copying (or deleting) a copy of the edited macro back into the glossary via the scrap. The specific steps needed to edit a macro are as follows:

1. Move to a blank space in the document (preferably the end).
2. The appropriate glossary file must be loaded.
3. Press Esc, I, to select the Insert command.
4. Press F1 to list the current glossary buffers.
5. Highlight the glossary buffer containing the macro program and press ^, Return. The text of the macro is inserted into your document.
6. Edit the macro as you would edit text in a document.
7. Highlight the entire macro.
8. Press Esc, C, to select the Copy command.
9. Type in the name of the edited macro and press Return. If you use the same name as before, the old macro will be replaced by the edited macro.

An alternate and slightly faster method for inserting a macro into the document is to type the macro name followed by a caret and press F3. For example, typing movsent^<F3> would insert the macro text for the movement macro program. You can use this method instead of steps 3, 4, and 5 above to insert a macro into a document for editing purposes.

Testing and debugging macros

Although the macros you have been writing might seem simple, macros can be very complex, especially when you begin to use macro command words. Testing and debugging macros are facts of life. Macro testing consists of running the macro and observing what happens on the screen. You can run the program normally, or you can execute the macro one step at a time. Executing a program step-by-step is often the best way to debug it, because Word runs macros too quickly for you to see what is happening on the screen. Follow the directions given earlier to run a macro program normally.

To run a macro one step at a time, press Ctrl-F3. Word displays **ST** on the status line to indicate that step mode is turned on. Run the macro. Word performs the first step and pauses. Press any key (other than Esc or Ctrl-F3) to process the next step. Word pauses at the end of each step, waiting for you to press a key before continuing. If you want to cancel the macro at any time, press Esc. If you want to stop the step mode and run the macro at normal speed, press Ctrl-F3.

Macro debugging means reading over the macro program to check for errors. Proper comments and formatting of a macro program help you read and check for errors (see the next section for formatting instructions).

You can place the command Ctrl-F3 in a macro to activate and deactivate step mode. This technique is useful when you have a very large macro and know that the first half of the macro works and therefore only need to step through the second half of the macro.

Macro formatting and notes about macros

The following paragraphs hold some tips that might help you write long macros.

A space in a macro program is interpreted as a space keystroke. Thus, a space in a macro program causes a space to be inserted into the document or cause the menu cursor to move. Macro programs, however, ignore paragraph marks, newline characters, tab symbols, page breaks, and division breaks in the macro program. Thus, you can (and should) format your macro program by judiciously using tabs and paragraph breaks. Formatting makes it easier to read and understand macro programs, thereby facilitating the debugging process.

Mouse actions cannot be placed in macros.

Macros can be used to execute the Library Run command and run a DOS command. After the DOS command is run, the macro resumes at the appropriate place without displaying Press any key to resume Word.

Macros can also run the Spell, Thesaurus, and Learning Word programs. The macro runs one of these programs, but you must enter commands to control these programs when they are running by hand. When you exit the program, the macro resumes at the appropriate place.

Turning off the menu display

If you do not turn off the menu display, it flashes at the bottom of the screen as the macro program is executed. If you find this bothersome, use the menu setting on the Options menu to turn off the Word main menu display. The menu is always displayed when testing with the step mode, or when a Pause macro command is encountered.

The instructions to turn off the display of a menu can be inserted at the beginning of a macro program. The following line turns off the menu display:

<esc>o<up 6>n<enter>

And the following line can be placed at or near the end of the macro to turn the menu back on:

<esc>o<up 6>y<enter>

Autoexecuting macros

An autoexecuting macro is automatically run when the glossary file containing it is loaded. Each glossary file can contain one and only one autoexecuting macro. A macro is made an autoexecuting macro by giving it the name AUTOEXEC. Thus, if you have a glossary file called MANUSCRIPT, and it contains a macro program called AUTOEXEC, the macro runs automatically every time you load the glossary with the Transfer Glossary Merge command.

An autoexecuting macro can also be given a macro control code. The autoexecuting macro can be run at any time by the same method as other macros are run (that is, by entering the macro control code, typing AUTOEXEC and pressing F3 or using the Insert command).

The NORMAL.GLY glossary file is automatically loaded whenever you start Word. Therefore, if you put an autoexecuting macro in the NORMAL.GLY glossary file, the macro is run whenever you start Word.

Adding comments to a macro

Comments do not affect how a macro program runs. They can, however, explain what a particular macro does. Comments are useful when sharing a macro with another person because they can explain the macro's function. A comment can be placed between any two keystrokes in a program. More than one comment can be placed in a program. Comments can be created in two different manners, either

　　《COMMENT text》

or

　　《COMMENT》 text 《ENDCOMMENT》

The 《 and 》 characters are entered by pressing Ctrl-[and Ctrl-] respectively. Comments are actually a type of macro command. You will see the similarity between comments and other macro commands later.

Summary

Macros are so easy to run that even beginners can use them. Writing macros, however, requires much experience with Word. This chapter covered the following:

- What macros can do.
- How to run macros.
- How to write macros by recording keystrokes.
- How to write and edit macros by writing them in a document.
- How to enter key names in a macro.
- Saving and retrieving macros.
- Testing and debugging macro programs.
- Formatting and adding comments to macros.

CHAPTER 33

Macro instructions

A macro can contain instructions directing it to carry out complex tasks. Macro instructions are very similar to merge commands. The main difference is that macro instructions take place during the execution of a macro program. Macro instructions can only be entered when writing or editing a macro. Like merge commands, macro instructions are surrounded by chevrons (« and »), which are entered by pressing Ctrl-[and Ctrl-], respectively (or by typing Alt-174 and Alt-175).

The Ask instruction

The *Ask* instruction is used to obtain input from the user during the execution of a macro. It assigns the user's response to a variable specified in the instruction. This variable can be used as a counter or as part of a conditional statement. The Ask instruction is written in the following form:

«ask variable=?prompt»

When executed, the macro displays the prompt in the message line and assign the user's response to the variable. The Ask instruction could appear like this in a macro program:

<f8>

«ask response=?Do you want to delete this word (y/n)»

«if response ="y"»<del>

«endif»

In this example, the macro displays Do you want to delete this word (y/n) on the message line. The user types either Y and hit Return or N and hit Return, and that response is assigned to the variable response. The question mark is always required in the Ask command. A prompt such as Do you want to delete this word (y/n), on the other hand, is not necessary, but it is helpful.

The Ask instruction has some limits. It cannot be used within a menu. For example, if you were in the Format Division Margins menu, the Ask command could not be executed. There can be up to 64 different variables in a macro (including the variables in *nested* macros, or macros called by the running macro). Each variable name can be any combination of letters or numbers, but the variable must start with a letter. Underscores, hyphens, and periods are not allowed in variable names. Some examples of incorrect variable names are listed below:

2letter

letter_two

letter-two

letter.two

There are also different variable types. Responses in date format such as mm/dd/yy, where the separator is a slash, hyphen, or period, are treated as dates. Numbers are treated as such and all other responses are treated as text. Note that the Ask instruction does not calculate expressions such as 1+1, but treats a formula as if it were text.

The Comment-Endcomment instruction

The *Comment* and *Endcomment* instructions allow you to place nonexecuting code in your macro. In other words, when Word encounters the Comment instruction, it ceases operation, simply scanning the macro until it encounters the Endcomment instruction. What is the good of an instruction that doesn't do anything? It is for your convenience. If you are like most people, you might probably forget the purpose of a section of code shortly after writing it. Rather than risk spending precious minutes trying to figure out the purpose of a routine, place a comment in it:

«comment this routine changes the word "utilize" to the word "use" throughout a document»«endcomment»

The If-Else-Endif instruction

The *If* instruction is a conditional instruction that executes one set of commands if the condition is met and another set of commands if the condition is not met. The *If-Else-Endif* instruction is written in the following forms:

«if condition»result1«endif»

«if condition»result1«else»result2«endif»

In the first form, the macro performs result1 if the condition is true. Otherwise, result1 is skipped entirely. In the second example, the macro performs result1 if the condition is true and performs result2 if the condition is false. The example below demonstrates the usefulness of the If instruction:

<f8>

《ask response=?Do you want to delete this word(y/n)》

《if response="y"》<del>

《endif》

If response is equal to y, then the macro deletes the word. Note that the desired macro command is between the If statement and the Endif statement. An Endif statement must always follow an If statement, but an Else statement is not always necessary. If you expand upon the above example, you can see the use of the else statement:

<f8>

《ask response=?Do you want to delete this word (y/n)》

《if response="y"》<del>

《else》<f8>

《endif》

Now if response does not equal y, the macro highlights the next word. However, if response does equal y, the macro deletes the words, but does not highlight the next word. Once again, the Endif statement must follow the If and Else statements.

The equal sign in the If statement is known as an *operator*. The If statement can use different types of operators. The accepted operators are as follows:

```
 =   equals
 <>  not equal
 <   less than
 >   greater than
 <=  less than or equal
 >=  greater than or equal
```

These operators work with dates, numbers, and text. When two expressions are compared, they must be the same type. An expression can be a constant date, number or text, a variable, or a combination of variables and constants comprising a mathematical expression. For example, consider the following:

wage*hours/20

This would be a valid expression. An example of an incorrect comparison of variable types would be:

《if 10>"hello"》

Constants are text strings (anything enclosed by quotation marks), numbers, or dates. Anything not designated by a variable (like 10 and "hello" in the last example) are constants. Also certain variables and constants in the If-Else-Endif instruction are reserved:

selection   The highlighted text.

scrap   The current contents of the scrap.

field   The value of the currently active menu field. For example, if the show non-printing symbols field of the Options command is set to Partial, then field="Partial".

found, notfound   These are Boolean variables that allow you to test the result of a search. For example,《if found》<f9>《endif》《 is one possible use of the found variable.

save   Save is used to indicate whether Word is prompting you to save your work. If this variable is true, the prompt to save your document is at the bottom of the screen and you should save your document. Therefore you can put an instruction in your macro to use the Transfer Allsave command to save your document before making massive changes in it: 《if save》<esc><esc><shift tab 3>a《endif》.

window   This variable can be used with Set to make an indicated window active or with If to make an action conditional on the active window. 《set window = 1》 would make window 1 active. 《if window = 1》 would make the following action contingent on window 1 being open. If you the instruction 《set window = 8》 and only two windows are open, the highest numbered window (2) would be made active.

echo   This variable turns screen refresh on and off. 《set echo = "on"》 causes all of the macro's actions to show on the screen. Because this action takes processing time, it slows down the computer somewhat. To speed up your macros, you might want to 《set echo = "off"》.

promptmode   Use this variable to tell Word from where responses to prompts should come. The basic command structure is 《set promptmode = source》 where source may be "user", "macro", or "ignore", if prompts Word should proceed without a response.

wordversion   This command allows you to adapt your macros to work with future versions of Word, which might have different commands in the menus, as well as different keypresses and codes. At the very least, you might include in your macro the instruction 《if wordversion <>5.0》《quit》endif》 to prevent accidentally running your macro on Word 6.0 when you upgrade. Unfortunately, this variable is not recognized by versions prior to Word 5.0.

zoomedwindow   Detects whether the active window is zoomed. It cannot be set with the Set instruction.

Special characters in macro commands, such as the paragraph marker, are indicated by a caret and the first letter of the special character. For example, ^p indicates a paragraph marker and ^t represents a tab. These codes are used to place the special characters in an expression. See Chapter 11 for the complete list of special characters and details on their usage.

The Message instruction

The Message instruction is used to display messages on the message line at the bottom of the screen when the macro is running. Its form is as follows:

《message text》

When a macro encounters this instruction, it displays the text until another Message instruction is encountered, or until the macro runs a command that uses the message line for a message of its own.

Messages can be up to 80 characters long and are useful to indicate what the macro is doing at a particular point in time. Note that messages are displayed if the menu display is turned off in the Option command. If you add a message to the example program, it might look like this:

《message Running word_delete macro》

<f8>

《ask response=?Do you want to delete this word? (y/n)》

《if response="y"》<del>

《else》<f8>

《endif》

The Pause instruction

The *Pause* instruction allows the user to format or edit a document or enter commands during the execution of a macro. It is written in this fashion:

《pause prompt》

When a Pause instruction is encountered by a macro, the macro execution pauses to allow the user to make changes in the document, to enter text in a command field, such as Transfer Save. The macro resumes after the user types Return.

Basically, the Pause instruction allows the user to edit or format a document by temporarily stopping the macro. The prompt appears in the message line and can be up to 80 characters long. In the sample macro, suppose you wanted to save the document after making our changes. You would add a Pause instruction like this:

《message Running word_delete macro》

<f8>

《ask response=?Do you want to delete this word (y/n)》

{if response="y"》<del>

《else》<f8>

《endif》

<esc>ts

《pauses Enter filename text is to be saved under》 <enter>

Notice that the <enter> at the end of the line is required after the Pause instruction because when you type <enter> during the Pause instruction, it only tells the macro to run the next line in the macro program. The <enter> after the Pause instruction enters the filename itself in the Transfer Save command.

The Quit Instruction

The *Quit* instruction ends the execution of the macro immediately. It is encountered in the following form:

«quit»

Quite simply, the macro is ended when Quit is executed.

The Quit instruction is useful in conditional statements such as the If-Else-Endif instruction or the While-Endwhile instruction, but it is rarely used in macros. However, suppose you want to find a specific word in a document, and you do not want to check it word by word, as our example program does. If the word were not found, you would want the macro to terminate. The program would look like this:

<ctrl pgup>

<esc>s

«pause Enter text to delete»<enter>

«if notfound»«quit»

«else»<del>

«endif»

First, the macro moves up to the beginning of the document and then executes the Search command. The Pause instruction allows the user to enter the text to be deleted. If the text is found, it is deleted and the macro continues. If not, the macro ends.

The Repeat-Endrepeat instruction

The *Repeat-Endrepeat* instruction is used to carry out repetitive instructions in a macro. Instead of typing the same instruction over and over again, you could use the Repeat-Endrepeat instruction to execute that instruction the number of times you desired. It is used in the following manner:

«repeat n . . . «endrepeat»

All the instructions between the Repeat and the Endrepeat commands are executed n number of times. The n can be a constant, a variable, or a mathematical expression. For example, the program below deletes addresses from a mailing list database:

«ask number=?How many addresses to delete»

«repeat 5•number»

«shift f9»«del»

«endrepeat»

This macro program assumes that each address is four lines long and that there is a blank line between each address. If you had ten or more addresses to delete, the Repeat-Endrepeat instruction could be very useful indeed.

The Set instruction

The *Set* instruction assigns values to variables. It is very similar to the Ask instruction. But, while you must input something from the Ask instruction, the Set instruction allows a macro to increase or decrease the value of a variable. The Set instruction can be encountered in three different ways:

set variable=expression»

«set variable=?»

«set variable=?prompt»

The first form of the Set instruction changes the value of the variable. For example, consider the following:

«Set counter=counter+1»

This would increment the variable counter by one. In the second form, the macro prompts you for input and assigns whatever you enter to the variable name. The third is a variation of the second form with the additional option to let you enter your own prompt.

The Set instruction can also be used with the reserve variables. For example:

<esc>fdm

<tab 2>

«set left=field»

This would assign the value of the left margin to the variable left. As with the Ask instruction, the Set instruction cannot be executed within an active menu.

The While-Endwhile instruction

The *While-Endwhile* instruction is used to create a loop in which the instructions between the While and the Endwhile are processed as long as a certain condition is true. The While-Endwhile instruction is written in the following form:

«while condition»task«endwhile»

First the condition is tested. If it is true, the task is carried out. The Endwhile sends the macro back to the While condition line, where the condition is tested again. If the condition remains true, the task is executed again. The task is repeated until the condition becomes false.

You should always make sure that somewhere in the While-Endwhile loop, the condition is changing. Otherwise, the loop never ends, and the task is repeated forever (or until the computer is turned off). The While-Endwhile loop is a conditional instruction, so all the restrictions on the If-Else-Endif instruction also apply to the While-Endwhile instruction. All the special variables can also be used. For example, if you recall the old example macro program, you can add a While-Endwhile loop that deletes all occurrences of a word in the document, as shown:

<ctrl pgup>

<esc>s

《pause Enter text to delete》<enter>

《while found》

<del><esc>s<enter>

《endwhile》

Combining macro commands in macro programs

Macro commands can best be demonstrated in a real-life macro. Two moderately long macro programs are shown in this section, and an explanation of each line in the program is given. Not only are these macros educational, but they also might be helpful in your business.

The first program is designed to assist in the production of form letters. The second macro is designed to print an address in a letter on an envelope.

A macro to generate form letters

Suppose you have typed a letter that you want to send to several different people, but you don't have their addresses in a data file you can use. If you are sending the letter to only ten people (or fewer), it would be foolish to use the merge feature to generate a form letter. The macro "formlet" enables you to address the same letter to different people. The macro uses your input (in this case, the address), and inserts it where the macro is executed, as well as inserting the appropriate greeting. Thus, if you want to quickly send out a small batch of form letters, formlet would be useful. Figure 33-1 shows the macro program formlet in full.

The first two lines of the program illustrates the Comment command and the message command:

《comment This macro makes form letters》

《message running formlet》

The *Comment* command allows you to insert useful explanations in the macro program describing various parts of the program. The *Message* command displays the text running formlet in the message line. This is to indicate that the macro formlet is running. The next line sets the variable to y:

《set again="y"》

```
《comment This macro makes form letters》
《message running formlet》
《set again="y"》
《while again="y"》
《pause enter name》<enter>
《ask company=?Is there a company name (y/n)》
《if company="y"》《pause enter company name》<enter>
《endif》
《pause enter street》<enter>
《pause enter town,state,zip》<enter>
《if company<>"y"》<enter>
《endif》
<enter>Dear
《ask gender=?Is the addressee male (y/n)》
《if gender="y"》 Mr. <enter>
《else》 Ms. <enter>
《endif》
<up 6><end><f7><esc>c<enter>
<down 5>
<end>
<ins>,<enter>
<esc>pp
<up 6>
《repeat 7》
<shift f9><del>
《endrepeat》
《ask again=?Do you want to print another letter (y/n)》
《endwhile》
```

33-1 The lines in the form letter generating macro program.

This initializes again to y so the following While-Endwhile loop is executed at least once. It is this variable that determines whether to continue to print form letters or not:

《while again="y"》

This line begins the While-Endwhile loop that is executed as long as again is equal to y. When again is not equal to y, all the commands within the loop are skipped and the remaining part of the macro is executed.

The next lines prompt the user to enter the address:

《pause enter name》<enter>

《ask company=?Is there a company name (y/n)》

《if company="y"》

《pause enter company name》<enter>

《endif》

《pause enter street《<enter>

Macro instructions

《pause enter town,state,zip》<enter>

The Pause command allows you to enter text into the letter itself. When you are finished entering the appropriate text as prompted by the macro, merely press Return. The <enter> following in the program inserts a paragraph marker to move the highlight down to the next line. For example, consider the first line, 《pause enter name》<enter> as an example. The macro displays enter name in the message line and then pauses for you to enter the name of the recipient of the letter. After you type in the recipient's name, press Return. The macro then adds an <enter> after the name you just typed. The line 《ask company name (y/n)》 asks whether the address contains a company name. The If-Endif command determines whether the response was y or not. If the response is y, the macro pauses to allow you to enter the company name. Now the macro moves down a line and starts the greeting with Dear:

《if company<>"y"》<enter>

《endif》

<enter>Dear

Note that if there were no company name (《if company<>"y"》<enter>), another blank line is inserted to ensure that the address is four lines long.

After inserting the word Dear into the text, the macro asks the user about the gender of the addressee and determines the appropriate title:

《ask gender=?Is the addressee male (y/n)》

《if gender="y"》Mr.<enter>

《else》Ms.<enter>

《endif》

The user types in y and hits Return or N and hits Return depending on the gender of the addressee. The If-Else-Endif command analyzes the response. If the response was a Y, then the macro adds a blank space, the title Mr. and another blank. All other responses are regarded as an N response, and the macro adds a blank space, the title Ms. and another blank space. The next line,

<up 6><end><f7><esc>c<enter>

goes up six lines (<up 6>) to the beginning of the address and highlights the last name of the addressee with <end><f7>. The line copies the last name to the scrap with <esc>c<enter>. The next three lines insert the last name into the greeting:

<down 5>

<end>

<ins>,<enter>

<down 5> moves the highlight down five lines to the greeting and <end> moves the highlight to the end of the greeting. <ins> inserts the last name from the scrap. A comma is inserted and a paragraph marker is inserted before the previous paragraph marker to put a blank line between the letter and the greeting.

Finally, the letter is printed with this line:

<esc>pp

The Repeat-Endrepeat command is used to delete the address and greeting from the text after the highlight has been moved up to the beginning of the address with <up 6>:

<uop>

《repeat 7》

<shift f9><del>

《endrepeat》

The current line is highlighted and deleted using <shift f9><del>, and this line of the program is executed seven times using the Repeat-Endrepeat command.

The user is asked whether he or she wants to continue the macro, and the loop is ended in the last two lines of the program:

《ask again=?Do you want to print another letter (y/n)》

《endwhile》

The Ask command asks the user whether to print another form letter and therefore remain in the macro. The 《endwhile》 command sends the macro back to the first part of the While-Endwhile loop where again is checked to see if it is equal to y by 《while again="y"》. If this is not the case, the macro ends.

The form letter macro can be used with the macro envelope, if you wish to print both a letter and an envelope for each form letter. The code for the envelope macro appears in the next section. This macro can be nested in the formlet macro by merely inserting envelope<f3> into the formlet macro program after the letter has been printed. The inserted line would look like this:

<esc>pp

envelope<f3>

<up 6>

A macro to print envelopes

The envelope macro finds the address in a letter and prints it onto an envelope. The address is found by searching for nonblank lines from the beginning of the document. When a nonblank line is found, it is checked to see if there are numbers in it. If there are numbers, the program assumes the line is the date. If there are no numbers, the program assumes this is the start of the address. Figure 33-2 shows how the envelope macro finds the address in a typical letter.

The envelope macro demonstrates the versatility of macro commands, and can save time and effort. Figure 33-3 shows the code for the macro program envelope. We analyze what each line of the macro does here. The first three lines summarize what the macro does:

《comment This macro prints envelopes》

Macro instructions

```
┌[········1·········2·········3·········4·········5·········]·········7······┐
│ December 2, 1988¶──── This line contains numbers, so it is considered the date
│ ¶──── Program checks each line to determine whether it is blank or not
│ ¶
│ Mr. Richard Byer¶──── First nonblank line without numbers is considered start of address
│ President¶
│ Mickey Mouse Products¶
│ Wayne, NJ  07673¶
│ ¶──── Blank line marks end of address
│ ¶
│ ¶
│
│ Dear Mr. Byer:¶
│ ¶
│ Make-It-Gold wants you to know about our new car gold
│ plating service in the New York Metro area.  Make-It-Gold is
│ prepared to gold plate your car at the amazingly low price
│ of $997.95.  Imagine how you will be the talk of the town as
│ you cruise by in a gold plated car.  Whether your car is a
│ Cadillac or a Chevette, your car will look like a million as
│ passerbys ooh and aah as you drive by.▮
│                                                              ─MACFIG.DOC─
COMMAND: Copy Delete Format Gallery Help Insert Jump Library
         Options Print Quit Replace Search Transfer Undo Window
Edit document or press Esc to use menu
Pg1 Li19 Co39    {}                                    Microsoft Word
```

33-2 A demonstration of how the envelope macro program finds the address in a letter and then prints the address.

```
«comment This macro prints envelopes»
«message running envelope»
«pause insert envelope in printer, press enter when ready»
<ctrl pgup>
1<left><del>
«while scrap<>0»
<shift f9><esc>c<enter>
«if scrap="^p"»
1<left><del>
«else»<f2>
«endif»
<down>
«endwhile»
«message found address»
«set number=1»
<shift f9><esc>c<enter>
«while scrap<>"^p"»
<down><shift f9><esc>c<enter>
«set number=number+1»
«endwhile»
<up><f6>
«repeat number»
```

33-3 The lines for the envelope-printing macro program.

```
<f9>
《endrepeat》
《repeat 5》
<alt n>
《endrepeat》
<esc>po<down 3>s<enter>p
<esc>po<down 3>a<enter><esc>
《repeat 5》
<alt m>
《endrepeat》
```

33-3 Continued

《message running envelope》

《pause insert envelope in printer, press enter when ready》

When the macro is run, the comment line does not appear, but the message running envelope appears in the message line. Then, the Pause command asks you to insert the envelope in the printer, and waits for you to press Return before continuing with the macro program. The next two lines are as follows:

<ctrl pgup>

1<left><del>

The <ctrl pgup> line moves the highlight to the beginning of the document. In the next line, 1<left><del> places the number 1 in the scrap. The envelope macro uses the scrap while searching for the address in the document. It assumes that the first line of the address will not contain a number. (If your first line does contain a number, write out the number in words.) The macro looks for the first line in the document that does not contain numbers and assumes that the line is the start of the full address.

The next eight lines comprise a While-Endwhile loop:

《while scrap<>0》

<shift f9><esc>c<enter>

《if scrap="^p"》

1<left><del>

《else》<f2>

《endif》

<down>

《endwhile》

This loop actually performs the search for the address. In the loop, <shift f9><esc>c<enter> highlights a line and copies it to the scrap. The scrap is then checked with an If-Else-Endif command. If the scrap (the current line) contains a paragraph marker, the number 1 is placed into the scrap by 1<left><del>. Otherwise, the value of that line is "calculated" by the calculate function key <f2>. If the line is the date, some figure other than zero is placed into the scrap because the date contains numbers.

The While-Endwhile loop continues its search until the scrap equals zero:

《message found address》

《set number=1》

<shift f9><esc>c<enter>

Once the first line of the address has been found, the macro displays the message found address. Now, the macro counts how many lines are in the address with a While-Endwhile loop and a counter. Because the highlight is already on the second line of the address, the counter variable number is initialized to 1 using the Set command. In other words, the first line of the address has been counted already. The second line of the address is then highlighted and copied to the scrap.

The second While-Endwhile loop counts the number of lines in the address until it reaches a line containing only the paragraph symbol, signaling the end of the address:

《while scrap<>"^p"》

<down><shift f9> <esc>c<enter>

《set number=number+1》

《endwhile》

As each line of the address is highlighted, 1 is added to the counter variable number using the Set command.

Once the number of lines has been counted, the Repeat-Endrepeat command is used with the extend function key <f6> to highlight the address:

<up><f6>

《repeat number》

<f9>

《endrepeat》

<up f6> moves the highlight back up the last line of the address and activates the extend function. The 《repeat number》 line commands the macro program to press the F9 key number times, because number was the counter used to count the number of lines in the address. This highlights the entire address from bottom to top.

Then the program indents the entire address (which is now highlighted) five tabs to the right (2.5 inches, if you are using the tabs preset in Word) with the Repeat command:

《repeat 5》

<alt n>

《endrepeat》

<alt n> moves the highlighted section to the next tab, and 《repeat 5》 instructs the

program to carry out this task five times. Note that the macro assumes that the address is along the left margin.

    <esc>po<down 3>s<enter>p

    <esc>po<down 3>a<enter><esc>

The next line of the program prints just the address (highlighted section) on the envelope by setting the Print Options Range to Selection and then selecting the printer command. When printing is finished, the Print Options Range is put back to the All setting.

Finally, the address is returned to its original position using the repeat command and <alt m> (for backtab):

    《repeat 5》

    <alt m>

    《endrepeat》

Arrays

In addition to using variables, you can use *arrays* of variables. For example, you can have a series of variables called record1, record2, record3 or you could have record《x》 in which x could contain a value of 1 through 3. Using ordinary variables, you must refer to each variable individually each time it is used. By implementing arrays, however, you can refer to any of the variables simply by changing the value of x.

Functions

Four functions to use with variables in macros can be extremely valuable as your expertise with variables and macros increases. The functions are int, len, mid, and a concatenation function that does not actually have a function name but is implied by syntax. Those familiar with the BASIC language will recognize the functions because they are the same as their BASIC keyword counterparts.

The int function

The *int* function simply turns a floating-point number into an integer. If the value of a variable number is 1.5, then 《set value=int(number)》 means that the value in the variable value is 1. This assists in rounding numbers as well. Add .5 to the value being rounded and use the int function to round a value. If the value is 4.5, it is rounded correctly to 5. If it is 4.4999, it is rounded correctly to 4. If you want to round at a value behind the decimal point, add .05 for tenths, .005 for thousandths, and so on.

The len function

The *len* function returns the length of a text variable. If you place the word string in variable text, the macro command 《set stringlength=len(text)》, the value 6 is placed in the variable stringlength. Other options are to substitute the reversed variables selection and field for the variable name. Using selection returns the number of characters (including spaces) in the selected part of the document. Field returns the number of characters entered in the field in the menu (such as the filename field in the Transfer Load and Transfer Save commands).

The mid function

Simply put, the *mid* function tells Word to look at a specific place in a text variable, take a specific number of characters, and assign them to a second variable. If the variable text contained the text able was I ere I saw Elba, the command «set sample =mid(text,3,6)» would cause the variable sample to contain the text le was, the third through the ninth characters in the variable text. This function only works on the first 255 characters of a string.

The concatenation function

This function is not given a name like the others but is implied from the syntax of the command. A typical concatenation is to combine fields into a name or address. To combine four variables street, city, state, and zip into a single variable address, use the following command:

«set address=street city state zip»

Strings can only be concatenated up to 255 characters in length. Here is an example of concatenating variables. Note how literal text (the commas and spaces in quotation marks) can be inserted into the concatenation.

«set street="6144 E. Broadway"»

«set city="Mt. Pheasant"»

«set state="Michigan"»

«set zip="49959"»

«set address=street ", " city ", " state " " zip»

«address»

This macro prints out a formatted address when it is run.

Summary

Upon completing this chapter, you should be familiar with the macro instructions and how to combine them in macro programs. The macro instructions, their functions, and important related topics are as follows:

- The Ask instruction assigns user inputs to a variable.
- The Comment-Endcomment command places explanations in the macro.
- The If-Else-Endif instruction conditionally executes lines in a macro.
- How to create conditions for If and While instructions.
- The Message instruction displays information to the message line.

- The Pause instruction to allow users to edit and format a document.
- The Quit instruction to terminate a macro.
- The Repeat-Endrepeat instruction performs a task a certain number of times.
- The Set instruction sets or changes the value of a variable.
- The While-Endwhile instruction performs a task until a certain condition is false.
- How to write programs using one or more of these commands.

CHAPTER 34

Page layout

Page layout represents the most advanced use of Word: as a desktop publishing system. Only a few pages are devoted to this aspect in the manual, despite its heavy emphasis in Microsoft advertising. This chapter shows how Word can be teamed with a laser printer and a graphics package to produce publications that rival those from a professional press.

Importing graphics

Central to Word's page layout facility is its ability to incorporate graphics from other packages. Word can import graphics in the following formats:

    Lotus PIC
    PC Paintbrush PCX and PCC
    Microsoft Pageview
    HPGL (a Hewlett-Packard plotter format)
    PostScript and EPS files
    Compressed or uncompressed TIFF black and white
    Uncompressed TIFF gray-scale
    Files created in lieu of printing (printed to disk)
    Files created with the Word utility CAPTURE.COM
    Windows clipboard files, if they are in bitmap format

PostScript and EPS files cannot be previewed, though they can be printed, if you own a PostScript printer.

Basically, the quick and easy way is to type .G.GRAPHIC.TIF;4";3"TIFF and hit Return and then format the first three characters (.G.) as hidden text. Immediately, Word sets aside the space for the graphic according to settings in the Format Paragraph and Format pOsition menus. The text contains the call for a graphic (.G.), the name of the graphic file (GRAPHIC.TIF;), the width and height of the graphic (4";3";) and the graphics format (TIFF).

Another way to call for a graphic is to use the Library Link command. You are given the option of linking a document, a graphic, or a spreadsheet. Select Graphic, and you see the menu shown in Fig. 34-1. (Document and spreadsheet linking is discussed in Chapter 35.)

```
LIBRARY LINK GRAPHICS filename:
      file format:                    alignment in frame: Centered
      graphics width: 7"              graphics height: 7"
      space before: 0"                space after: 0"
Enter filename or press F1 to select from list
Pg2 Li14 Co21    {.}              ?            LY          Microsoft Word
```

34-1 The Library Link Graphics menu is used to import graphics into the document.

This menu provides the opportunity to enter the name (and path) of the graphic file. If you want to select graphics images from a directory, press F1 to see the files in the selected subdirectory or on the selected disk. If you are importing from the Windows Clipboard, select Clipboard.

Generally, the graphics file should be in the same subdirectory or on the same disk as the document to which it is being linked. The next option provides the format. This is generally intuited by the program from the file extension. If nothing appears in this field, press F1 to pick a format from a list. Next is the position of the graphic on the page. A graphic can be centered, right-aligned, or left-aligned.

The next selection is to enter the height and width of the graphic. You can enter values into these areas, or you can press F1 to select between Same as frame width or Natural size. Generally, when you stretch or shrink a bitmap graphic, you do so at your peril because the bitmap appears on paper as a checkerboard plaid or a washed-out imitation of itself. This isn't supposed to happen with TIFF-format graphics, but it does.

You have another problem when you select natural size. For some reason, Word seems to think some graphics are extremely tiny, often fractions of an inch in "natural size." This means that the program cannot figure out what size it is supposed to be. You have to enter figures in these fields. It would be helpful to know the size from the graphics package (some provide this kind of information). When you tab to the width option, you can enter a value or press F1 for a series of options that includes an approximation of a proportion to the height, a value equal to the height, or the natural size of the graphic, subject to all the same caveats as the natural height setting.

The next two options, space before and space after, allow you to specify the amount of white space surrounding the graphic in text.

A better way to import graphics (and text) is to use the CAPTURE.COM program in conjunction with your graphics program (covered in the section labeled "CAPTURE.COM").

Providing a caption

You usually want to provide a caption with a graphic. To do so, position your cursor at the end of the graphics call, on the paragraph marker. Press Shift-Return to create a Newline character. Type in your caption. Use the bookmark command to place a reference to the graphic in text. (It is considered good form to refer to a graphic in text.)

Viewing your graphic

You will want to see where your graphic appears in text, and you might want to see what the finished page will look like. To see the position of your graphic, choose the Show Layout command. Press Alt-F4. A dotted line appears, encompassing the area where the graphic will appear.

Another option, designed to show what the printed page will look like, is the Print preView option, which creates a graphic depiction of the printed page.

CAPTURE.COM

You need to place CAPTURE.COM in the same subdirectory as the Word program. It is located on the Program 1 disk (it might have been moved on your version). When you run CAPTURE.COM the first time, you should use the /S option (CAPTURE /S) to set it up for your particular computer and graphics capabilities.

Either from the DOS prompt (CAPTURE.COM won't word with OS/2) or by pressing Esc, L, and then R to run DOS, type CAPTURE /S. This runs the setup part of the program. A menu allows you to select graphics hardware, use "reverse video" (photographic negative), and other settings. One setting, the ability to use clipping, ought to be turned off when you are taking screen shots of Windows screens. If you are using the IBM 8514 display, select option 18 (screen.vid) when you set up CAPTURE.COM. If you are using the Wyse 700, you won't be able to use CAPTURE.COM to capture screens. You will probably want to use option 05 for a Hercules monochrome card.

When you leave the setup component, CAPTURE.COM is installed. Henceforth, you can simply enter CAPTURE at the command line to install the program, so long as none of the settings need to be changed. You must make the changes while you are in the same subdirectory as the CAPTURE.COM program or your changes won't be recorded. To remove CAPTURE from memory, use the command CAPTURE /E. To take a screen shot with CAPTURE.COM in memory, press Shift-Keypad * (most keyboards identify this key as the PrtSc or Print Screen key).

Start your application, load up the screen you want to capture, and press

Shift-PrtSc. If you are taking a screen shot of a graphics screen (other than a Windows screen), you have the option of using a special property called *clipping*. This property allows you to take a screen shot of a smaller piece of the screen. The arrow keys adjust the *clipping lines*, either the top and left lines or the bottom and right lines. Press Tab to change the lines you control. If you prefer to operate the top and bottom lines as a unit, and the left and right lines as a unit, press Ins. To return to the top-right, bottom-left control, press Del. The keypad Plus and Minus keys increase and decrease the rate of clipping line movement, respectively. When all is ready, press Return to take the screen shot. If you are using clipping, or taking a shot of a text screen, you are prompted for a filename. To back out of taking a screen shot, press Esc.

Text screens are given an .LST extension by CAPTURE.COM, and graphics screens are given the extension .SCR.

Positioning and formatting graphics

You can use the Format pOsition command to place the graphic on the screen. Select the graphic call as a paragraph and type Esc, F, O. The first option is horizontal frame position as shown in Fig. 34-2. Press F1 to make a choice among Left, Centered, Right, Outside, and Inside. These options are all positions relative to the column, the margins, or the page (the next option). Inside means close to the binding in a bound document. The Inside option places the graphic on the left side of a right-hand page and on the right side of a left-hand page. Outside has the opposite meaning, placing the graphic away from the binding.

```
FORMAT POSITION
        horizontal frame position: Left         relative to:(Column)Margins Page
        vertical frame position: In line        relative to:(Margins)Page
        frame width: Single Column              distance from text: 0.167"
Enter measurement or press F1 to select from list
Pg4 Li13 Co9          {¶}              ?                LY           Microsoft Word
```

34-2 The Format pOsition menu provides additional layout tools.

Vertical frame position places the graphic frame In line, Top, Centered, or Bottom, relative to the margins or the page. Frame width can be set for Single column or Width of graphic. Single column makes the graphic frame the width of the text in the current column, allowing you to "wrap" text around the graphic. If the graphic is narrower than the width of the text column, it is possible to wrap the text around the figure. *Wrapping text* means making the column narrower and placing text in the same column as the figure, to the right or left of the graphic. If the graphic is centered in a wide column, you can even have lines begin to the left of the graphic and end to the right. Word is very flexible when it comes to placing graphics and text on the page.

You can also enter values in the horizontal and vertical frame positions, for fine control.

The last option in the Format pOsition menu is distance from text. Essentially, this places a region of white space around the graphic. Most graphics look better if a small amount of white space is allowed.

Technically, Word considers your paragraph to be a graphic. Therefore, you can use all the Format Border commands to format the graphic. For example, you can place rules around the graphic or put shading behind it, depending on the capabilities of your printer, of course.

You should explore the dozens of combinations of text and graphics. Some of the most interesting involve placing text into a separate frame. This can be used to set apart sidebars and other informative text, like callouts. To set text apart, write the text to appear in a separate frame. Select the paragraphs containing the text and select the Format pOsition option. Place the frame on the page as if it were a graphic. If you adjust the frame width with the Format pOsition command, text wraps tightly around the text box (leaving little white space to appear around the text in the frame).

If you place your frame on the edge of the paper, the on-screen representation of the page is adjusted to show the frame. That means the text is moved right slightly when the frame is placed tightly against the left edge of the paper. This is not a problem with the Format Division or Format Paragraph menus, but just a way of showing text that might be partly invisible.

If the frame includes text, you should select the text in the frame with Esc, F, and then P to go to the Format Paragraph menu and then set line spacing to Auto. These settings cause Word to respect the text. Under certain circumstances, Word might overwrite the text in a separate frame. You can create under wider margins to place text in the margins without crowding the page.

When you have text in a frame, it has its own ruler. If you click on the text on the page, you can edit it, add to it, put in tabs, and change the margins, just as if it were ordinary text.

Summary

On completion of this chapter, you should have a working knowledge of the following:

- Importing graphics.
- Previewing a graphic and providing a caption for it.
- Setting up and using CAPTURE.COM.
- Positioning and formatting graphics.
- Creating sidebars and callouts.

35
CHAPTER

Importing data from other programs

Word can import data from various spreadsheet programs or any print file. Word is designed to import spreadsheet data from 1-2-3, Symphony, Multiplan, and Excel. Word can also import print files from any software package.

Figures 35-1 and 35-2 show how a 1-2-3 spreadsheet can be inserted in a document. Figure 35-1 shows how the spreadsheet appears on the screen. Figure 35-2 shows how the spreadsheet looks when printed.

Any number of spreadsheet tables can be included in a Word document. The hidden text format is used in codes that determine the placement of the spreadsheet tables and print files in the Word document.

312 *Importing data from other programs*

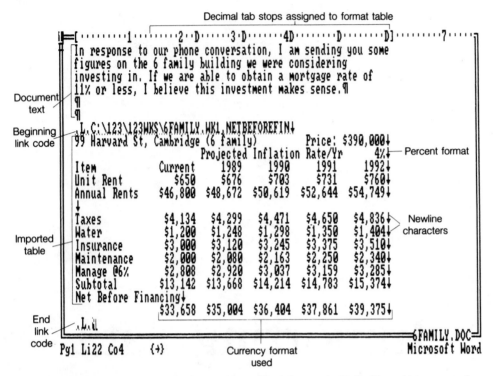

35-1 Spreadsheets can be imported into a Word document with the Library Link command. The codes at the beginning and end of the table control updates to the spreadsheet.

```
In response to our phone conversation, I am sending you some
figures on the 6 family building we were considering
investing in. If we are able to obtain a mortgage rate of
11% or less, I believe this investment makes sense.

99 Harvard St, Cambridge (6 family)           Price: $390,000
                     Projected Inflation Rate/Yr         4%
Item             Current    1989    1990    1991    1992
Unit Rent           $650    $676    $703    $731    $760
Annual Rents     $46,800 $48,672 $50,619 $52,644 $54,749

Taxes             $4,134  $4,299  $4,471  $4,650  $4,836
Water             $1,200  $1,248  $1,298  $1,350  $1,404
Insurance         $3,000  $3,120  $3,245  $3,375  $3,510
Maintenance       $2,000  $2,080  $2,163  $2,250  $2,340
Manage @6%        $2,808  $2,920  $3,037  $3,159  $3,285
Subtotal         $13,142 $13,668 $14,214 $14,783 $15,374
Net Before Financing
                 $33,658 $35,004 $36,404 $37,861 $39,375
```

35-2 The printed version of the document shown in Fig. 35-1.

Placing a spreadsheet in a Word document

The Library Link Spreadsheet command enables you to transfer all or part of a spreadsheet into a Word document. Spreadsheets are imported into a Word document by first pressing Esc, then L, L, and S for the Library Link Spreadsheet command. The two fields of the Library Link Spreadsheet menu are filename and area.

Enter the name of the spreadsheet file you want to link in the filename field. If the spreadsheet is in a directory other than the Word directory, include the path name. You can list all the files in the current directory by typing *.* into the filename field and pressing F1. If you want to list only Lotus 1-2-3 files from version 1a, type *.WKS in the filename field and press F1. If you are importing a 1-2-3 version 2 file, type *.WK1 and press F1.

Finally, enter a range name or the range of cells into the area field. Again, you can press F1 to list the range names attached to the spreadsheet. If you do not specify a range name or a range of cells, Word imports the entire spreadsheet.

When the filename and area settings are correct, press Return to process the Library Link Spreadsheet command. Word imports the spreadsheet and displays it on the screen. The spreadsheet might not look like the spreadsheet in the original document because Word does not preserve all cell formats and column sizes when data is imported. Therefore, you might have to edit the spreadsheet table to suit your needs.

Updating imported spreadsheets

When Word imports a spreadsheet, it includes special spreadsheet codes at the beginning and end of the spreadsheet in the Word document. The codes are in hidden text format so the Options show hidden text setting must be Yes for you to see the codes. The code .L. *filename,area*<newline> appears at the beginning of the spreadsheet in Word. The code .L. appears at the end of the spreadsheet. These codes enable Word to update all the spreadsheet tables in a document when the original spreadsheet files are modified. Thus, the codes link a spreadsheet table to the spreadsheet file by enabling Word to modify the spreadsheet tables when the spreadsheet files are changed.

The Library Link Spreadsheet command also updates imported spreadsheets. To update one or more spreadsheet tables in a document, first highlight all the spreadsheet tables to be updated. If you want to update all the spreadsheet tables in a document, press Shift-F10, and then the Esc, L, L, and S sequence to access the spreadsheet link. After executing the command, Word pauses at each highlighted spreadsheet table that is bounded by link codes and prompt you to enter a keypress if it should continue. At this point, press Y to update that spreadsheet and check the next spreadsheet.

Word does not update your imported spreadsheet tables if the corresponding link codes are missing, improperly altered, or not in hidden text format. If the link codes are damaged when you try to update the spreadsheet tables, Word either ignores the spreadsheet or displays a message that it cannot find the date. Therefore, it is advisable to leave the spreadsheet link codes in the document.

Formatting imported tables

When Word imports spreadsheets, it does not import all the spreadsheet formats. Word recognizes the currency format, the percent format, and the general format;

therefore, you should only use these formats in a spreadsheet that is imported. The percent and currency format allow you to set the number of decimal places for figures in the table. If you use the same number of decimal places for the numbers in a column, it is easier to align those numbers with a decimal tab stop. If you do not use the currency, percent, or general format, Word automatically uses one of these formats for cells.

If you want to use the general format and set the number of decimal places, use the general format to display spreadsheet data. Then, make a copy of the spreadsheet data on some open space on the 1-2-3 worksheet. Next, in the duplicate spreadsheet, use the @ROUND function to refer to the data in the original spreadsheet and set the required number of decimal places for each cell. Use @ROUND in a group of cells to be sure all values have the same number of decimal places. Note that this is not equivalent to formatting with the fixed decimal format.

When Word imports spreadsheet data, it separates spreadsheet columns with tabs. You can adjust the spreadsheet table columns by changing the tab stops (see Chapter 9). The Decimal Character setting on the Options menu determines whether Word considers a period or a comma as a decimal separator when manipulating decimal tabs. Word inserts newline characters after each line in the table. Therefore, the entire table is technically one paragraph and the tab stops can be changed easily.

The currency format figure (a dollar sign, pound sign, yen sign, or some other figure) depends on the version of DOS you are using. With DOS 2.0, the dollar sign is the default currency format. To change the currency format in DOS 3 or later, include the line COUNTRY statement in the CONFIG.SYS file on your boot disk (consult your DOS manual for further instructions).

Linking a document

The one other option on the Library Link menu is Document. To import text from one document into another, load the document from which you want to import text. Select the test and use the Format bookmark command to make the text a bookmark. You have to give the bookmark a unique name.

Load the document into which you want to insert the document. Press Esc, L, L, and D. You are prompted to enter the name of the donor document and the bookmark. If you are importing several bookmarks into the document, you might want to consult a list of the available bookmarks. If so, press F1 and select the bookmark to import. Another option is to leave the bookmark field blank. In this case, you import the entire document listed in the filename field. Press Return to import the text.

Like the spreadsheet import, your document import has a beginning and end code. The beginning code is .D. filename;bookmark, and the ending code is .D. followed by a Return.

Updating the imported documents is handled the same as updating an imported spreadsheet, with the exception that you use the Library Link Document command after highlighting text.

Never import a document within another linked document. The proliferation of document link codes confuses Word and could result in the loss of text.

Summary

In this chapter, you have seen how to:

- Link and update spreadsheet files in your Word document.
- Link and update document files in your Word document.

APPENDIX A

Macro keystrokes

A comprehensive list of keystrokes that can be written into a macro can be found in this appendix. These commands are broken down into categories by the type of keystroke.

Cursor keys

<home>   Home key
<end>   End key
<left>   Left arrow
<right> Right arrow
<up>   Up arrow
<down>   Down arrow
<pgdn>   Page Down key
<pgup>   Page Up key
<tab>   Tab key

Shift keys

<esc>   Escape key
<alt x>   Alt key with another key
<ctrl x> Ctrl key with another key
<shift x> Shift key with another key

<numlock>   Num Lock key (toggles keypad)
<scrolllock>   Scroll Lock key (toggles cursor key scrolling)
<capslock>   Caps Lock key (toggles caps lock condition)

Control keys

<enter>   Return key
<ins>   Ins key
<del>   Del key
<backspace>   Backspace key

Keypad

<keypad x>   Used with numbers or *, −, + keys on keypad

Function keys

<f1>   Next window; List choices when in menu
<shift f1>   Undo
<ctrl f1>   Zoom
<alt f1>   Set tab
<f2>   Calculate
<shift f2>   Outline view
<ctrl f2>   Header
<alt f2>   Footer
<f3>   Expand glossary name
<shift f3>   Record macro
<ctrl f3>   Step mode
<alt f3>   Copy to scrap
<f4>   Repeat last action
<shift f4>   Repeat search
<ctrl f4>   Toggle uppercase/lowercase; Recompile list (document retrieval mode)
<alt f4>   Show layout
<f5>   Overtype/insert mode toggle
<shift f5>   Outline edit/Outline organize toggle (Outline mode)
<ctrl f5>   Line drawing mode toggle
<alt f5>   Goto page
<f6>   Extend selection
<shift f6>   Column selection
<ctrl f6>   Thesaurus
<alt f6>   Spell
<f7>   Previous word selection
<shift f7>   Previous sentence selection
<ctrl f7>   Load
<alt f7>   Show line breaks toggle

<f8>	Next word selection
<shift f8>	Next sentence selection
<ctrl f8>	Print
<alt f8>	Font name
<f9>	Previous paragraph selection
<shift f9>	Current line selection
<ctrl f9>	Print preview
<alt f9>	Display mode toggle (between last two modes)
<f10>	Next paragraph selection
<shift f10>	Entire document selection
<ctrl f10>	Save
<alt f10>	Record style
<f11>	Collapse heading
<shift f11>	Collapse body text
<f12>	Expand heading
<shift f12>	Expand body text
<ctrl f12>	Expand entire outline

APPENDIX B

Editing commands

The commands used in editing a document are listed here. These commands, or keystrokes, are grouped by categories. A brief description follows each command.

Entering text

The following keys aid in designating lines, paragraphs, pages, hyphenation and tabs in a document.

Return   Marks beginning of a new paragraph.
Shift-Return (Newline)   Begins a new line without ending paragraph.
Ctrl-Return (Division break)   Marks beginning of a new division.
Ctrl-Shift-Return (Page break)   Marks beginning of a new page.
Tab   Moves to the next tab stop.
Ctrl-Hyphen (Nonrequired hyphen)   Enters a nonrequired hyphen that is visible only if the word must be hyphenated at the end of the line.
Ctrl-Shift-Hyphen (Nonbreaking hyphen)   Enters a nonbreaking hyphen that joins two inseparable words.
Alt-Keypad char   Enter ASCII characters not on keyboard.
Ctrl-Space   Enters a nonbreaking space that joins two inseparable words.

Selecting text

The keys listed here highlight text. The highlighted text is placed in the scrap by the copy and delete commands. Highlighted text can also be formatted by the direct format keys and the format commands.

Home   Moves cursor to the first character in line.
End   Moves cursor to the last character in line.
Ctrl-End   Moves cursor to bottom of window.
F6 (extend key)   Switches the extend toggle (on/off). When on, the highlighted section is extended with cursor movement.
Shift-F6   Switched the column extend toggle on and off.
F7 (word left)   Highlights the next word to the left.
Shift-F7   Highlights the previous sentence.
F8 (word right)   Highlights the next word to the right.
Shift-F8   Highlights the next sentence
F9 (Previous paragraph)   Highlights the previous paragraph.
Shift-F9 (line)   Highlights the current line.
F10 (Next paragraph)   Highlights the next paragraph.
Shift-F10 (Whole document)   Highlights the entire document.
Shift-Ctrl-Home   Highlights to the top of the current window.
Shift-Ctrl-End   Highlights to the bottom of the current window.
Esc (Cancel)   Cancels command and returns you to the main menu.

Scrolling text

The cursor keys or the numeric keypad move the cursor for viewing and editing purposes.

PgUp (Page Up)   Moves up one screen in document.
PgDn (Page Down)   Moves down one screen in document.
Ctrl-PgUp (Document Top)   Moves up to beginning of document
Ctrl-PgDn (Document Bottom)   Moves down to end of document.
Ctrl-Left (Page Left)   Moves document left one word.
Ctrl-Right (Page Right)   Moves document right one word.
Scroll Lock+Up   Moves up one line.
Scroll Lock+Down   Moves down one line.
Scroll Lock+Left   Moves left one third of the window.
Scroll Lock+Right   Moves right one third of the window.
F1 (Next window)   Moves to the next window.
Shift-F1   Moves to the previous window.

Choosing commands

The choosing commands aid in selecting settings in menus, options, and command fields.

F1   Displays a list of choices in the command field.

Space   Moves to next item in menu, or to next setting in a list.
Backspace   Moves to previous item in menu, or previous setting in a list.
Tab or Right   Moves to next item.
Shift-Tab (Backtab) or Left   Moves to previous item.
F4 (Redo)   Repeat the last command.
Shift-F4   Repeat the last search command.
F7 (Word left)   Highlights the word to the left of the cursor when in a command field.
F8 (Word right)   Highlights the word to the right of the cursor when in a command field.
F9 (Char left)   Moves the cursor one character to left in menu text field.
F10 (Char right)   Moves the cursor one character to right in menu text field.
Return   Execute the command.
Esc   Cancel command and return to main menu.
Alt-H (Help)   Presents appropriate Help information on screen.
Ctrl-Esc   Returns to command menu.

Direct formatting

The direct formatting commands determine the type of characters that are displayed on the screen and printed on a printer. The commands are equivalent to the Format Character command on the edit menu. The commands may be used in combination so that the bold command and underlined can result in words that are both bold and underlined.

Alt-Space   Normal characters.
Alt-B   Bold characters.
Alt-I   Italic characters.
Alt-K   Small caps characters.
Alt-s   Strikethrough characters.
Alt-u   Underline characters.
Alt-D   Double underline characters.
Alt-E   Hidden text.
Alt-Plus or Alt-Equal   Superscript characters.
Alt-Hyphen   Subscript characters.

Paragraph format keys

The paragraph format keys format a paragraph in the document.

Alt-C   Centers paragraph.
Alt-F   Indents first line to next tab.
Alt-J   Justifies paragraph.
Alt-L   Flush left paragraph.
Alt-M   Reduces left indent to previous tab.
Alt-N   Increases left indent to next tab.
Alt-O   Inserts line between paragraphs.

324 *Editing commands*

Alt-P   Sets the normal paragraph format.
Alt-R   Flush right paragraph.
Alt-T   Creates hanging indent.
Alt-2   Double-spaced paragraph.

Page format keys

The page format keys format the page layout.

Alt-F1   Sets tab.
Ctrl-F2 Creates header.
Alt-F2   Creates footer.
Alt-F4   Sets margins.
Ctrl-F9 Repaginates document.

Shortcut keys

F2   Calculates highlighted equation.
Shift-F1   Cancels last action.
Alt-F3   Copies highlighted text to the scrap.
Alt-F8   Changes font.
Alt-F5   Jumps to specified page number.
Ctrl-F6 Opens thesaurus.
Alt-F6   Checks spelling.
Ctrl-F7 Loads a document.
Ctrl-F10 Saves a document.
Ctrl-F8 Prints a document.
Alt-F10 Saves a style.
Ctrl-F4 Updates retrieval list.
Shift-F3 Saves a macro.
F3   Runs a macro.
Ctrl-F3 Steps through a macro.

Line drawing keys

Ctrl-F5   Toggles line drawing option.
Left, Right, Up, and Down   Draw lines.
Home   Draws from cursor to left indent.
End   Draws from cursor to right indent.

Window keys

Alt-F7   Toggles printer display.
Alt-F9   Switches between last two graphics modes.
Ctrl-F1 Zoom/Unzoom.

Edit text

The following keys aid editing or making corrections by providing various methods of deleting and inserting text.

Backspace   Deletes character to the left of cursor.
Del (Delete)   Deletes highlighted text and places text in scrap.
Shift-Del   Deletes highlighted text but does not place text in scrap.
Ins (Insert)   Inserts text from scrap into document at cursor position
Shift-Ins   Inserts text from scrap into document after deleting highlighted text.
F3 (Glossary Reference)   Insert glossary text into document at cursor position.
F5 (Overtype)   Switches between overtype mode and insert mode.
F4 (Redo)   Repeats last editing command.

Main menu

These commands are options you can use from the main menu. The boldface commands are what Word shows you in the menu.

Copy   Places a copy of a highlighted text in scrap { } or glossary.
Delete   Deletes highlighted text from the document and places text in scrap { } or glossary.
Format   Specifies the format of characters, paragraphs, divisions, tabs and other document elements.
Character   Sets formatting attributes of characters, such as italics and boldface.
Tab   Sets tabs.
Footnote   Sets footnote formatting.
Border   Sets paragraph border, including outline and rules.
Division   Sets formatting attributes of divisions, such as, page length and margins.
Running-head   Formats running head.
Stylesheet   Transfers formatting to stylesheet.
sEarch   Searches for formatting in text.
repLace   Replaces one formatting scheme with another.
revision-Marks   Controls redlining: accepting or refusing editing changes.
pOsition   Places frame in text.
Annotation   Formats a special-case footnote called an annotation.
bookmark-   Inserts a bookmark.
Gallery   Moves to Gallery menu for creating, reviewing, or editing style sheets.
Copy   Copies a style.
Delete   Leaves the Gallery menu.
Format   Opens up the formatting menus for inserting special formatting into the style.
Help   Provides information on using the Gallery menu.
Insert   Inserts a style from the scrap.
Name   Allows you to name a style.
Print   Prints the stylesheet for future reference.
Transfer   Loads, saves, merges stylesheets.
Undo   Undoes the last change.

Help   Presents information about Microsoft Word.
Exit   Leaves the Help menu.
Next   Selects next topic.
Previous   Selects previous topic.
Basics   Basic information about the operation of Word.
Index   List of help modules.
Tutorial   Starts a training module on a part of Word.
Keyboard   Assistance with keyboard options.
Mouse   Assistance with mouse options.
Insert   Places text, taken from either the scrap {} or glossary, in front of the cursor.
Jump   Moves quickly to a specific place in a document, for instance, a page and footnote.
Page   Jumps to a specified page.
Footnote   Jumps to a footnote mark or to footnote text matching footnote mark.
Annotation   Jumps to specified annotation.
Bookmark   Jumps to specified bookmark.
Library   Moves to the Library menu which contains additional tools for word processing.
Autosort   Sorts lists according to your settings.
Document-retrieval   Retrieves documents according to your criteria.
Hyphenate   Hyphenates a document.
Index   Inserts index codes.
Link   Links documents, graphics, or spreadsheet files to the document.
Number   Provides sequential numbers in a document.
Run   Allows access to DOS commands from within Word.
Spell   Provides access to the speller utility.
Table   Provides for table of contents.
thEsaurus   The thesaurus utility helps you find the right word.
Options   Reviews and sets a wide variety of options for Word.
Print   Offers a set of subcommands for producing hard copies.
Printer   Prints the active document in Word.
Direct   Sends all characters typed from the keyboard directly to the printer.
File   Saves a formatted printer version of a document in a file on disk for later printing. Printer file can be printed with the DOS copy command on a remote printer.
Glossary   Prints out the current glossary.
Merge   Prints multiple versions of a document, such as form letters. A main document is combined with variable or customized text to print unique documents.
Options   Sets options that control printing, such as manual or continuous feeding.
Queue   Controls the printing queue, stopping or restarting the printing of documents.
Repaginate   Updates page breaks in the active document, but does not print the document.
preView   Provides on screen a facsimile of the printout of a document.
Quit   Ends the editing session and exits from the Word program.

Replace Searches for specified text pattern and substitutes it with text entered by the user.
Search Searches for occurrence of specified text in the document.
Transfer Offers a set of subcommands that load, save, clear, and perform other actions on documents, glossaries, and other files.
Undo Reverses the effect of the last editing command.
Window Offers a set of window operations.
Split Splits a window in two.
Close Closes a window.
Move Allows you to resize the window.

APPENDIX C

Useful DOS commannds

Although you do not need to know DOS commands to run Word, you do need to know DOS commands to organize the files created by Word. The DOS DIR command lists all the files on a disk. The DOS COPY and DISKCOPY commands are used to backup files and move files from one disk to another.

The DOS directory command

The DIR command produces a directory of all the files on the disk. The last name, first name, date of last modification, and time of last modification are listed on the screen. The DIR command can tell you the name of a file you are looking for just as the jacket of a record album tells you the songs on the album. The DIR command can also be used to check if a disk has any information stored on it. To illustrate the DIR command, type the following line:

    DIR

(Hit Return after typing the command.) The result is a directory of all the files on the disk in the current drive.

To get a directory of a disk in a drive other than the current one, type in the following:

DIR x:

where x represents the disk from which the directory will be read.

If a disk has absolutely no files on it, the DIR command does not list any files. Requesting a directory for a disk that has not been formatted causes the following message to appear:

Not ready error reading drive A

Abort, Retry, Ignore

In this case, abort the search by typing A.

The DOS COPY command

Another DOS command that you should know is COPY. The COPY command:

COPY A:ACCOUNTS.WKS B;

copies a file called ACCOUNTS.WKS from drive A to drive B.

The COPY command is entered while you are in DOS or while using the Library Run command within Word. The command example orders the computer to find a file called ACCOUNTS.WKS on the disk in drive A. Once the file is located, it copies onto the disk residing in drive B. The new file has the same name as the original file. If the file does not reside on the disk in drive A, the computer prints 0 files copied to the screen. If the computer was able to carry out your orders, it responds 1 files copied.

Some special characters enable you to copy entire families of files from one disk to another. These characters are the *wildcards* * *and* ?. The ? represents any single character. The * represents any chain of characters. SALES8?.WKS can represent SALES 80.WKS, SALES 81.WKS, and SALES82.WKS, but not SALES81A.WKS. SALES8*.WKS represents all the aforementioned files, but not SALES79.WKS or SALES81.PIC.

The wildcards make it very easy to copy groups of files. Copying all the files from one disk to another can be condensed to one line:

COPY *.* B:

Because the asterisks (*) represent all possible combinations of letters before and after the period, the command copies all the files listed in the directory on the current drive to drive B.

The DOS DISKCOPY command

The DISKCOPY command is a little like COPY *.* B:. DISKCOPY makes an exact copy of one disk on another disk. This erases any previous information on the duplicated disk. COPY *.* B: does not copy certain hidden files on disks containing the DOS commands, but DISKCOPY does.

Before using DISKCOPY, find either a blank disk or one without any files worth saving. Then put the DOS disk in drive A (if you have a hard drive, change the default drive to the hard drive by typing x: where x is the hard drive). Affirm that DOS has been loaded into your computer (the A> prompt should be visible at the bottom of the screen). Then enter the following at the DOS prompt:

DISKCOPY A: B:

This orders the computer to copy all the information from a disk in drive in drive A to a disk in drive B. The computer instructs you to:

Insert source diskette in drive A:

Insert target diskette in drive B:

Strike a key when ready. . .

The *source* diskette is the disk from which you want to copy; it is the original diskette. The *target* diskette is the disk to which you want to copy; it is the duplicate copy. Place the disk to be copied in drive A, the source drive. Seat the disk to receive the files in drive B, the target drive. Close the disk drive doors and press Return.

APPENDIX D

Starting Word

There are a number of methods to start Word besides simply typing word. The various options are listed below:

    word

Starts Word with no documents loaded.

    word *filename*

Word starts normally, but with the listed document file loaded. If Word cannot find the document, it asks permission to create a new document file by that name.

    word/L

Word starts normally, then loads the last document file loaded in window #1. If the document file cannot be located, Word begins as if the /L option was not selected.
    The /C option starts Word in text mode:

    word/C

The /# option

    word/H

uses a Hercules Graphics card to create a 90 character by 43 line display.

    word/G

starts Word in graphics mode. When you type:

    word/M

Word uses an EGA monitor and card to start in high-resolution monochrome mode.

At the end of the last line, Word scrolls up by half a window (as in Word 4.0) with this command:

    word/Y

At the end of the last line, Word wraps the text and starts a new line at the bottom of the window.

    word/Z

Some of these ways to begin Word cannot be combined, but others can be. The filename and /L options cannot be combined. The combination word /L/C, for example, would start Word in text mode and then load the last document loaded in window #1.

E
APPENDIX

The mouse

With the mouse, you can do a variety of things quickly and intuitively. You can select various amounts of text, scroll through a document, or work with windows and ???. This appendix explains the keys or buttons to press with the mouse in order to use it most effectively.

Selecting text

To select text, move into the text window.

Left button—Selects a single character. If the left button is held down, a sequence of characters can be selected by moving the mouse.
Right button—Selects a single word. If the right button is held down, a sequence of words may be selected.
Both buttons—Selects a single sentence. Selects a sequence of sentences when both buttons are held down and the mouse moved.
With Shift—Copies previously selected text to destination.
With Ctrl—Moves previously selected text to destination.
With Alt—Formats selected text in the same manner as previously selected text.

Selecting commands

Move the mouse to the menu area to select commands.

Left button—Chooses a command, subcommand, option, or command field from the menu. The command is executed when the pointer is on the command the button is pressed.

Right button—If pointing to a command, Word carries out both the command and the default selection in that submenu. For example, pressing the right mouse button when the pointer is on the Format command chooses the Format Character command. Equivalent to pressing left mouse button and then pressing Return. If pointing to an empty command field, the right mouse button causes a list of valid responses for the field to be displayed. If pointing to an option in an option field, the option is selected and the command is then carried out. Equivalent to pressing left mouse button and then Return.

Both buttons—Cancels current command when pointing to command area.

The selection bar

To use the selection bar, the mouse must be moved close to the left window border. When the mouse is on the selection bar in graphics mode, the mouse pointer points to the upper right corner of the screen.

Left button—Selects line next to the mouse pointer.
Right button—Selects paragraph next to the mouse pointer.
Both buttons—Selects entire document.
ALT–Right button—Assigns paragraph format of selected paragraph to previously selected text.

Scrolling vertically

To use the scroll bar, move the mouse to the left window border. When the mouse is over the scroll bar, the mouse pointer resembles a vertically oriented double-headed arrow.

Left button—Scrolls the document up a distance relative to the mouse's position on the scroll bar.
Right button—Scrolls the document down a distance relative to the mouse's position on the scroll bar.
Both buttons—Jumps to a position in the document relative to the location of the mouse pointer on the scroll bar. For example, if the mouse pointer is at the top of the scroll bar, the window jumps to the top of the document.

Scrolling horizontally

The document must be wider than the window before the scroll bar can be used to scroll the window to the left or to the right. To use the horizontal scroll bar, move the mouse to the bottom window border. When the mouse is over the scroll bar, the mouse pointer appears like a horizontally oriented double arrow.

Left button—Scrolls the document left a distance according to the mouse's position on the scroll bar.

Right button—Scrolls the document right a distance according to the position of the mouse on the scroll bar.
Both buttons—Window jumps to a position in the document relative to the position of the mouse pointer on the scroll bar. For example, if the mouse pointer is at the far left of the scroll bar, the window jumps to the far left of the document.

Opening and closing horizontal windows

Move the mouse to the right window border to open or close horizontal windows. The mouse pointer resembles an empty box when in the correct position.

Left button—Splits window horizontally at mouse pointer.
Right button—Opens footnote window at mouse pointer.
Both buttons—Closes horizontal window split.

Opening and closing vertical windows

Move the mouse to the top window border to open or close vertical windows. The mouse pointer looks like an empty box when in the correct position.

Left button—Splits window vertically at mouse pointer.
Both buttons—Closes vertical window split.

Moving windows

Move the mouse pointer to the lower left corner of the window. The mouse pointer resembles a cross with arrows when the mouse is in the correct position.

Left button—Move window corner while holding down button.
Right button—Move window corner while holding down button.

Turning the ruler on and off

Move to the upper right corner of the window to activate or deactivate the ruler line. When the mouse is in place, the mouse pointer looks like three vertical lines.

Left buttons—Activate ruler for window.
Both buttons—Deactivate ruler for window.

Setting tab stops on the ruler.

Tab stops can be manipulated with the mouse when the Format Tabs command is selected. After the Format Tabs command is chosen, point to the ruler line at the top of the window and use the mouse buttons to move the tabs.

Left button—Select tab stop, or set left flush tab stop.
Right button—Move tab stop.
Both buttons—Clear tab stop.

In the selection area (at the extreme left of ruler) clicking in the first space changes the leader character and clicking in the right changes the type of tab (right, left, decimal, and so on).

F
APPENDIX

Network notes

What is a network? Generally, a network is a way to share resources such as printers and disk drives. Because it is tied up primarily with input and output, these network notes have to do with loading files, saving files, and printing files. The first note, however, has to do with setting up Word to work with a network.

Setting up Word on a network

Setting up Word on a network is a two-step process. First, Word has to be installed, and then the individual workstation must be installed.

Installing Word

Installation of the program is not very different from the procedure outlined earlier in this book. You are given the opportunity within the SETUP program to install a network. Simply take that option.

Installing a workstation

& To install the individual workstation, place the Utilities 1 disk in drive A of the workstation and type A:SETUP USER.

Loading and Saving Files

A puzzling byproduct of a network is the ability for more than one person to work on a single file. This means that if person A saves his file with changes, and then person B saves her file with changes, the B version is the only one on the shared disk. When A looks at the file again, not only are his changes be gone, but he will see unfamiliar changes. (This can cause disorientation and loss of morale.) Fortunately, Word was written with network users in mind. This kind of accident cannot happen with Word.

The way to prevent person B from saving her changes to the file when person A is using it is to mark the file read only in the Transfer Save menu. This does not really lock anyone out of the file. It only serves to prevent users from saving the file under the same name, thus overwriting changes.

If the file is read-write (not read only), any user can load it, but then other users are locked out of the file until it is saved again.

You can use a utility like PC Tools to look at the file's attributes, or you can use the operating system command ATTRIB -R FILE.DOC either from the command line or using Word's Library Run command. This command turns off the read only attribute. To turn on the read only attribute, making it impossible to overwrite a file, use the operating system command ATTRIB +R FILE.DOC. Your network administrator might have to assist you in this operation.

The conditions described in this section also apply to files being used for merging and to files being searched with the Document Retrieval command. Glossary files can also be affected. Users should have their own versions of glossary files, though, as these are generally very individual and tailored to the user by the user. Have your network administrator place NORMAL.GLY in your directory. Save it as read-write (not read only) and change it as you wish. No one else should take an interest in your glossary (unless it has an effect on the network as a whole, in which case the administrator might want to look at it). You should also have access to your own spelling dictionary.

A file can be changed to read only status by running the program RDONLY. This DOS program does not work with OS/2. The ATTRIB command should be used in OS/2. Simply type RDONLY FILENAME and hit Return on the command line or using Word's Library Run command. FILENAME stands for the name of the file whose status is being changed.

A file can be changed back to read-write status by running the program RDWRITE. This DOS program does not work with OS/2. Again, the ATTRIB command should be used in OS/2. Simply type RDWRITE FILENAME and hit Return on the command line or using Word's Library Run command. FILENAME stands for the name of the file whose status is being changed.

Network printing

The major problem in printing on a network is that the network server has its own print queue. Therefore, you are not be able to spool printing from a workstation. Networks often have several printers attached, such as a laser printer for high quality printouts and a dot matrix printer for drafts. Changing printers is accomplished with the Print Options menu, just like changing printers in the individual computer.

Index

A
active windows, 126
Alt key, 8, 21
annotations, 140, 154, 325, 326
arrays, 301
arrow keys, 29, 92, 231
ascending sort, 239
ASCII characters, 321
ASCII files, 167, 193
Ask instruction macro, 287
Ask merge command, 203-205
AUTOEXEC.BAT files, Word installation and, 19
autoexecution, macro, 285
automatic hyphenation, 223-225
autosave option, 142, 144
Autosort command, 237-241, 326

B
background shading, 235
Backspace key, 9, 21, 28-29
backups, 13-16, 167
black box printer connection, 4
blank lines, 67, 144, 323
blocking text, 35, 39-41, 101-112
  columns, 41
  copying, 102
  entire document, 40
  extending selections, 41
  glossary and, 105-111
  mouse for, 40-41, 103
  overtype option, 103-105
  paragraphs and sentences, 40, 62
  replacing, 103
  scrap contents management, 102-103
body text, outlines, 247, 249, 252-253
boldface, 78, 323
bookmarks, 140, 154-155, 325, 326
booting up, 11-13
borders, 144, 233-235, 325

C
calculator, 243-246, 324
cancelling commands, 50, 324
Caps Lock key, 9, 25
captions, 307
CAPTURE.COM, 307
centering text, 63, 64, 93
central processing unit (CPU), 1-2
characters, 77-84
  boldface, 78, 323
  combination formats for, 79
  double underline, 78, 323
  downloadable fonts for, 83
  font color for, 83
  font names, 83
  font size (point size), 81
  formatting, 78-80, 325
  hardware capability constraints on, 77-78
  hidden, 78, 82, 129, 170, 171, 264, 323
  italics, 78, 323
  near letter-quality fonts, 83
  selecting, 78
  small caps, 78, 323
  strikethrough, 78, 323
  super- and subscripts, 79
  underline, 78, 323

342 *Index*

choosing commands, text, 322-323, 322
clipping lines, 308
collapsing outlines, 252-253
colors, 143, 235
columns, 148-149
   indexes with, 272
   mathematical calculations on, 245
   multiple, side-by-side option for, 73-75
   selecting, 41
   sorting, 240
   vertical lines in, 97
command area, 24-25
command letter, 48
commands, 48-51, 335
Comment macro instruction, 288
comments, macro, 286, 288
compilation, table of contents and indexes, 268-269
concatenation, 302
condition testing, macro, 288-290
conditional messages, merging, 205
CONFIG.SYS file, Word installation and, 19
control keys, 8, 318
COPY command, 13, 225, 330
cursor, 23, 30
   extending, 37
   extending, search and replace and, 117
   macro, 317
   mouse movement of, 31
   movement of, 29-31, 140, 322, 323
   speed of, 143
   stretching, 38
cut and paste, windows, 133-134

D

data files (see also merging), 193, 195-200
date, 12-13, 109, 142, 261
debugging macro, 284
decimal places, 93, 144
Delete key, 21, 28-29
descending sort, 239
desktop publishing (see importing graphics), 305-309
dictionaries (see spell checker)
DIR command, 329-330
direct formatting, 62-63, 323
directories, 163
disk drives, 5, 162
DISKCOPY command, 13, 16, 330-331
diskettes, 10-11
   backups, 13-14, 13
   care and handling, 10
   copying (DISKCOPY), 16, 330
   formatting, 17-18
   print to, 169-170
   source and target designations, DISKCOPY, 16
   write protection, 10
display mode, 143
divisions, 25, 321, 325
   creating, 145-146
   division marks (::::), 90
   document, 91
   entering and deleting, 86-87
document dictionary, 218
document retrieval system, 255-262
   changing arrangement of document list for, 262
   creation and revision dates, 261
   document text field, 261
   documents, printing, 257-258
   loading documents, 256
   menu for, 256
   Query command to select files, 260
   summary sheets, 255-260
documents (see also files; text)
   annotations in, 154
   automatic scrolling, 27-28
   autosave, 142, 144
   bookmarks in, 154-155
   clearing, 57-58, 166
   columns in, 148-149
   combining, 209
   copying (COPY), 330
   cursor movement through, 29-31
   cut and paste, 133-134
   divisions in, 91, 147-149
   editing keys (Backspace; Delete) for, 28-29
   editing text in, 35-45
   entering text, 26-28
   entry of, 21-33
   footnotes in, 149-154
   formatting, stylesheets for, 179
   gutter margins for, 147-148
   jumping between locations in, 137-140
   linking, 314-315
   list of (DIR), 329
   loading, 164-165, 256, 324
   merging (see merging), 168-169, 208
   naming, 56, 167
   outlines directly from, 253
   oversized, 165-166
   page numbers in, 98
   previewing, 173, 326
   printing, 53-56, 169-174, 257-258, 324, 326
   protecting, read-only command, 165
   recording styles from, 188
   retrieval (see also document retrieval), 58-59, 255, 326
   revision marks in, 275
   running heads, 155-158
   saving, 56-57, 142, 144, 166-167, 324
   scrolling, 31-33
   selecting (blocking) entire, 40
   sequential numbers in, 155
   simultaneous editing of, windows for, 134
   spreadsheets into, importing, 312-313
   status line report of, 165
   subcommands for, 327
   summary sheets, 255
   update styles in, variants for, 186
   word wrap, 26-27
DOS, 2, 225, 329-331
   access to 326
   floppy disk drive operation, 11
   hard drive operation, 11-12
   loading, 11, 16
dot matrix printers, 2, 3
double underline, 78, 323
double-spacing, 67, 324
drivers, installation of, 18-19
duplex printing, 170, 171

E

editing, 321-327
editing keys, 28-29
EDLIN command, 225

F

End key, 30
end mark, 23
Endcomment macro instruction, 288
Enter key, 9
envelope printing macro, 297-301
Escape key, 8, 21, 50
exiting Word, 59, 326
expanding outlines, 252-253
Extended mode, 25, 37, 117
extensions, 167

F

fields, data file, 195
files (see also documents; text), 161-169
  ASCII, 167
  autosave, 142, 144
  backups, 167
  clearing, 166
  copying (COPY), 330
  data (see data files; merging)
  date stamp, 261
  default drive, changing, 162
  deleting, 168
  extensions, 167
  glossary, 109-111
  header (see header files; merging)
  list of (DIR), 163, 191, 329
  loading, 164-165
  merging (see merging), 168-169
  naming, 56, 167
  network, loading and saving, 339
  overwriting, 167
  print to disk, 169-170
  printing, 169-173
  programming and, 167
  protecting, read-only command, 165
  renaming, 168
  retrieving (see document retrieval system)
  revision, date stamp for, 261
  RTF, 167
  saving, 56-57, 142, 144, 166-167
  selecting, Query command for, 260
  summary sheets, 255
  unformatted, 167

floating point numbers, 246, 301
floppies (see diskettes)
fonts, 324
  color of, 83
  downloadable, 83
  names of, 83
  near letter-quality, 83
  size of (point size), 81
  type of, 80-81
footers, 324
footnotes, 149-154, 325, 326
  glossary insertion of, 108-109
  jumping to, 139-140, 151
  reference marks in text for, 149
form letters (see also merging), 193, 209, 294-297
Format Character command, 79-80
FORMAT command, 18, 225
Format Division command, 86-91
Format Division Layout command, 146-147
format keys, 78, 181
Format Paragraph command, 62-63, 67-68, 87, 91
Format Stylesheet command, 180
Format Tab command, 87, 91-97
formatting, 325
  characters (see characters)
  date and time, 142
  direct, 62-63, 323
  disks, 17-18
  divisions for, 86-87
  format keys for, 78
  graphics, 308
  indexes, 269-272
  indirect, stylesheets for, 175
  macro for, 283, 284
  pages (see page formatting)
  paragraphs (see paragraphs)
  search and replace for, 120-122
  spreadsheets, 313-314
  stylesheets for, 179, 325
  tables of contents, 269-272
frames, 129
function keys, 9, 21, 35-36
  blocking, 35-36
  extend cursor, 37
  glossary references (F3), 107-108
  macro, 318-319
  Redo search and replace, 120

repeat search and replace, 119
stretch cursor, 38
text selection with, 35-36
functions, 301-302

G

Gallery menu, 177, 183-184, 192, 325
glossary, 105-111
  clearing buffer, 111
  F3 glossary reference key for, 107-108
  files in, 109-111
  footnotes in, 108-109
  insert, 325
  macros in, 279
  merging files in, 110-111
  nextpage, date, dateprint, time, timeprint, 109
  page numbers in, 108-109
  printing buffer, 111, 326
  retrieving files in, 110-111
  retrieving text, 105-107
  saving files in, 110
graphics, 129
  captions for, 307
  CAPTURE.COM for, 307
  clipping, 308
  display modes, 143
  formatting, 308
  importing, 305-307
  positioning, 308
  previewing, 307
  resolution of, 170, 171
  switch modes, 324
gutter margins, 147-148

H

hanging indents, 65, 324
hard disks, formatting, 17-18
header files, 198-199, 324
headings, outline, 247, 249, 249-253
Help screens, 25, 50-53, 326
hidden text, 78, 82, 129, 170, 171, 264, 323
Home key, 30
hyphenation, 69-71, 115-116, 223-225, 321, 326

I

If merge command, 205-208

If-Else-Endif macro instruction, 288-290
illustrations lists, 266
importing data, 305-307, 311-315
Include command, merging, 209
indentation, 64-66, 68, 323, 324
indexes, 267-272, 326
indirect formatting, stylesheets for, 175
ink jet printers, 3
installation, 15-20
int function, 301
integers, 301
italics, 78, 323

J
Jump command, 137-140, 151
justification, 63, 64, 223-225, 323

K
key codes, 179, 184-186
keyboards, 8-10, 21
  printing direct from (typewriter style), 169
keynames, macro, 283
keypad, macro, 318
keyword fields, summary sheets, 259, 260

L
laser printers, 2, 3
leader characters, 86, 95
len function, 301
letter quality printers, 2, 3
Library menu, 326
line drawing, 97, 144, 231-236, 324
line numbers, 143, 273-275
line spacing, 67-68, 144, 323-324
linking documents, 314-315, 326
Load command, 58
loops, 293

M
macro, 279-303, 279, 317-319
  arrays, 301
  Ask instruction, 287
  autoexecution, 285
  canceling, 280
  combining macro commands in macro programs, 294
  Comment instruction, 288
  comments in, 286, 288
  control codes for, 281
  control keys, 318
  creation, recording keystrokes for, 281
  cursor keys, 317
  debugging, 284
  editing, 282, 283
  Endcomment instruction, 288
  envelope printing with, 297-301
  form letters with, 294-297
  formatting, 283-284
  functions, 301-302
  function keys, 318-319
  If-Else-Endif instruction, 288-290
  key names, 283
  keypad, 318
  Message instruction, 291
  mouse actions in, 285
  naming, 280, 281, 283
  Pause instruction, 291
  Quit instruction, 292
  Repeat-Endrepeat instruction, 292
  retrieving, 282
  running, 280, 324
  saving, 282, 324
  Set instruction, 293
  shift keys, 317
  step through, 324
  testing, 284
  turn off menu display during, 285
  user queried for input (Ask), 287
  variables, 301
  While-Endwhile instruction, 293
  writing, 282
main menu, 325-327
margins, 63, 64, 68, 85, 86, 88-90, 147-148, 324, 325
mathematical calculations, 243-246
measure option, 142
memory, 6, 25
menus, 9, 49, 142
merging, 168-169, 193-210, 326
  Ask merge command, 203-205
  combining documents (Include), 209
  commas and quotation marks in, 197-198
  conditional (If), 205
  data file creation, 195-196
  data files from other programs, 199-200
  glossary files, 110-111
  header files, 198-199
  If merge command, 205-208
  Include command, 209
  merge command designation, < >, 194-195
  Next command, 208
  printing after, 197
  printing to disk file, 197
  Set merge command, 201-203
  several records into single document, 208
  Skip record command, 208
  steps in, 194
  variables in, 195
message line, 24
Message macro instruction, 291
mid function, 302
monitors, 2
mouse, 4-5, 335-338
  blocking text and, 103
  command selection with, 48-49, 335
  cursor movement with, 31, 140
  delete text, 43
  drivers, installation, 19
  insert text, 43
  installation, 19
  macro and, 285
  moving windows, 135, 337
  open and close windows, 135, 337
  pointer, 23
  ruler on and off, 337
  scrolling with, 31-32, 336
  selection bar, 336
  tabs with, 337
  text selection (blocking) with, 40-41, 335
  windows with, 135
mute option, 141-142

N
nesting paragraphs, 64

Index 345

networks, 339-340
newline, 70, 321
Next command, merging, 208
nextpage, glossary, 109
non-impact printers, 2, 3
nonbreaking hyphens, 71
nonbreaking space, 70, 321
NORMAL.GLY, 109
Num Lock key, 9, 10, 25
numbers (see also mathematical calculations)
   decimal places, 93, 144
   floating point to integer, 301
   page numbers (see page numbers)
   testing conditions of (IF), 206
numeric keypad, 10, 21

O

opening screen, Word, 22
operating systems, 2, 11-12, 16, 225
Options command, 141-144
OS/2, loading, 16
outlines, 129, 134, 247-254, 325
   body text, 247, 249
   collapsing, 252-253
   converting document into, 253
   editing headings, 251
   expanding, 252-253
   headings, 247, 249
   levels in, 249
   paragraph numbering for, 249-250
   printing, 254
   stylesheets for, 254
   subheadings, 247
   table of contents from, 267
oversized documents, 165-166
overtype option, 103-105, 325
overwrite mode, 25, 167

P

page breaks, 146, 321
   Keep option and, 72
   paragraphs and, 72, 73
   setting, 138
   updating after editing, 139, 172-173
page formatting, 145-160, 324
   annotations, 154
   bookmarks, 154-155
   columns, 148-149
   divisions in, 145-149
   footnotes, 149-154
   Format Division Layout command, 146-147
   gutter margins for bound documents, 147-148
   page breaks, 146
   running heads, 155-158
page layout, 145, 305-309
   captions, 307
   CAPTURE.COM for, 307
   importing graphics for, 305-307
   positioning and formatting graphics, 308
   previewing graphics, 307
page length, 325
page numbers, 25, 85, 98-99, 146
   default settings, 86
   glossary insertion of, 108-109, 108
   index with, 270-271
   jumping to, 137-138
   location of, 98
   odd and even, 147
   order of numbering, 99
   printing, 170, 171
   running heads using, 157
   style of numbers in, 99
pagination, 142, 172-173, 324, 326
paragraphs, 61-75, 321
   advanced formatting, 71-75
   alignment of, 63-64
   blank lines between, 67
   borders for, 233-235
   centering text, 63, 64
   combination formats in, 66
   double-spacing in, 67
   formatting, 61-63, 67-68, 323-324
   hyphenation, 69-71, 69
   indentation, 64-66, 68
   joining, 68-69
   justification, 63, 64
   line spacing in, 68
   margins, 63, 64, 68
   multiple column printing, side-by-side option, 73-75
   numbering, outlines and, 249-250
   page breaks in, 72, 73
   selecting, 40, 62
   sorting, 240
   splitting, 68-69
   word spacing, 69, 70
   word wrap, 63, 64, 69, 70
parallel ports, 55, 56
Pause macro instruction, 291
PgUp-PgDn keys, 30
point size, 81
ports, printer, 55, 56
previewing, 173, 307, 326
Print command, 169-174
printers, 2, 3, 4, 18, 53-56, 324
printing, 53-56, 169-174, 324, 326
   columns, side-by-side option, 73-75
   copies of, 170, 171
   direct from keyboard (typewriter style), 169
   documents, 257-258
   draft quality, 170, 171
   duplex, 170, 171
   envelopes, macro for, 297-301
   glossary buffer, 111
   graphics resolution setting, 170, 171
   hidden text, 170, 171
   line numbers, 273-275, 273
   merged documents, 197
   networks, 340
   options for, 170-171
   outlines, 254
   page breaks and repagination, 172-173
   page numbers, 170, 171
   previewing, 173
   queues, 170-172, 326
   range, 170, 171
   revision marks, 275-276
   sending document to printer for, 169
   summary sheet, 170-171, 257-258
   to disk, 169-170
   widows and orphans, 170, 171
punctuation, 220-221, 265, 267-268

Q

Query command, 260-262

queues, 170-172, 326
Quit command, 59
Quit macro instruction, 292

R

ragged right, 223-225
RAM, 6, 225
records, data files, 195
redlining, 325
redo command, 325
remark, 179, 186
repagination (see also page numbers), 172-173, 326
Repeat-Endrepeat macro instruction, 292
retrieval list, update, 324
Return key, 9, 21
revision marks, 275-277
RTF files, 167
ruler line, 87-88, 135, 325, 337
running heads, 155-158, 325

S

scrap file, 25, 102-103, 324
scroll bar, 32-33, 140
Scroll Lock key, 10, 25
scrolling, 27-28, 31-33, 131-133, 322, 336
search and replace, 113-122, 277, 325, 327
selection bar, mouse, 336
sequential numbers, 155, 326
serial ports, 55, 56
Set macro instruction, 293
Set merge command, 201-203
shading, 235
Shift keys, 8, 9, 317
shortcut keys, 324
side-by-side option, multiple column printing with, 73-75
Skip command, merging, 208
small caps, 78, 323
sorting, 237-241
sound, mute option for, 141-142
spacing, word, 69, 70, 321
spell checker and dictionary, 213-221, 324, 326
  adding words to dictionary, 218
  alternatives for, 220
  capital letters, 220
  changing corrections in, 217-218
  dictionaries for, 218-219
  editing dictionaries, 221
  path entry, 143
  punctuation, 220, 221
  usage of, general principles, 219
spreadsheets, documents using, 312-314
status line, 24, 25, 165
stretching cursor, 38
strikethrough, 78, 323
strings, text, 301-302
style bar, 129
styles, 178-179, 186-188
  copying, 189, 325
  default, 182
  deleting, 189
  editing, 189
  format key assignment of, 181
  inserting, 325
  moving, 189
  naming, 325
  recording from documents, 188
  revising, 189
  saving, 324
  search and replace for, 120-122
stylesheets assignment of, 180
stylesheets, 175-192, 325
  assigning styles to, 180
  attaching, 176-177, 179
  changing, 189-190
  default styles, 182
  detaching, 176-177, 179
  editing styles, 189
  formatting documents with, 179
  Gallery meny for, 177, 183-184, 192, 325
  indirect formatting with, 175
  key codes, 179, 184-186
  loading, 177, 192, 325
  merging, 325
  outlines, 254
  printing, 325
  recording styles from documents to, 188
  remarks, 179, 186
  retrieving, 190-191
  revising styles, 189
  saving, 190-191, 325
  selecting text for, 180
  style composition in, 178-179, 186-188
  undo, 190
  unloading, 177
  usages, 179, 185
  variants, 179, 185, 186
sub menus, 49
subheadings, outlines, 247, 252-253
subscripts, 79
summary sheets, 143, 170, 171, 255, 258-260
superscripts, 79
synonyms, 229-230
system requirements, Word, 1-6

T

Tab key, 8, 9
table of contents, 264-272, 326
tables, 97, 313
tabs, 8, 85, 91-97, 144, 324, 325, 337
teletype (TTY), 55
text (see also documents; files)
  autosave, 142, 144
  background shading for, 235
  blocking, 35, 39-41, 101-112
  boldface, 78, 323
  centering, 63, 64, 93
  choosing commands, 322-323
  color for, 235
  columnar, 41, 148-149
  concatenation of, 302
  copying, 102, 325
  cursor movement through, 29-31, 322, 323
  delete, 28-29, 35-37, 39, 41-42, 325
  display modes, 143
  double underline, 78, 323
  editing, 35-45, 325
  entering, 26-28, 321
  extending cursor, 37, 41
  font selection for, 80-81, 83
  framing, 325
  function keys to edit, 35-36
  glossary for, 105-111
  hidden, 78, 129, 170, 171, 264, 323
  insert, 42-43, 325, 326
  italic, 78, 323
  jump through, 326
  length of string, 301
  mouse insert-delete, 43

mouse selection, 335
moving, 101
overtype option, 103-105, 325
placement of string in, 302
printing, 169-174
redlining and revisions, 325
redo command, 325
replacing blocks of, 103
saving, 56-57, 142, 144
scrap, 102-103
scrolling, 27-28, 31-33, 322
search and replace, 113-122, 325, 327
selecting, 40, 78, 180, 322
simultaneous editing of, windows for, 134
small cap, 78, 323
stretching cursor, 38
strikethrough, 78, 323
super- and subscripts, 79
underline, 78, 323
undo command, 43-45
word wrap, 26-27
wrapping, 308
thesaurus, 227-230, 324, 326
thumb line, 140
time, 13, 109, 142
timeprint, glossary, 109
toggle keys, 9, 25, 37
training modules, 326

Transfer command, 131, 161-169
Transfer Load command, 58
Transfer Save command, 56-57
tutorial, Word, running, 52-53
type in mode, 47, 48

U

underline, 78, 323
Undo, 43-45, 102, 190, 325, 327
unformatted files, 167
unit of measurement, 142
usage, 179, 185
user dictionary, 219

V

variables, 301
variants, 179, 185, 186

W

While-Endwhile macro instruction, 293
widows and orphans, printing, control of, 170, 171
wildcards, 114, 163, 330
Window Split command, 123-125
windows, 23-24, 123-136, 324, 327
  active, 126
  borders around, shut off, 144
  clearing, 125, 131

closing, 130-131, 135, 327
cut and paste, 133-134
footnote, 152
frames, 129
graphics, 129, 324
mouse control of, 135, 337
moving between, 126-127, 135
opening, 123-126, 135
options for, 129-130
number of, 23
printer display, 324
resizing, 327
scrolling, 131-133
show layout of, 129
simultaneous editing with, 134
sizing, 127-128, 133
splitting, 123-125, 130, 131, 327
zooming, 133, 324
word wrap, 26-27, 63, 64, 69, 70
WordStar, 211-212
wrapping text, 308
write protection, 10

X

XCOPY command, 13

Z

zooming, 133, 324

Other Bestsellers of Related Interest

ADVANCED MS-DOS® BATCH FILE PROGRAMMING—Dan Gookin

Batch file programming is a way of communicating with your computer . . . a way of transforming DOS into a system that works the way you want it to. In this book, Dan Gookin explains unique methods of using batch files to crate a work environment that will improve your efficiency, productivity, and overall relationship with your computer. All the necessary tools, batch file structures, commands, and helpful techniques can be found here. 400 pages, 733 illustrations. Book No. 3197, $29.95 paperback, $34.95 hardcover

THE BEST OF SHAREWARE: IBM® PC UTILITIES—Mark R. Sawusch

This unique resource provides complete documentation for over 100 of the best IBM PC public domain and shareware utilities. Sawusch presents the advantages and limitations of each program as well as showing how to use it most effectively. He supplies command and feature summaries and example applications for each. A much-needed listing of the programs' distributors is also included. In addition, 75 of the most useful programs are included on a disk that comes with the book. 240 pages. Book No. 3006, $29.95 paperback only

COMPUTER VIRUSES: What They Are, How They Work, and How to Avoid Them—Jonathan L. Mayo

The Trojan horse, the worm, and the logic bomb—all these are programs that move silently from computer to computer destroying and changing files. Now, you can protect your computer from these and other ailments. Mayo explains how viruses get into your computer, and examines the parts of DOS that are most susceptible to infection. Many commercial anti-viral programs discussed. with this book you'll receive a disk containing some of the best shareware and public domain anti-viral programs available, including top-rated FLU_Shot+! 160 pages, 40 illustrations. Book No. 3382, $29.95 paperback only

NORTON UTILITIES™ VERSION 4:0: An Illustrated Tutorial—Richard Evans

". . . a handy guide for evaluating the features of the Norton Utilities before buying . . . and important desk reference after purchase." **Midwest Book Review**

This book is a practical, easy-to-read instruction manual for using Peter Norton's powerful utility programs. Extremely well illustrated, it explains each of the 25 individual utilities. Every MS/PC-DOS microcomputer user will appreciate this easy-to-follow reference and instruction manual which also shows how to combine these utilities with DOS batch processing techniques for truly efficient management of your computer system. 176 pages, 89 illustrations. Book No. 2929, $15.95 paperback only

NORTON UTILITIES™ 4.5: An Illustrated Tutorial—Richard Evans

This completely revised edition of Richard Evans' bestselling guidebook demonstrates the vast capabilities of the Norton Utilities package, and features the exciting new additions to release 4.5. You'll find straightforward, step-by-step instruction on using every program in the Norton Utilities, for every version from 3.0 to the current 4.5. All the details of the command structure and common applications are presented. 224 pages, 98 illustrations. Book No. 3359, $16.95 paperback only

DOS VSAM FOR APPLICATION PROGRAMMERS—Lana J. Chandler

Lana Chandler gives you the background knowledge and the expert tips and techniques you need to apply the powers of VSAM to your database applications. This invaluable guide covers: portability of data between operating systems, conversion of ISAM files to VSAM, centralized space management control, simplified file reorganization, and more. Includes popular VSAM commands and options with sample output, job streams, and AMS control statements. 240 pages, 41 illustrations. Book No. 3251, $21.95 paperback only

INVITATION TO DOS LIBRARY SERVICES FOR APPLICATION PROGRAMMERS—Lana J. Chandler

Here's expert guidance in using support software to access and control DOS libraries and their directories. Using clear, easy-to-understand language supported by numerous illustrations, Lana Chandler defines DOS libraries and shows you how simple it can be to access and control them once related software is mastered. Comparisons are made to core images, relocatable, source statement, and procedural libraries and their directories. 192 pages, Illustrated. Book No. 3261, $21.95 paperback only

MS-DOS® BEYOND 640K: Working with Extended and Expanded Memory—James Forney

Find out how some relatively inexpensive hardware and software enhancements can give your 8088, 80286, or 80386-based computer the ability to run larger applications, create multiple simultaneous work environments, maintain larger files, and provide all the memory you need. This book provides a clear picture of all the alternatives and options available. even up-to-the-minute tips and techniques for using Lotus 1-2-3® , Release 3.0, in extended memory! 248 pages, Illustrated. Book No. 3239, $19.95 paperback, $29.95

80386: A Programming and Design Handbook—2nd Edition—Penn Brumm and Don Brumm

"This book has all the information you require to design, build, and program your own 80386-based system." —*Computing Magazine*

Now, with the guidance of system applications experts Penn and Don Brumm, you can exploit this advanced processor. Revised and expanded, this book explains and demonstrates such advanced features as: 32-bit instruction enhancements, memory paging functions, debugging applications, and Virtual 8086 Mode. 480 pages, 108 illustrations. Book No. 3237, $24.95 paperback only

80386 MACRO ASSEMBLER AND TOOLKIT—Penn Brumm and Don Brumm

Now you can expand your programming horizons with MASM 5.1. This practical guide to writing and using assembly language on 80386-based computers centers on the Microsoft Macro Assembler (MASM), Version 5.1. It is designed to help you become a proficient programmer—able to write effective code and solve problems efficiently. A collection of useful macros is provided to illustrate the concepts presented. There is also a detailed discussion of MASM syntax and grammar, plus coverage of the options and their usage. 608 pages, 284 illustrations. Book No. 3247, $25.95 paperback, $35.95 hardcover

MS-DOS® UTILITY PROGRAMS: Add-On Software Resources—Ronny Richardson

Combining the most useful features of a product catalog and magazine reviews, this book is the most comprehensive guide available for finding the utility programs you need to optimize your DOS-based computer system. Richardson candidly describes the capabilities and operation of virtually every DOS utility on the market. He clearly explains what each package does, who might benefit from the package, and what specific problems it can solve. 672 pages, Illustrated. Book No. 3278, $24.95 paperback, $34.95 hardcover

ASSEMBLY LANGUAGE SUBROUTINES FOR MS-DOS® COMPUTERS—Leo J. Scanlon

This collection of practical, easy-to-use subroutines is exactly what you need for performing high-precision math, converting code, manipulating strings and lists, sorting data, reading user commands and responses from the keyboard, and doing countless other jobs. If you consider your time a valuable asset, you won't want to miss this handy quick-reference to a gold mine of subroutines. 350 pages, 43 illustrations. Book No. 2767, $21.95 paperback only

80386 ASSEMBLY LANGUAGE: A Complete Tutorial and Subroutine Library—Penn Brumm and Don Brumm

An invaluable sourcebook that offers array manipulation routines and one of the most complete descriptions of MS-DOS and BIOS interrupts available. You'll find fast sort routines, fixed- and variable-length strings, 80386 programs, BCD packages, direct I/O to monochrome graphics adapters, MS-DOS error code, internal program documentation, and more! 656 pages, 248 illustrations. Book No. 3047, $24.95 paperback, $34.95 hardcover

Prices Subject to Change Without Notice.

Look for These and Other TAB Books at Your Local Bookstore

To Order Call Toll Free 1-800-822-8158
(in PA, AK, and Canada call 717-794-2191)

or write to TAB BOOKS, Blue Ridge Summit, PA 17294-0840.

Title	Product No.	Quantity	Price

☐ Check or money order made payable to TAB BOOKS

Charge my ☐ VISA ☐ MasterCard ☐ American Express

Acct. No. _____ Exp. _____

Signature: _____

Name: _____

Address: _____

City: _____

State: _____ Zip: _____

Subtotal $ _____

Postage and Handling
($3.00 in U.S., $5.00 outside U.S.) $ _____

Add applicable state and local
sales tax $ _____

TOTAL $ _____

TAB BOOKS catalog free with purchase; otherwise send $1.00 in check or money order and receive $1.00 credit on your next purchase.

Orders outside U.S. must pay with international money order in U.S. dollars.

TAB Guarantee: If for any reason you are not satisfied with the book(s) you order, simply return it (them) within 15 days and receive a full refund.
BC